Quick Business Math

Wiley Self-Teaching Guides teach practical skills from accounting to astronomy, management to mathematics. Look for them at your local bookstore.

Other Wiley Self-Teaching Guides on Business Skills:

Accounting: A Self-Teaching Guide, by Neal Margolis and N. Paul Harmon

Effective Meetings: A Self-Teaching Guide, by Clyde W. Burleson

Listening: The Forgotten Skill, A Self-Teaching Guide, Second Edition, by Madelyn Burley-Allen

Making Successful Presentations: A Self-Teaching Guide, by Terry C. Smith

Managing Assertively: A Self-Teaching Guide, Second Edition, by Madelyn Burley-Allen

Managing Behavior on the Job: A Self-Teaching Guide, by Paul L. Brown

Quick Business Math: A Self-Teaching Guide, by Steve Slavin

Selling on the Phone: A Self-Teaching Guide, by James Porterfield

Quick Business Math
A Self-Teaching Guide

Steve Slavin

John Wiley & Sons, Inc.

New York • Chichester • Brisbane • Toronto • Singapore

Contents

Part IV   Statistics and Graphing Techniques

How to Use This Book

Business math cuts a wide swath across arithmetic, algebra, accounting, personal finance, graphing, and statistics. Its focus is solving practical problems encountered in these fields. Because a lot of the work you will be doing is very technical, you won't want to rush through each chapter without taking the time needed to fully digest its contents.

Each chapter is broken into numbered sections, or frames. After every few frames you'll take a quick quiz to provide you with an instant progress report. When you've gotten every problem right, you'll know that you've mastered the material in the previous frames and can safely go on to the next topic. But when you get more than one problem wrong, it would be an excellent idea to repeat the previous frames. It would be great if every reader could breeze through this book in just a couple of weeks, but not every concept can be mastered immediately, so don't worry about repeating sections.

The book's 13 chapters are organized into four parts—a basic math review, retailing applications, general business applications, and statistics and graphs. Ideally, you'll work your way through the book, problem by problem.

When you're confident that you can do the problems without even reading the relevant frames, feel free to go directly to the quick quiz. Similarly, if you think that you can skip an entire chapter, just take the self-test at the end of that chapter.

I've tried to define all new terms as we go along, but have also included a glossary of terms at the back of the book for your reference.

Now let's look at each of the book's four parts to get a better idea of what we'll be doing.

Part I.   Basic Math Review

Chapters 1, 2, and 3 provide a review of the basic arithmetic and algebraic skills you'll need to do business math. The mere mention of algebra is known to cause panic among some students. "How much algebra do I have to know?" "I've forgotten what I learned in high school—and I didn't learn that much to begin with."

The chances are that the arithmetic and algebra that you *do* remember will be sufficient to get you through most of the later chapters of this book. In Chapter 1, you'll have a chance to brush up on your basic arithmetic skills, and in Chapter 2, we'll review all the elementary algebra you'll need. And then, in Chapter 3, we'll go over percentages in great detail. The ability to work with percentages is crucial in doing business math, so we'll cover everything you need to know about this arithmetic tool.

What about calculators? I recommend you try to get along without using one for at least the first two chapters. However, when you get into repetitive calculations, like those you'll encounter in Chapter 3, a calculator will save you a lot of time.

Part II.   Retailing Applications

You don't have to own a store, or even to work in one, to make use of the concepts we'll be covering in this part of the book. In Chapter 4, we'll learn what it really means to say that goods are marked up by 70 percent or marked down by 50 percent. Then, in Chapter 5, we'll look at trade discounts and chain discounts to find out what retail stores really pay for their inventory.

In Chapter 6, we'll talk about the three main methods of taking inventory—FIFO (first in, first out), LIFO (last in, first out), and the retail method. These three methods will also provide an introduction to accounting, a topic we'll cover in more depth in the next section.

Part III.   General Business Applications

Calculating interest and depreciation and working with financial statements are the basic applications of business math. Chapter 7 covers simple interest, and Chapter 8 introduces compound interest and an important concept known as present value. In Chapters 9, 10, and 11, we'll go over the basics of business accounting: depreciation, the balance sheet, and the income statement.

Part IV.   Statistics and Graphing Techniques

In Chapter 12, you'll be finding the means, medians, modes, and ranges of different groups of numbers. These statistical tools will serve you well long after you've completed this book. Chapter 13 will teach you how to read and draw bar graphs, line graphs, and pie charts from frequency distributions that you will compile.

You may be able to work your way through this book in just three or four weeks, but then again, you may need to take three or four months. Try working at a comfortable pace, skipping parts of chapters or even entire chapters if your skills are really sharp.

So what are we waiting for? Let's get started!

Acknowledgments

I want to thank Judith McCarthy for doing such a fine job of editing this book. Not only did she suggest that I write it, but she also saw it through the entire production process. I would also like to thank Hazel Staloff for quickly and accurately transforming a cut-and-pasted pile of pages into a clean manuscript.

Linda Weidemann, the project manager at A-R Editions, arranged for the copyediting, design, and typesetting of the book. Robin Gold, the copyeditor, smoothed out the rough edges of the manuscript without impinging on my mellifluous prose, while Dennis Weidemann corrected dozens of mathematical errors. And finally John Cook, a managing editor at John Wiley & Sons, saw to it that the book was printed and delivered to our warehouse, from which it was shipped to your bookstore.

Part I Basic Math Review

1 Basic Arithmetic

Here you are at the very beginning of the first chapter and we're hitting you with a test. Here's the deal: If you do well on this test, you get to skip the next part of the chapter. Let's talk about that again after the test. Right now, you'd better fasten your seat belt because here comes the test.

1. Do these problems:

    a. 15,000
       × 8,000
       (handwritten: 120,000,000)

    b. 350,000
       × 100,000
       (handwritten: 35,000,000,000)

    c. 1,500,000
       × 800,000
       (handwritten: 1,200,000,000,000)

2. Now do these problems:

    a. 3,000)48,000 (handwritten quotient: 16)

    b. 40,000)1,000,000 (handwritten quotient: 25)

    c. 90,000)360,000 (handwritten quotient: 4)

    d. 500,000)125,000,000 (handwritten quotient: 250)

Answers to Pretest 1.1

1.	a.	15,000	b.	350,000	c.	1,500,000
		× 8,000		× 100,000		× 800,000
		120,000,000		35,000,000,000		1,200,000,000,000

3

2. a. $\overset{1\ 6}{3\overline{)4^18}}$ b. $\overset{2\ 5}{4\overline{)10^20}}$ c. $\overset{4}{9\overline{)36}}$ d. $\overset{2\ 50}{5\overline{)12^250}}$

Did you get them all right? If you did, then you can proceed to Pretest 1.2 later in this chapter. If you didn't, then we need to review a bit, so please keep reading here.

1 FAST MULTIPLICATION

Do this problem however you would normally do it.

$$\begin{array}{r} \overset{2}{1,}700 \\ \times\ 300 \\ \hline \end{array}$$

Solution: 510,000   *510,000*

$$\begin{array}{r} 1,700 \\ \times\ 300 \\ \hline 0\ 000 \\ 00\ 00 \\ 510\ 0 \\ \hline 510,000 \end{array}$$

Is it really necessary to write out all those zeros? Definitely not! I'm going to show you a couple of shortcuts. Let's do this problem over again:

$$\begin{array}{r} 1,700 \\ \times\ 300 \\ \hline 510,000 \end{array}$$

The first shortcut is to multiply 1,700 by 0 and to write down 0. Then multiply 1,700 again by 0 and write down 0 again as shown in the two steps following:

$$\begin{array}{r} 1,700 \\ \times\ 300 \\ \hline 0 \end{array} \qquad \begin{array}{r} 1,700 \\ \times\ 300 \\ \hline 00 \end{array}$$

Then multiply 1,700 by 3 to get 5,100, and write this next to the left zero:

$$\begin{array}{r} 1,700 \\ \times\ 300 \\ \hline 510,000 \end{array}$$

We'll be doing another trick in a couple of minutes, but right now, work out these three problems taking the same shortcut I took:

1.	420	2.	800	3.	2,000
	× 500		× 600		× 9,000
	21 0,000		*480p 00*		*18,000,000*

Solutions:

1.	420	2.	800	3.	2,000
	× 500		× 600		× 9,000
	210,000		480,000		18,000,000

2

Ready for our second trick? How much is $4,000 \times 7,000$? Watch this closely: Multiply 4×7. That's 28. Now add six zeros: 28,000,000.

What's the rule? When you want to multiply two numbers that both end in zeros, just multiply the numbers and tack on the sum of the zeros.

Try this one:

$$
\begin{array}{r}
12,000 \\
\times\, 500 \\
\hline
\end{array}
$$
6p 00p 00

Solution:

$$
\begin{array}{r}
12,000 \\
\times\, 500 \\
\hline
6,000,000
\end{array}
$$

Ready for another set of problems? O.K., find the solution to each of these:

1.	16,000	2.	200,000	3.	14,000,000
	× 9,000		× 12,000		× 4,000
	144,000,000		*24 00p00,000*		*56 000,000,000*

Solutions:

1.	16	2.	2	3.	14
	× 9		× 12		× 4
	144,000,000		4		56,000,000,000
			2		
			2,400,000,000		

3

Now suppose you wanted to multiply a number by 10. All you have to do is tack on a zero. And if you want to multiply a number by 100, tack on two zeros.

How much is 10 times

1. 157 ?	2. 2,300 ?	3. 1,562 ?
1,570	*23,000*	*15,620*

Solutions:

  1. 1,570   2. 23,000   3. 15,620

And now how much is 100 times

  1. 36 ?   2. 175 ?   3. 4,000 ?

Solutions:

  1. 3,600   2. 17,500   3. 400,000

When you work with numbers frequently, you learn to manipulate them. This takes time. But over the course of the next few chapters, I can promise you that you get plenty of practice working with numbers.

4   FAST DIVISION

Occasionally you can take a shortcut in division. For instance, suppose you need to divide 1,500 into 23,000. You can get rid of some of the zeros. How many?

The answer is four. You can get rid of the two zeros in the 1,500, reducing it to 15, and you can get rid of two of the zeros in 23,000, reducing it to 230. Keep in mind that you are taking *the same number* of zeros from 1,500 and 23,000. It's a lot easier dividing 230 by 15 than it is dividing 23,000 by 1,500.

$$
1{,}500\overline{)23{,}000} = 15\overline{)230} \quad
\begin{array}{r}
15R5 \\
\hline
230 \\
-15 \\
\hline
80 \\
-75 \\
\hline
5
\end{array}
$$

What's R5? R5 means that we have a remainder of 5. So—how many times does 15 go into 230? It goes in 15 times, with a remainder of 5. Another way to answer this question is to say that 15 goes into 230 15 and $\frac{5}{15}$ times, or $15\frac{1}{3}$ times.

Time to do some problems:

  1. $5{,}000\overline{)125{,}000}$ 2. $10{,}000\overline{)200{,}000}$

  3. $18{,}000\overline{)54{,}000}$ 4. $170{,}000\overline{)510{,}000{,}000}$

Solutions:

1. 5,000)‾125,000‾

    $\frac{2\ 5}{5)12^25}$

2. 10,000)‾200,000‾

    $\frac{20}{1)20}$

3. 18,000)‾54,000‾

    $\frac{3}{18)54}$

4. 170,000)‾510,000,000‾

    $\frac{3,000}{17)51,000}$
    $\frac{-51}{}$

5

As you've observed, getting rid of all those zeros can save you a lot of work. Just one more fast division trick and we'll be ready for the next Pretest. How much is 117,000 divided by 10?

[handwritten: 11,700]

Solution:

Just lop off that last zero from 117,000 and you've got your answer: 11,700.

Divide each of these numbers by 10:

1. 195,000   2. 460   3. 3,010   4. 10

Solutions:

1. 19,500   2. 46   3. 301   4. 1

6

Remember, when you divide a number by 10, that number loses its last zero. Ready to divide by 100? Divide each of these numbers by 100:

1. 5,000   2. 100,000   3. 18,500   4. 401,000

Solutions:

1. 50   2. 1,000   3. 185   4. 4,010

PRETEST 1.2

Do the following problems.

1. a. $\begin{array}{r} ^2\ 1.4 \\ \times 2.6 \\ \hline \end{array}$ *[handwritten: 8 4 28 364]*

   b. $\begin{array}{r} 1.33 \\ \times 1.5 \\ \hline \end{array}$ *[handwritten: 665 133 1.995]*

   c. $\begin{array}{r} ^3\ ^{11}\ 2.67 \\ \times 3.05 \\ \hline \end{array}$ *[handwritten: 1335 0000 8.1435]*

2. a. $\begin{array}{r} 2.797 \\ \times 1.5 \\ \hline \end{array}$ *[handwritten: 13985 27970 4.1955]*

   b. $\begin{array}{r} 3.012 \\ \times 1.44 \\ \hline \end{array}$ *[handwritten: 12048 120188 301200 4.33428]*

   c. $\begin{array}{r} 10.295 \\ \times 1.533 \\ \hline \end{array}$

3. a. $0.253\overline{)1.17}$ b. $1.166\overline{)4.8}$ c. $0.395\overline{)2}$

4. Carry your division in these problems to one decimal place:

   a. $0.39\overline{)6}$ b. $1.533\overline{)4.1}$ c. $0.954\overline{)3}$

Answers to Pretest 1.2

1. a.
```
     1.4
   × 2.6
   ─────
     84
   2 8
   ─────
   3.64
```
b.
```
     1.33
   × 1.5
   ─────
    665
   1 33
   ─────
   1.995
```
c.
```
      2.67
   × 3.05
   ──────
    1335
   8 010
   ──────
   8.1435
```

2. a.
```
     2.797
   × 1.5
   ──────
   1 3985
   2 797
   ──────
   4.1955
```
b.
```
     3.012
   × 1.44
   ──────
   12048
   1 2048
   3 012
   ──────
   4.33728
```
c.
```
     10.295
   × 1.533
   ───────
    30885
    30885
   5 1475
   10 295
   ───────
   15.782235
```

3. a.
```
                      4R158
0.253)1.17 = 253)1170
              −1012
              ─────
               158
```

b.
```
                      4R136
1.166)4.8 = 1166)4800
            −4664
            ─────
              136
```

c.
```
                    5R25
0.395)2 = 395)2000
          −1975
          ─────
            25
```

4.a.
```
                       15.38 = 15.4
0.39)6 = 39)600.00
           −39 x xx
           ───────
             210
            −195
            ────
             15 0
            −11 7
            ─────
              3 30
```

b.
```
                         2.67 = 2.7
1.533)4.1 = 1533)4100.00
              3066 xx
              ───────
               1034
               −919 8
               ──────
               114 20
```

c.
```
                       3.14 = 3.1
0.954)3 = 954)3000.00
            −2862 xx
            ────────
              138 0
             −95 4
             ─────
              42 60
```

Did you get everything right? If so, you're ready to take Pretest 1.3, later in this chapter. If you got all the division problems right but one or more of the multiplication problems wrong, please read frames 7 and 8. If you got all the multiplication right but are still not up to par on division, then read frames 9 to 11.

7 MULTIPLYING DECIMALS

Here's something that can't be done very easily on a calculator, even though calculators have floating decimals. Multiplying with decimals probably leads to more mistakes than any other arithmetic operation. But if you follow just one simple rule, you can avoid all that grief.

We'll work out a simple problem and then apply the rule.

Problem:

$$\begin{array}{r} 1.2 \\ \times\, 1.6 \\ \hline \end{array}$$

Solution:

$$\begin{array}{r} 1.2 \\ \times\, 1.6 \\ \hline 72 \\ 1\,2 \\ \hline 1.92 \end{array}$$

This was really a two-part problem. The first part was straight multiplication. The second part was to figure out where to place the decimal point.

Here's the rule: Add the number of places to the *right* of the decimals in the numbers being multiplied and place the decimal point that number of places to the *left* in the answer. For instance, 1.2 has one number to the right of the decimal point, and 1.6 also has one number to the right of the decimal point. That gives us two numbers to the right of the decimal point. In our answer, we placed our decimal point two places to the left. After you have a few problems under your belt, you'll be able to place your decimal points without even *thinking* about it.

See what you can do with this problem:

$$\begin{array}{r} 2.94 \\ \times\, 1.35 \\ \hline \end{array}$$

Solution:

$$\begin{array}{r} 2.94 \\ \times\, 1.35 \\ \hline 1470 \\ 882 \\ 2\,94 \\ \hline 3.9690 \end{array}$$

Remember that equations with decimals are *two*-part problems. Before you even worry about where to place the decimal point, it's important to get your multiplication right.

Here's another problem:

$$\begin{array}{r} 2.143 \\ \times\,.22 \end{array}$$

Solution:

$$\begin{array}{r} 2.143 \\ \times\,.22 \\ \hline 4286 \\ 4286 \\ \hline .47146 \end{array}$$

8

Are you getting better at placing the decimal point? Here's a trick that may help you check your answer. Refer back to the first multiplication problem we did in frame 7: 1.2 × 1.6. How much is 1 × 1? It's 1, of course. So what kind of an answer were we looking for here? Both multipliers are higher than one, so we can expect something more than 1. But how much more than 1? Well, 2 × 2 = 4, and since 1.2 and 1.6 are both less than 2, we know our answer has to be less than 4. OK, so our answer will be between 1 and 4. That sounds about right because our answer came out to 1.92. If we had placed the decimal point in the wrong place, our answer would have been either .192, which is too low, or 19.2, which is too high.

In the next problem we multiplied 2.94 by 1.35. Now 3 × 1 = 3. Our answer should be around 3, maybe a bit more. It came out 3.696. So as long as the answer is reasonably close to our estimate, we're doing fine.

In the last problem we multiplied 2.143 by .22. Because .22 is less than 1, we want an answer that is less than 2.143. What did we get? We got .47196.

All we're looking for is a very rough estimate so we know where to place the decimal point. Try a problem set. Use estimating to check the decimal position.

1. $\begin{array}{r} 1.903 \\ \times\,2.231 \end{array}$ 2. $\begin{array}{r} 4.725 \\ \times\,3.64 \end{array}$

3. $\begin{array}{r} 89.02 \\ \times\,4.263 \end{array}$ 4. $\begin{array}{r} 7.856 \\ \times\,1.24 \end{array}$

Solutions:

1.
$$
\begin{array}{r}
1.903 \\
\times\,2.231 \\
\hline
1903 \\
5709 \\
3806 \\
3\,806 \\
\hline
4.245593
\end{array}
$$

2.
$$
\begin{array}{r}
4.725 \\
\times\,3.64 \\
\hline
18900 \\
2\,8350 \\
14\,175 \\
\hline
17.19900
\end{array}
$$

3.
$$
\begin{array}{r}
89.02 \\
\times\,4.263 \\
\hline
26706 \\
5\,3412 \\
17\,804 \\
356\,08 \\
\hline
379.49226
\end{array}
$$

4.
$$
\begin{array}{r}
7.856 \\
\times\,1.24 \\
\hline
31424 \\
1\,5712 \\
7\,856 \\
\hline
9.74144
\end{array}
$$

9 | DIVIDING DECIMALS

Division is a lot easier than multiplication. All you have to do is align your numbers, and the placement of the decimal point will take care of itself.

See what you can do with this problem:

$$9)\overline{18.00}$$

Solution:

$$
\begin{array}{r}
2.00 \\
9)\overline{18.00}
\end{array}
$$

Here's one that's a little tricky. See if you can work it out, and then check my solution below.

$$1.5)\overline{4.50}$$

Solution:

$$
\begin{array}{r}
3.0 \\
1.5)\overline{4.50} = 15)\overline{45.0}
\end{array}
$$

I wanted to get rid of the decimal point in the 1.5, so I moved it one place to the right; then to keep things even, I had to move the decimal point one place to the right in the 4.50. It's a lot easier to divide 15 into 45 than it is to divide 1.5 into 4.50.

What we did, then, by moving the decimal point one place to the right was to multiply each of these numbers by 10. Whenever you want to multiply a number by 10, just move its decimal point one place to the right. For instance, if you had $10.00 and moved its decimal one place to the right, how much money would you end up with? You'd end up with $100.0, or $100.00. (You can always tack on zeros after, or to the right of, the decimal point without changing the value of the number.)

Now let's set up the original problem as a fraction:

$$\frac{4.50}{1.5}$$

When you have a fraction, you always divide the denominator, or bottom, into the numerator, or top. Always!

So we have the fraction: $\frac{1.5}{4.50}$ Now if we multiplied the numerator 1.5 by 10, we would get 15. And if we multiplied the denominator, 4.50 by 10, we would get 45.0. What gives us the right to do this? That old law of arithmetic that says, what you do to the top of a fraction you must do to the bottom, or vice versa.

Now let's apply all this information by doing this problem:

$$1.23\overline{)9.84}$$

Solution:

$$1.23\overline{)9.84} = 123\overline{)984} \quad \begin{array}{r} 8 \\ \underline{-984} \end{array}$$

Now do another group of problems:

1. $1.6\overline{)9.6}$ 2. $0.41\overline{)1.354}$

3. $4.06\overline{)10.7}$ 4. $0.35\overline{)5}$

Solutions:

1. $1.6\overline{)9.6} = 16\overline{)96}$ (quotient 6)

2. $0.41\overline{)1.354} = 41\overline{)135.4}$ 3.3 R1

$$\begin{array}{r} 3.3\ R1 \\ 41\overline{)135.4} \\ \underline{-123}\ x \\ 12\ 4 \\ \underline{-12\ 3} \\ 1 \end{array}$$

3. $4.06\overline{)10.7} = 406\overline{)1070}$ 2 R258

$$\begin{array}{r} 2\ R258 \\ 406\overline{)1070} \\ \underline{-812} \\ 258 \end{array}$$

$$\begin{array}{r} 14\ R10 \\ 4.\quad 0.35\overline{)5} = 35\overline{)500} \\ \underline{-35x} \\ 150 \\ \underline{-140} \\ 10 \end{array}$$

11 When we divide, we sometimes need to carry out our division to just one or two decimal places. Suppose we want to round off a number to one decimal, or tenth. For example, the decimal .66 rounded off to the nearest tenth would be .7. Carry your division to one decimal place in this problem set:

1. $0.52\overline{)9.1}$ 2. $1.33\overline{)6}$

3. $10.5\overline{)12}$ 4. $0.357\overline{)1.6}$

Solutions:

$$\begin{array}{r} 17.5 \\ 1.\quad 0.52\overline{)9.1} = 52\overline{)910.0} \\ \underline{-52x\ x} \\ 390 \\ \underline{-364} \\ 26\ 0 \\ \underline{-26\ 0} \end{array}$$

$$\begin{array}{r} 4.51 = 4.5 \\ 2.\qquad 1.33\overline{)6} = 133\overline{)600.00} \\ \underline{-532\ xx} \\ 68\ 0 \\ \underline{66\ 5} \\ 1\ 50 \\ \underline{-1\ 33} \end{array}$$

$$\begin{array}{r} 1.14 = 1.1 \\ 3.\quad 10.5\overline{)12} = 105\overline{)120.00} \\ \underline{-105\ xx} \\ 15\ 0 \\ \underline{-10\ 5} \\ 4\ 50 \\ \underline{-4\ 20} \end{array}$$

$$\begin{array}{r} 4.48 = 4.5 \\ 4.\quad 0.357\overline{)1.6} = 357\overline{)1600.00} \\ \underline{-1428\ xx} \\ 172\ 0 \\ \underline{-142\ 8} \\ 29\ 20 \\ \underline{-28\ 56} \end{array}$$

PRETEST 1.3 Change the following fractions into decimals:

1. a. $\dfrac{7}{8}$ 2. a. $\dfrac{29}{100}$ 3. a. $\dfrac{319}{1000}$

  b. $\dfrac{6}{10}$ b. $\dfrac{8}{10}$ b. $\dfrac{44}{100}$

  c. $\dfrac{5}{16}$ c. $\dfrac{83}{100}$ c. $\dfrac{699}{1000}$

4. Convert these improper fractions to decimals and carry out your division to one decimal place:

a. $\dfrac{15}{7}$ b. $\dfrac{7}{3}$ c. $\dfrac{22}{5}$

Answers to Pretest 1.3

1. a. .9 (or .88, or .875) b. .6 c. $16\overline{)5.00}$ gives $.31 = .3$
   $$-4\,8x$$
   $$20$$

2. a. 2.9
   b. .8
   c. .83

3. a. .319
   b. .44
   c. .699

4. a. $7\overline{)15.^{1}0^{3}0}$ gives $2.1\ 4 = 2.1$
   b. $3\overline{)7.^{1}0^{1}0}$ gives $2.3\ 3 = 2.3$
   c. $5\overline{)22.^{2}0}$ gives $4.\ 4$

If you got everything right on Pretest 1.3, go directly to frame 16. If not, then work your way through frames 12 through 17.

12 CONVERTING PROPER FRACTIONS INTO DECIMALS

Coverting a fraction into a decimal is a simple problem of division. For instance, try converting $\frac{1}{4}$ into a decimal. Were you able to do it? Did you get .25? Here's how I did it:

$$\frac{1}{4} = 4\overline{)1.00} = .25$$

The big question is why do we divide the 4 into the 1? The rule is, whenever you have a fraction, it may be read as follows: divide the top number by the bottom number, or the numerator by the denominator.

You may raise the objection that you can't divide 4 into 1. It doesn't fit. Although it's true that 4 doesn't go into 1 completely, it does go in one-quarter of the way. For example, if a 400-foot train went through a 100-foot tunnel, only one-quarter of the train would be in the tunnel. So we could say that 400 goes into 100 one-quarter (or $\frac{100}{400}$) of the way.

When you divide a large number into a smaller one, your quotient, or answer, will be less than 1.

Try another one. Convert $\frac{3}{5}$ into a decimal.

Solution:

$$\frac{3}{5} = 5\overline{)3.0} = .6$$

Here are some fractions to be converted into decimals:

1. $\dfrac{5}{8}$ 2. $\dfrac{3}{4}$ 3. $\dfrac{5}{12}$

Solutions:

1. $\dfrac{5}{8} = 8\overline{)5.0^20^40}$ .625

2. $\dfrac{3}{4} = 4\overline{)3.0^20}$ .75

3. $\dfrac{5}{12} = 12\overline{)5.000}$ .416 = .42

$$
\begin{array}{r}
.416 = .42 \\
12\overline{)5.000} \\
-4\ 8\text{xx} \\
\hline
20 \\
-12 \\
\hline
80 \\
-72 \\
\hline
\end{array}
$$

13

Do you always have to divide the denominator into the numerator to convert a fraction into a decimal? The answer is yes. But sometimes you can take a shortcut. We'll take that shortcut when we convert the fraction $\frac{3}{10}$ into a decimal.

When we divide a number by 10, we move the decimal point one place to the left. For example, we get .5 when we divide 5 by 10. What we really did was this: .5.0. The fraction $\frac{3}{10}$ may be read as 3 divided by 10. If we took the number 3, or 3.0, and divided it by 10, we'd end up with .3, or .30.

Now change the fraction $\frac{7}{10}$ into a decimal. Did you get .7? Good.

We're ready to move on to hundredths. The fraction $\frac{19}{100}$ is read as nineteen-hundredths. Can you change it into a decimal?

Solution:

$$\frac{19}{100} = .19$$

What we did was take the 19, or .19, and move the decimal two places to the left: .19.0. So when you want to divide a number by 100, just move the decimal two places to the left.

Are you ready to apply all the knowledge you've acquired so far? Try this group of problems.

Convert each of these fractions into decimals:

1. $\dfrac{4}{10}$ 2. $\dfrac{9}{10}$ 3. $\dfrac{23}{100}$ 4. $\dfrac{47}{100}$

Solutions:

1. .4   2. .9   3. .23   4. .47

14

We've talked so far about tenths and hundredths. One tenth is ten times the size of one one-hundredth. And one one-hundredth is ten times the size of one one-thousandth, which may be written as a fraction: $\frac{1}{1000}$.

Can you convert the fraction $\frac{329}{1000}$ into a decimal?

Solution:

$$\frac{329}{1000} = .329$$

Now change the fraction $\frac{821}{1000}$ into a decimal. Do it right here:

Solution:

$$\frac{821}{1000} = .821$$

Try one more set of problems before we go on. Convert these fractions into decimals:

1. $\frac{416}{1000}$ 2. $\frac{8}{10}$ 3. $\frac{333}{1000}$ 4. $\frac{17}{100}$

5. $\frac{932}{1000}$ 6. $\frac{717}{1000}$ 7. $\frac{89}{100}$ 8. $\frac{503}{1000}$

Solutions:

1. .416   2. .8   3. .333   4. .17
5. .932   6. .717   7. .89   8. .503

15 CONVERTING IMPROPER FRACTIONS INTO DECIMALS

Improper fractions—such as $\frac{9}{2}$, $\frac{14}{9}$, and $\frac{5}{3}$—are called "improper" because they have larger numerators than denominators. Now we'd like to convert these fractions into decimals. When we converted proper fractions into decimals, we divided the denominator into the numerator, or the bottom of the fraction into the top. So how do we convert improper fractions into decimals? We do it exactly the same way—by dividing the denominator into the numerator.

Convert $\frac{9}{2}$ into a decimal. I'm going to take a break for a minute or two, and maybe grab a diet soda. So go ahead and try to convert $\frac{9}{2}$ into a decimal and I'll be right back.

How did you do? Did you get 4.5?

Solution:

$$2\overline{)9.^10}^{\,4.\,5}$$

Are you ready for a problem set? Here we go. Convert these improper fractions into decimals (Carry out your division to one decimal place):

1. $\dfrac{14}{9}$ 2. $\dfrac{5}{3}$ 3. $\dfrac{21}{14}$

Solutions:

a. $\dfrac{14}{9} = 9\overline{)14.^50^50}\quad \dfrac{1.\ 5\ 5 = 1.6}{}$

b. $\dfrac{5}{3} = 3\overline{)5.^20^20}\quad \dfrac{1.\ 6\ 6 = 1.7}{}$

c. $\dfrac{21}{14} = \dfrac{3}{2} = 2\overline{)3.^10}\quad \dfrac{1.\ 5}{}$

---

16 CONVERTING MIXED NUMBERS INTO DECIMALS

So far we've converted proper fractions and improper fractions into decimals. While we're at it, we might as well convert mixed numbers into decimals. A mixed number is a whole number with a proper fraction. Examples are $1\frac{2}{3}$, $4\frac{3}{8}$, and $5\frac{1}{4}$.

Have you got any ideas about how to convert mixed numbers into decimals? Think about it for a while. Maybe I'll take another break and finish that can of soda.

All right, how can we convert a mixed number into a decimal? Believe it or not, there are two ways. First, we can convert the mixed number into an improper fraction, which can then be converted into a decimal. For instance, $1\frac{2}{3} = \frac{5}{3}$. And we know how to convert $\frac{5}{3}$ into a decimal. But a second way of converting a mixed number into a decimal may be even better. Start with $1\frac{2}{3}$. Leave the 1 alone and just convert $\frac{2}{3}$ into a decimal:

Solution:

$\dfrac{2}{3} = 3\overline{)2.0^20}\quad \dfrac{.6\ 6 = .7}{}$

So $\frac{2}{3} = .7$. Now we bring back the 1. The number 1 plus .7 = 1.7.

Which way is easier? For most people, the second way of converting mixed numbers into decimals is easier than the first. But both ways are correct.

OK, it's your turn to convert a mixed number into a decimal. Convert $1\frac{3}{8}$ into a decimal.

Solution:

$$\frac{3}{8} = 8\overline{)3.0^60} \qquad .3\ 7 = .4 \qquad 1 + .4 = 1.4$$

Are you ready for another problem set? Change these mixed numbers into decimals:

   1. $5\frac{1}{4}$ 2. $6\frac{5}{6}$ 3. $4\frac{3}{5}$

Solutions:

  1. $\dfrac{1}{4} = 4\overline{)1.0^20} \qquad .2\ 5 = .3 \qquad 5.3\ (\text{or } 5.25)$

  2. $\dfrac{5}{6} = 6\overline{)5.0^20} \qquad .8\ 3 = .8 \qquad 6.8$

  3. $\dfrac{3}{5} = 5\overline{)3.0} \qquad\ \ .6 = 6 \qquad\ \ 4.6$

17 | CONVERTING DECIMALS INTO FRACTIONS

To change fractions into decimals, we had to do some division. But changing decimals into fractions is a lot easier. Start by changing .7 into a fraction. Now it happens that .7 may be read as seven-tenths. And seven-tenths in fraction form is $\frac{7}{10}$.

When we change a number from a decimal to a fraction, it's still the same number. Just its form changes. But it still has the same numerical value.

The number .7 is changed into $\frac{7}{10}$ in two steps. The first step is to move the decimal point one place to the right: 7. By moving the decimal one place to the right, we have multiplied the number by 10. Step 2 is to put the 7 over 10: $\frac{7}{10}$. Whenever we put a number over 10, we are dividing that number by 10. So in step 1, we multiplied .7 by 10 (from .7 to 7), and in step 2 we divided 7 by 10 ($\frac{7}{10}$).

If you multiply a number by 10 and then divide it by 10, do you change its value? Not at all!

Another way of putting it is this:

$$.7 = \frac{.7}{1} = \frac{.7 \times 10}{1 \times 10} = \frac{7}{10}$$

Are you ready to convert another decimal into a fraction? Convert .33 into a fraction.

Solution:

$$.33 = \frac{.33}{1} = \frac{.33 \times 100}{1 \times 100} = \frac{33}{100}$$

It works the same way with thousandths. Convert .489 into fractional form:

Solution:

$$.489 = \frac{.489}{1} = \frac{.489 \times 1000}{1 \times 1000} = \frac{489}{1000}$$

Did you get that one right? Let me summarize what we're doing. When we have a decimal, like .5, its fractional form is $\frac{5}{10}$. So we move the decimal one place to the right and then place the number over 10. When we change a decimal like .43 to a fraction, we move the decimal point two places to the right and place the number over 100: $\frac{43}{100}$. And when we change a decimal like .974 to a fraction, we move the decimal three places to the right and put the number over 1000: $\frac{974}{1000}$.

Let's put that all together by doing this problem set. Convert these decimals to fractions:

    1. .9   2. .61   3. .807   4. .92   5. .763   6. .5

Solutions:

1. $.9 = \frac{.9}{1} = \frac{.9 \times 10}{1 \times 10} = \frac{9}{10}$

2. $.61 = \frac{.61}{1} = \frac{.61 \times 100}{1 \times 100} = \frac{61}{100}$

3. $.807 = \frac{.807}{1} = \frac{.807 \times 1000}{1 \times 1000} = \frac{807}{1000}$

4. $.92 = \frac{.92}{1} = \frac{.92 \times 100}{1 \times 100} = \frac{92}{100}$ or $\frac{23}{25}$

5. $.763 = \frac{.763}{1} = \frac{.763 \times 1000}{1 \times 1000} = \frac{763}{1000}$

6. $.5 = \frac{.5}{1} = \frac{.5 \times 10}{1 \times 10} = \frac{5}{10}$ or $\frac{1}{2}$

PRETEST 1.4   Ready for another pretest? Do these problem sets:

1. a. Add –4 and –9.

   b. Add –11 and –8.

   c. Add –5 and –12.

2. a.   –8   b.   +5   c.   –11
         +1   –2   + 4
         –9   –9   – 7
         +4   +3   + 2

3. a. Subtract –6 from –5.

   b. Subtract –8 from +3.

   c. Subtract –12 from –4.

   d. Subtract –15 from +9.

   e. Subtract –14 from –6.

Answers to Pretest 1.4

1. a. –13   b. –19   c. –17
2. a. –12   b.   –3   c. –12
3. a.   +1   b. +11   c.   +8   d. +24   e. +8

Adding and subtracting negative numbers is done not just in business math, but in algebra as well. If you got everything right in Pretest 4, then you may skip frames 18, 19 and 20 and go directly to the Chapter 1 Self-Test. If you did get a perfect score, but would still like a review of negative numbers, then finish the last few pages of this chapter before taking the Chapter 1 Self-Test.

18 ADDING NEGATIVE NUMBERS

Negative numbers can be added, subtracted, multiplied, and divided. Just like positive numbers. First we'll do addition.

Add –2 plus –3. What did you get? Your answer should be –5. Let's say I already owed you two cups of sugar. If I borrowed three more, then I'd owe you five.

Suppose you were playing poker with your buddies. It was just before you were going to call it a night, and you were $5 in the hole.

You played double or nothing. And lost. How much would you owe? You would owe $10. Or, arithmetically: –5 (+) –5 = –10.

Doesn't that look a lot like subtraction? It should, because when you start with one number and add to it a negative number, the number you end up with is lower than the number you started with.

How much is +3 and –7? Do it right here:

The answer is –4. If this is not clear, then we'll go back to the poker game. You arrive with $3 in your pocket. During the evening you lose $7. How much do you go home with?

Well, that $3 you brought is gone. But if you lost a total of $7, then you still owe $4. So you go home owing $4. In other words, you started the evening with +$3 and ended it with –$4.

Now do this group of problems:

1. Add 3 and –9.   2. Add 5 and –6.

3. Add –8 and +5.   4. Add –5 and +2.

Solutions:

   1. –6   2. –1   3. –3   4. –3

That wasn't so hard now, was it? If it was, go back to the beginning of this section and start over again. If not, then I've got some more problems for you to do:

1. Add –3 and –8.   2. Add –5 and –7.   3. Add –10 and –15.

Solutions:

   1. –11   2. –12   3. –25

As you've observed, adding two negative numbers is very easy. Just add the numbers and keep the negative sign.

One more set of problems and we'll be ready to go on to subtraction. Add each of these set of numbers:

1.	–2	2.	+3	3.	+8	4.	–5
	+5		–7		–4		+3
	+4		+2		+3		–9
	–1		–1		–6		+6

Solutions:

You can do these a couple of ways. One way is to add the positive numbers and then add the negative numbers. In (1) we'd take +9 and subtract 3, getting +6. In (2) we take +5 and add –8 getting –3.

A second way to do these is to keep a running total in your head. In (3) we have $+8 - 4 = +4$; $+4 + 3 = +7$; $+7 - 6 = +1$. And in (4) $-5 + 3 = -2$; $-2 - 9 = -11$; $-11 + 6 = -5$.

Either way our answers come out the same:

1. +6   2. −3   3. +1   4. −5

19   SUBTRACTING NEGATIVE NUMBERS

Ready for some subtraction? Subtract −7 from −3. What's your answer? It should be +4. That's right! Imagine that you did your income taxes and figured out that you owed the government $3,000. You didn't have the money, so you enclosed a note with your tax return saying that you'd send them the money in a few months. But a few months later the Internal Revenue Service informed you that you had made a $7,000 mistake on your tax return, and that it was sending you a $4,000 refund.

Here's another problem. Subtract −5 from −9. What did you get? The right answer is −4. Here's the orthodox way of doing this: $-9 - (-5) = -9 + 5 = -4$. In other words, subtracting a −4 is really the same thing as adding a +4.

And finally, one last subtraction example. Subtract −6 from −4. Do it right here:

Solution: $-4 - (-6) = -4 + 6 = +2$

Let's recap. Start with −4. Subtract −6. Which is like adding +6. So, $-4 + 6 = +2$.

This gives us a rule of subtraction. When you subtract a negative number, it's the same as if you were adding the same number, but with a plus sign. For example, subtracting −5 is the same as adding +5.

Here's a chance to apply all the knowledge you've just acquired:

1. Subtract −8 from −7.   2. Subtract −5 from +3.

3. Subtract −3 from −7.   4. Subtract −9 from −7.

5. Subtract −10 from +4.   6. Subtract −12 from −7.

Solutions:

1.	+1	2.	+8	3.	−4
4.	+2	5.	+14	6.	+5

20

Business math is basically arithmetic. After taking the pretests in this chapter, you have a pretty good idea whether or not your arithmetic skills are up to par. If you'd like some extra help, I recommend a couple of books, both available from John Wiley & Sons, Inc. or your local bookstore. *Quick Arithmetic* by Robert and Marilyn Carmen, and *All the Math You'll Ever Need* by Steve Slavin (who happens to be me), will quickly bring your arithmetic skills up to par.

Before going on to algebra in the next chapter, you've got just one more test to take. This will not only test your knowledge but also serve as a review of the work we have covered in this chapter.

SELF-TEST

1. a. $\begin{array}{r} 24{,}000 \\ \times\,3{,}000 \\ \hline \end{array}$ b. $\begin{array}{r} 2{,}800{,}000 \\ \times\,700{,}000 \\ \hline \end{array}$

2. a. $5{,}000\overline{)125{,}000}$ b. $90{,}000\overline{)4{,}500{,}000}$

3. a. $\begin{array}{r} 7.8 \\ \times\,1.9 \\ \hline \end{array}$ b. $\begin{array}{r} 6.33 \\ \times\,2.08 \\ \hline \end{array}$

4. a. $0.89\overline{)1.916}$ b. $1.174\overline{)12}$

5. Change these fractions into decimals:

   a. $\dfrac{7}{10}$ b. $\dfrac{49}{100}$ c. $\dfrac{613}{1000}$

6. Convert these improper fractions to decimals and carry out your division to one decimal place:

   a. $\dfrac{13}{6}$ b. $\dfrac{41}{5}$

7. Do these problems:

   a. Add –5 and –8.   b. Add –3 and –14.

   c. $\begin{array}{r} -3 \\ +2 \\ +8 \\ -10 \\ \hline \end{array}$ d. $\begin{array}{r} +4 \\ -9 \\ -5 \\ +2 \\ \hline \end{array}$

   e. Subtract –5 from –14.

   f. Subtract –4 from +3.

ANSWERS

1. a. 24
    ×3
    ‾‾‾‾‾‾‾‾
    72,000,000

   b. ^{5}28
    × 7
    ‾‾‾‾‾‾‾‾‾‾‾‾‾‾
    1,960,000,000,000

2. a. 2 5
    5)12^{2}5

   b. 50
    9)450

3. a. 7.8
    ×1.9
    ‾‾‾‾‾
    702
    78
    ‾‾‾‾‾
    14.82

   b. 6.33
    ×2.08
    ‾‾‾‾‾
    5064
    12 660
    ‾‾‾‾‾
    13.1664

4. a. 2.15 = 2.2
    89)191.60
    −178 xx
    ‾‾‾‾‾‾‾
    13^{1}6
    −8 9
    ‾‾‾‾‾
    4 70
    −4 45
    ‾‾‾‾‾

   b. 10.22 = 10.2
    1174)12000.00
    −1174x xx
    ‾‾‾‾‾‾‾‾
    260 0
    −234 8
    ‾‾‾‾‾‾
    25 20
    −22 48
    ‾‾‾‾‾‾

5. a. $\dfrac{7}{10}$ = .7

   b. $\dfrac{49}{100}$ = .49

   c. $\dfrac{613}{1000}$ = .613

6. a. 2. 1 6 = 2.2
    6)13.^{1}0^{4}0

   b. 8. 2
    5)41.^{1}0

7. a. −13   b. −17   c. −3

   d. −8   e. −9   f. +7

2 Simple Algebra

How much algebra have you forgotten since you were in school? Well, I have some good news and some bad news. The bad news is that you're going to need to know some algebra to do business math. But the good news is that you'll need to know just a few concepts that are usually covered in elementary algebra.

We're going to follow the same procedure that we followed in the last chapter. You'll take some pretests. And when you get all the answers right, you can skip the work in the next section and go directly to the next pretest. When you get some wrong, you should read the frames that come after the pretest. Here's the first one.

PRETEST 2.1

1. In each of these problems, solve for *x*:

   a. $x - 5 = 9$ b. $x + 4 = 13$
   c. $x + 10 = 12$ d. $x - 5 = 18$

2. Solve for *x* in each of these problems:

   a. $x + 4 = -2$ b. $x + 3 = -9$
   c. $x + 11 = 0$ d. $x + 6 = 3$

Answers to Pretest 2.1

1. a.
$$x - 5 = 9$$
$$x - 5 + 5 = 9 + 5$$
$$x = 14$$

   b.
$$x + 4 = 13$$
$$x + 4 - 4 = 13 - 4$$
$$x = 9$$

   c.
$$x + 10 = 12$$
$$x + 10 - 10 = 12 - 10$$
$$x = 2$$

   d.
$$x - 5 = 18$$
$$x - 5 + 5 = 18 + 5$$
$$x = 23$$

2. a.
$$x + 4 = -2$$
$$x + 4 - 4 = -2 - 4$$
$$x = -6$$

   b.
$$x + 3 = -9$$
$$x + 3 - 3 = -9 - 3$$
$$x = -12$$

   c.
$$x + 11 = 0$$
$$x + 11 - 11 = 0 - 11$$
$$x = 11$$

   d.
$$x + 6 = 3$$
$$x + 6 - 6 = 3 - 6$$
$$x = -3$$

We're going to get strict now. If you found the correct answer for each of these problems, then you're ready for Pretest 2.2. But if you got even one problem wrong, then you should read frames 1 through 4.

1   Isolating *x* by Adding and Subtracting

Remember that we have only one objective in this chapter—to find *x*. We can easily find *x* if it can be isolated.

Problem:

If $x - 5 = 3$, how much is *x*? Try to work it out right here. Don't worry about methodology—just write down your answer.

Solution:
$$x - 5 = 3$$
$$x - 5 + 5 = 3 + 5$$
$$x = 8$$

To isolate *x* we added 5 to both sides of the equation. Now let's check our work. Go back to the original equation, $x - 5 = 3$ and substitute your answer, 8, for *x*. Does it work?

Check:
$$x - 5 = 3$$
$$8 - 5 = 3$$
$$3 = 3$$

So it checks.

Problem:

If $x - 7 = 9$, how much is *x*?

Solution:
$$x - 7 = 9$$
$$x - 7 + 7 = 9 + 7$$
$$x = 16$$

Here we added 7 to both sides. Why are we allowed to do that? The rule is that what we do to one side of the equation, we must do to the other side as well. If it served our purposes in another problem, we could subtract the same number from both sides of an equation.

We found in the last problem that x is 16. Now check your work to make sure that 16 is the right answer.

Check:
$$x - 7 = 9$$
$$16 - 7 = 9$$
$$9 = 9$$

Problem:

$x - 6 = 11$. How much is x?

Solution:
$$x - 6 = 11$$
$$x - 6 + 6 = 11 + 6$$
$$x = 17$$

Now check your work:

Check:
$$x - 6 = 11$$
$$17 - 6 = 11$$
$$11 = 11$$

Problem:
$$x + 4 = 18$$

Solution:
$$x + 4 = 18$$
$$x + 4 - 4 = 18 - 4$$
$$x = 14$$

I won't continue to show how we check answers, but it would be a good idea for you to keep checking.

Problem:

$x + 9 = 10$. How much is x?

Solution:

$$x + 9 = 10$$
$$x + 9 - 9 = 10 - 9$$
$$x = 1$$

2

Still a little confused about whether to add or subtract? Then remember, we want to isolate x. In the last problem, $x + 9 = 10$, we had to get rid of the +9. We did that by adding −9 to both sides of the equation. In the first three problems, we needed to add positive (+) numbers to both sides of the equation so we could isolate x.

Well, we're finally ready for our first problem set:

1. $x - 5 = 16$ 2. $x + 8 = 14$

3. $x + 5 = 12$ 4. $x - 12 = 21$

Solutions:

1.
$$x - 5 = 16$$
$$x - 5 + 5 = 16 + 5$$
$$x = 21$$

2.
$$x + 8 = 14$$
$$x + 8 - 8 = 14 - 8$$
$$x = 6$$

3.
$$x + 5 = 12$$
$$x + 5 - 5 = 12 - 5$$
$$x = 7$$

4.
$$x - 12 = 21$$
$$x - 12 + 12 = 21 + 12$$
$$x = 33$$

Try this problem: $x + 4 = 2$.

3

Solution:

$$x + 4 = 2$$
$$x + 4 - 4 = 2 - 4$$
$$x = -2$$

Here we did exactly what we did in every preceding problem to isolate x and then find its value. But its value happens to be negative. How can that be? Let's think of an example in which x can be negative.

Let x equal the money you owed (in millions of dollars) before you won the lottery. You won $4 million in the lottery. After you paid off your debts, you still had $2 million left from your lottery winnings. So, your debts had been $2 million—before the lottery you had −$2 million. The number is negative because it represents the money you owed.

The whole point is that x can certainly be negative. Now solve for x in this problem.

Solution:

$$x + 9 = -8$$
$$x + 9 - 9 = -8 - 9$$
$$x = -17$$

Hmmm, they seem to be getting a little harder. Actually, that's about as hard as they get—for now.

Do this group of problems:

1. $x + 7 = 5$ 2. $x + 6 = -16$

3. $x + 7 = 0$ 4. $x + 4 = -3$

Solutions:

1. $x + 7 = 5$ 2. $x + 6 = -16$
     $x + 7 - 7 = 5 - 7$ $x + 6 - 6 = -16 - 6$
     $x = -2$ $x = -22$

3. $x + 7 = 0$ 4. $x + 4 = -3$
     $x + 7 - 7 = 0 - 7$ $x + 4 - 4 = -3 - 4$
     $x = -7$ $x = -7$

4

Did you get all these right? If you did, go on to Pretest 2.2. And if you didn't? Well, then, it could be either of two things. If you got everything right in this chapter until we hit negative numbers, then try going back to frames 18 and 19 in the previous chapter, which happen to do a great job of explaining negative numbers. But if your problem is with the algebra, then you should try beginning this chapter over again. Work out each problem a second time. I think you'll find things much easier.

PRETEST 2.2

Solve for *x* in each of these problems:

1. a. $4x = 20$ $x = 5$ 2. a. $\dfrac{5x}{3} = 10$ $x = 6$ 3. a. $\dfrac{8x}{3} - 7 = 1$

   b. $8x = 56$ $x = 7$ b. $\dfrac{7x}{2} = 14$ $x = 4$ b. $\dfrac{3x}{7} - 4 = 2$

   c. $\dfrac{x}{2} = 10$ $x = 20$ c. $\dfrac{2x}{5} = 6$ $x = 15$ c. $\dfrac{5x}{9} + 4 = 2$

   d. $\dfrac{x}{4} = 32$ $x = 128$ d. $\dfrac{3x}{7} + 5 = 6$

Answers to Pretest 2.2

1. a. $4x = 20$ b. $8x = 56$
       $\dfrac{4x}{4} = \dfrac{20}{4}$ $\dfrac{8x}{8} = \dfrac{56}{8}$
       $x = 5$ $x = 7$

c. $\dfrac{x}{2} = 10$

$\dfrac{{}^{1}\cancel{2}}{1} \times \dfrac{x}{\cancel{2}_1} = 2 \times 10$

$x = 20$

d. $\dfrac{x}{4} = 32$

$\dfrac{{}^{1}\cancel{4}}{1} \times \dfrac{x}{\cancel{4}_1} = 4 \times 32$

$x = 128$

2. a. $\dfrac{5x}{3} = 10$

$\dfrac{{}^{1}\cancel{3}}{1} \times \dfrac{5x}{\cancel{3}_1} = 3 \times 10$

$5x = 30$

$x = 6$

b. $\dfrac{7x}{2} = 14$

$\dfrac{{}^{1}\cancel{2}}{1} \times \dfrac{7x}{\cancel{2}_1} = 2 \times 14$

$7x = 28$

$x = 4$

c. $\dfrac{2x}{5} = 6$

$\dfrac{{}^{1}\cancel{5}}{1} \times \dfrac{2x}{\cancel{5}_1} = 5 \times 6$

$2x = 30$

$x = 15$

3. a. $\dfrac{8x}{3} - 7 = 1$

$\dfrac{{}^{1}\cancel{3}}{1} \times \dfrac{8x}{\cancel{3}_1} - (3 \times 7) = 3 \times 1$

$8x - 21 = 3$

$8x - 21 + 21 = 3 + 21$

$8x = 24$

$x = 3$

b. $\dfrac{3x}{7} - 4 = 2$

$\dfrac{{}^{1}\cancel{7}}{1} \times \dfrac{3x}{\cancel{7}_1} - (7 \times 4) = 7 \times 2$

$3x - 28 = 14$

$3x - 28 + 28 = 14 + 28$

$3x = 42$

$x = 14$

c. $\dfrac{5x}{9} + 4 = 2$

$\dfrac{{}^{1}\cancel{9}}{1} \times \dfrac{5x}{\cancel{9}_1} + (9 \times 4) = 9 \times 2$

$5x + 36 = 18$

$5x + 36 - 36 = 18 - 36$

$5x = -18$

$x = -3\tfrac{3}{5}$

d. $\dfrac{3x}{7} + 5 = 6$

$\dfrac{{}^{1}\cancel{7}}{1} \times \dfrac{3x}{\cancel{7}_1} + (7 \times 5) = 7 \times 6$

$3x + 35 = 42$

$3x + 35 - 35 = 42 - 35$

$3x = 7$

$x = 2\tfrac{1}{3}$

Again we must reach perfection. If your answers were perfect, proceed to Pretest 2.3 later in this chapter. But if you got even one wrong answer, read frames 5 through 8.

5 | Isolating *x* by Dividing

Let's begin by repeating one of those universal rules of mathematics: What you do to one side of the equation, you must do to the other side as well. In the last section when we added a number to one side, we also had to add that number to the other side. And when a number was subtracted from one side of an equation, the same number was also subtracted from the other side.

Problem:

   $2x = 10$. Find x.

Solution:

   $2x = 10$
   $x = 5$

Problem:

   $3x = 21$

Solution:

   $3x = 21$
   $x = 7$

Solve for x in this group of problems by dividing these:

1. $5x = 100$ 2. $6x = 24$

3. $8x = 40$ 4. $7x = 56$

Solutions:

1. $5x = 100$ 2. $6x = 24$
   $x = 20$ $x = 4$

3. $8x = 40$ 4. $7x = 56$
   $x = 5$ $x = 8$

---

6 Isolating *x* by Multiplying

Remember that what we do to one side of the equation, we must do to the other side as well. So far in this section, we've been dividing both sides by the same number so we can isolate x.

Problem:

$$\frac{x}{2} = 9. \text{ Find } x.$$

Solution:

$$\frac{x}{2} = 9$$

$$\frac{1\cancel{2}}{1} \times \frac{x}{\cancel{2}_1} = 9 \times 2$$

$$x = 18$$

Problem:

$$\frac{x}{3} = 5$$

Solution:

$$\frac{x}{3} = 5$$

$$\frac{{}^1\cancel{3}}{1} \times \frac{x}{\cancel{3}_1} = 5 \times 3$$

$$x = 15$$

We're going to get a little fancier with the next problem:

Find x if $\dfrac{3x}{2} = 6$.

Solution:

$$\frac{3x}{2} = 6$$

$$\frac{{}^1\cancel{2}}{1} \times \frac{3x}{\cancel{2}_1} = 2 \times 6$$

$$3x = 12$$
$$x = 4$$

Let's try one more.

Find x if $\dfrac{4x}{3} = 12$

Solution:

$$\frac{4x}{3} = 12$$

$$\frac{{}^1\cancel{3}}{1} \times \frac{4x}{\cancel{3}_1} = 3 \times 12$$

$$4x = 36$$
$$x = 9$$

Do this group of problems:

1. Find x if $\dfrac{x}{4} = 2$

2. Find x if $\dfrac{x}{3} = 5$

3. Find x if $\dfrac{5x}{4} = 5$

4. Find x if $\dfrac{2x}{5} = 8$

Solutions:

1. $$\frac{x}{4} = 2$$

$$\frac{{}^1\cancel{4}}{1} \times \frac{x}{\cancel{4}_1} = 2 \times 4$$

2. $$\frac{x}{3} = 5$$

$$\frac{{}^1\cancel{3}}{1} \times \frac{x}{\cancel{3}_1} = 3 \times 5$$

$$x = 8$$
$$x = 15$$

3. $\dfrac{5x}{4} = 5$

$\dfrac{1\cancel{4}}{1} \times \dfrac{5x}{\cancel{4}_1} = 5 \times 4$

$5x = 20$

$x = 4$

4. $\dfrac{2x}{5} = 8$

$\dfrac{1\cancel{5}}{1} \times \dfrac{2x}{\cancel{5}_1} = 8 \times 5$

$2x = 40$

$x = 20$

7 Isolating *x* by Combining Addition, Subtraction, Multiplication, and Division

The title of this frame says it all. Let's get right into it.

Problem:

$$\text{Find } x \text{ if } \dfrac{3x}{4} + 2 = 11$$

Solution:

$$\dfrac{3x}{4} + 2 = 11$$

$$\dfrac{1\cancel{4}}{1} \times \dfrac{3x}{\cancel{4}_1} + (4 \times 2) = 11 \times 4$$

$$3x + 8 = 44$$

$$3x + 8 - 8 = 44 - 8$$

$$3x = 36$$

$$x = 12$$

Let's go over that problem step-by-step:

1. Multiply both sides by 4.

2. On the left side we're multiplying both terms by 4.

3. So we multiply $\frac{3x}{4}$ by 4 and we multiply 2 by 4.

4. We place 4×2 in parenthesis, (4×2), to make sure that we multiply the numbers inside those parentheses before we add them to $3x$. Why do we multiply before we add? It's another law of arithmetic.

5. The rest of the problem is straightforward.

That problem really gave you a chance to put it all together. Don't worry—this is as hard as it gets. And once you have a few more of these under your belt, you'll be able to do them with your eyes closed.

Problem:

$$\text{Find } x \text{ if } \frac{2x}{5} - 6 = 10$$

Solution:

$$\frac{2x}{5} - 6 = 10$$

$$\frac{1\cancel{5}}{1} \times \frac{2x}{\cancel{5}_1} - (5 \times 6) = 5 \times 10$$

$$2x - 30 = 50$$
$$2x - 30 + 30 = 50 + 30$$
$$2x = 80$$
$$x = 40$$

Let's summarize what we did here. First we multiplied both sides of the equation by 5. Note that once again we placed our multiplication, (5 × 6), in parenthesis. Why did we do this? To make sure that we multiplied 5 times 6 *before* we subtracted their product, 30, from *2x*. There's yet another law of arithmetic that tells us that we *must* multiply before we subtract. Or, to generalize, the law says that we must multiply before we either add or subtract.

Problem:

$$\text{Find } x \text{ if } \frac{3x}{4} + 3 = 0$$

Solution:

$$\frac{3x}{4} + 3 = 0$$

$$\frac{1\cancel{4}}{1} \times \frac{3x}{\cancel{4}_1} + (4 \times 3) = 0 \times 4$$

$$3x + 12 = 0$$
$$3x + 12 - 12 = 0 - 12$$
$$3x = -12$$
$$x = -4$$

You'll notice that we carried out this problem exactly like the previous ones. The only real difference was multiplying 4 times 0. *Any* number times 0 is 0.

Work out this group of problems:

1. $\dfrac{2x}{3} - 6 = 8$

2. $\dfrac{9x}{2} + 3 = 39$

3. $\dfrac{2x}{5} - 6 = 4$

4. $\dfrac{7x}{3} + 7 = 0$

Solutions:

1. $$\frac{2x}{3} - 6 = 8$$

$$\frac{\cancel{3}^1}{1} \times \frac{2x}{\cancel{3}_1} - (3 \times 6) = 8 \times 3$$

$$2x - 18 = 24$$
$$2x - 18 + 18 = 24 + 18$$
$$2x = 42$$
$$x = 21$$

2. $$\frac{9x}{2} + 3 = 39$$

$$\frac{\cancel{2}^1}{1} \times \frac{9x}{\cancel{2}_1} + (2 \times 3) = 39 \times 2$$

$$9x + 6 = 78$$
$$9x + 6 - 6 = 78 - 6$$
$$9x = 72$$
$$x = 8$$

3. $$\frac{2x}{5} - 6 = 4$$

$$\frac{\cancel{5}^1}{1} \times \frac{2x}{\cancel{5}_1} - (5 \times 6) = 5 \times 4$$

$$2x - 30 = 20$$
$$2x - 30 + 30 = 20 + 30$$
$$2x = 50$$
$$x = 25$$

4. $$\frac{7x}{3} + 7 = 0$$

$$\frac{\cancel{3}^1}{1} \times \frac{7x}{\cancel{3}_1} - (3 \times 7) = 0 \times 3$$

$$7x + 21 = 0$$
$$7x + 21 - 21 = 0 - 21$$
$$7x = -21$$
$$x = -3$$

8 Isolating *x* with Fractions

Not everything in life can be measured solely by whole numbers. That's why we have fractions and decimals. My friend Betsy says she's 5'2$\frac{3}{4}$". (Actually, I think she's 5'1".) And how much is your normal body temperature? It's 98.6°.

The answers to the remaining problems in this section all contain fractions. And in the next section, we'll work with decimals.

Problem:

$$\frac{9x}{4} + 7 = -12. \text{ Find } x.$$

Solution:

$$\frac{9x}{4} + 7 = -12$$

$$\frac{\cancel{4}^1}{1} \times \frac{9x}{\cancel{4}_1} + (4 \times 7) = 4 \times -12$$

$$9x + 28 = -48$$
$$9x + 28 - 28 = -48 - 28$$
$$9x = -76$$
$$x = -8\frac{4}{9}$$

Do this group of problems. In each case find x.

1. $\dfrac{7x}{2} - 6 = 3$

2. $\dfrac{2x}{3} + 1 = 4$

3. $\dfrac{7x}{9} - 4 = 12$

4. $\dfrac{4x}{5} + 2 = 0$

Solutions:

1.
$$\frac{7x}{2} - 6 = 3$$
$$\frac{{}^1\!\cancel{2}}{1} \times \frac{7x}{\cancel{2}_1} - (2 \times 6) = 3 \times 2$$
$$7x - 12 = 6$$
$$7x - 12 + 12 = 6 + 12$$
$$7x = 18$$
$$x = 2\tfrac{4}{7}$$

2.
$$\frac{2x}{3} + 1 = 4$$
$$\frac{{}^1\!\cancel{3}}{1} \times \frac{2x}{\cancel{3}_1} + (3 \times 1) = 3 \times 4$$
$$2x + 3 = 12$$
$$2x + 3 - 3 = 12 - 3$$
$$2x = 9$$
$$x = 4\tfrac{1}{2}$$

3.
$$\frac{7x}{9} - 4 = 12$$
$$\frac{{}^1\!\cancel{9}}{1} \times \frac{7x}{\cancel{9}_1} - (9 \times 4) = 9 \times 12$$
$$7x - 36 = 108$$
$$7x - 36 + 36 = 108 + 36$$
$$7x = 144$$
$$x = 20\tfrac{4}{7}$$

4.
$$\frac{4x}{5} + 2 = 0$$
$$\frac{{}^1\!\cancel{5}}{1} \times \frac{4x}{\cancel{5}_1} - (5 \times 2) = 0 \times 5$$
$$4x + 10 = 0$$
$$4x + 10 - 10 = 0 - 10$$
$$4x = -10$$
$$x = -2\tfrac{1}{2}$$

All right, I'll admit it. Some of these were pretty hard. So if you're not confident about doing these problems, why not go back to the beginning of this frame, reread it, and redo each of the problems?

PRETEST 2.3

Solve for x in each of these problems:

1. $5.3x = 9$

2. $.7x = 12$

3. $11.8x = 18$

Answers to Pretest 2.3

1. $5.3x = 9$

$$\frac{5.3x}{5.3} = \frac{9}{5.3}$$

$$x = 1.7$$

$$
\begin{array}{r}
1.7 \\
5.3\overline{)9} = 53\overline{)90.0} \\
-53 \\
\hline
370 \\
-371 \\
\end{array}
$$

2. $.7x = 12$

$$\frac{.7x}{.7} = \frac{12}{.7}$$

$$x = 17.1$$

$$.7\overline{)12} = 7\overline{)12^50.^10^30} \quad \begin{array}{c} 1\ 7.\ 1\ 4 = 17.1 \end{array}$$

3. $11.8x = 18$

$$\frac{11.8x}{11.8} = \frac{18}{11.8}$$

$$x = 1.5$$

$$11.8\overline{)18} = 118\overline{)180}$$

$$59\overline{)90.00} \quad \begin{array}{c} 1.52 = 1.5 \end{array}$$
$$\underline{-59\ \text{xx}}$$
$$31\ 0$$
$$\underline{-295}$$
$$15\ 0$$
$$\underline{-11\ 8}$$

How did you do? If you got each one right, go directly to Pretest 2.4 later in this chapter. If you didn't, and you'd like a little more practice, read frames 9 and 10.

9   Isolating *x* with Decimals

Now that you've been around the track a few times, I think you're ready to have a few decimals tossed at you. You're still after just one thing: You want to get *x* all alone.

Problem:

If $.2x = 6$, how much is *x*?

Solution:

$$.2x = 6$$

$$\frac{.2x}{.2} = \frac{6}{.2}$$

$$\frac{2x}{2} = \frac{60}{2}$$

$$x = 30$$

Let's take this problem step-by-step.

1. We divide both sides of the equation by .2 to help us isolate *x*.

2. That gives us $\frac{.2x}{.2} = \frac{6}{.2}$

3. We then multiply the numerators and denominators of both fractions by 10: $\frac{2x}{2} = \frac{60}{2}$

4. We did this to make our next step, division, much easier to carry out.

5. We carry out our division: $x = 30$.

Are you still checking your work? Checking is extremely important in algebra because you'll always know when you're right. Just to make sure we're clear on how to check our work, I'll check mine too for the next couple of problems.

Problem:

$3.5x = 19$. Find x.

Solution:

$$3.5x = 19$$

$$\frac{3.5x}{3.5} = \frac{19}{3.5} \qquad 3.5\overline{)19} = 35\overline{)190} = 7\overline{)38.^30^20}$$

$$x = 5.4$$

Check:

Before we do our check, keep in mind that 5.4 is only an approximate answer, because it was rounded off. The *real* value of x is slightly more than 5.4. So when we do our check, we'll end up with a value for $3.5x$ that is slightly less than 19.

$$
\begin{array}{r}
3.5x = 19 \\
3.5\,(5.4) = 19 \\
18.9 = 19
\end{array}
\qquad
\begin{array}{r}
5.4 \\
\times\ 3.5 \\
\hline
2\ 70 \\
16\ 2 \\
\hline
18.90
\end{array}
$$

Problem:

Find x when $4.9x = 12$.

Solution:

$$4.9x = 12$$

$$\frac{4.9x}{4.9} = \frac{12}{4.9}$$

$$x = 2.4$$

$$
\begin{array}{r}
2.448 = 2.4 \\
4.9\overline{)12} = 49\overline{)120.000} \\
-98\ \text{xxx} \\
\hline
22\ 0 \\
-19\ 6 \\
\hline
2\ 40 \\
-1\ 96 \\
\hline
440 \\
-392 \\
\end{array}
$$

Check:

$$4.9x = 12$$
$$4.9(2.4) = 12$$
$$11.76* = 12$$

$$
\begin{array}{r}
4.9 \\
\times\ 2.4 \\
\hline
196 \\
98 \\
\hline
11.76
\end{array}
$$

Solve for x in each of these problems and continue to check your work.

1. $4.2x = 15$

2. $.3x = 7$

3. $14.5x = 29$

4. $.8x = 14$

Solutions:

1. $4.2x = 15$

$$\frac{4.2x}{4.2} = \frac{15}{4.2}$$

$$x = 3.6$$

$$
4.2\overline{)15} = 42\overline{)150} = 21\overline{)75.00}
$$
$$
\begin{array}{r}
3.57 \\
\hline
-63\ \text{xx} \\
\hline
12\ 0 \\
-10\ 5 \\
\hline
1\ 50 \\
-1\ 47
\end{array}
$$

2. $.3x = 7$

$$\frac{.3x}{.3} = \frac{7}{.3}$$

$$x = \frac{70}{3}$$

$$x = 23.3$$

3. $14.5x = 29$

$$\frac{14.5x}{14.5} = \frac{29}{14.5}$$

$$x = 2$$

$$14.5\overline{)29} = 145\overline{)290}$$
$$
\begin{array}{r}
2 \\
\hline
-290
\end{array}
$$

4. $.8x = 14$

$$\frac{.8x}{.8} = \frac{14}{.8}$$

$$x = \frac{140}{8}$$

$$x = 17.5$$

$$\frac{140}{8} = \frac{70}{4} = \frac{35}{2}$$

$$
2\overline{)35.0}
$$
$$17.5$$

---

*If we had rounded to 2.5 and then checked, $4.9x$ would have come out to 12.005.

PRETEST 2.4

Set up equations to find the answers for the following problems:

1. Fred owns 15 percent of ABC Corp., Maxine owns 20 percent, Herb owns 25 percent, and Bill owns the rest. If each shares the profits in proportion to his or her percentage of ownership, how would they split $500,000 profits?

2. Farmer A owns three times as much land as Farmer B and twice as much land as Farmer C. Farmer D owns 100 acres more than Farmer A. If they own a total of 1,800 acres, how many acres does each farmer own?

3. Joe is twice as old as Irv and four times as old as Nancy. Nancy is three years older than Amy. If their combined age is 37, how old is each person?

4. Kathy earns twice as much as Terry and half as much as Melanie. Their combined income is $210,000. How much does each person earn?

5. Sherman earns $70 a week more than Diane. Diane earns $40 more than Lori. Lori earns $50 more than Sam. The four of them earn a total of $1,500. How much does each person earn?

6. One out of 20 employees at GGG Corporation has an advanced degree. In addition, one out of 10 is a college graduate, 2 in 10 have some college, and 3 out of 10 are high school graduates. If there are 175 other employees without high school diplomas, how many employees does the company have, how many have advanced degrees, how many have college degrees, how many have some college, and how many are high school graduates?

Answers to Pretest 2.4

1. Bill's share = 100% − (15% + 20% + 25%)
             = 100% − 60%
             = 40%
    Bill's share = .40 × $500,000 = $200,000
    Fred's share = .15 × $500,000 = $75,000
    Maxine's share = .20 × $500,000 = $100,000
    Herb's share = .25 × $500,000 = $125,000

2.   Let x = Farmer B's acreage
             Let $3x$ = Farmer A's acreage
             Let $\frac{3x}{2}$ = Farmer C's acreage
             Let $3x + 100$ = Farmer D's acreage
    $x + 3x + \frac{3x}{2} + 3x + 100 = 1800$
    $7x + \frac{3x}{2} + 100 = 1800$
    $7x + \frac{3x}{2} = 1700$
    $14x + 3x = 3400$
    $17x = 3400$
    $x = 200$
    $3x = 600$
    $\frac{3x}{2} = 300$
    $3x + 100 = 700$

3.
$$
\begin{aligned}
\text{Let } x &= \text{Nancy's age} \\
\text{Let } 4x &= \text{Joe's age} \\
\text{Let } 2x &= \text{Irv's age} \\
\text{Let } x - 3 &= \text{Amy's age} \\
x + 4x + 2x + x - 3 &= 37 \\
8x - 3 &= 37 \\
8x &= 40 \\
x &= 5 \\
4x &= 20 \\
2x &= 10 \\
x - 3 &= 2
\end{aligned}
$$

4.
$$
\begin{aligned}
\text{Let } x &= \text{Terry's earnings} \\
\text{Let } 2x &= \text{Kathy's earnings} \\
\text{Let } 4x &= \text{Melanie's earnings} \\
x + 2x + 4x &= \$210{,}000 \\
7x &= \$210{,}000 \\
x &= \$30{,}000 \\
2x &= \$60{,}000 \\
4x &= \$120{,}000
\end{aligned}
$$

5.
$$
\begin{aligned}
\text{Let } x &= \text{Sam's earnings} \\
\text{Let } x + \$50 &= \text{Lori's earnings} \\
\text{Let } x + \$90 &= \text{Diane's earnings} \\
\text{Let } x + \$160 &= \text{Sherman's earnings} \\
x + x + \$50 + x + \$90 + x + \$160 &= \$1{,}500 \\
4x + \$300 &= \$1{,}500 \\
4x &= \$1{,}200 \\
x &= \$300 \\
x + \$50 &= \$350 \\
x + \$90 &= \$390 \\
x + \$160 &= \$460
\end{aligned}
$$

6. Employees without high school diplomas = 100% − (5% + 10% + 20% + 30%) = 100% − 65% = 35%.

Let x = total employment
$$
\begin{aligned}
.35x &= 175 \\
\frac{35x}{.35} &= \frac{175}{.35} \\
x &= 500
\end{aligned}
$$
$$
\begin{aligned}
\text{advanced degrees} &= .05 \times 500 = 25 \\
\text{college degrees} &= .10 \times 500 = 50 \\
\text{some college} &= .20 \times 500 = 100 \\
\text{high school grads} &= .30 \times 500 = 150
\end{aligned}
$$

How did you do? If you got these right, you're ready to move into business math, so go directly to Chapter 3. But if you need more practice working out word problems, work your way through the rest of this chapter.

11 Setting up Equations to Solve for *x*

Once we figure out what it is we're trying to find and call it *x*, we set up an equation, then substitute numbers into the equation. Then, using simple arithmetic, we solve for *x*.

Problem:

Kelly is 5 years older than Jason. The sum of their ages is 21. How old is Kelly and how old is Jason?

Solution:

$$\text{Let Jason's age} = x$$
$$\text{Let Kelly's age} = x + 5$$
$$x + x + 5 = 21$$
$$2x + 5 = 21$$
$$2x + 5 - 5 = 21 - 5$$
$$2x = 16$$
$$x = 8$$
$$x + 5 = 13$$

We could have done this a somewhat different way:

$$\text{Let } x = \text{Kelly's age}$$
$$\text{Let } x - 5 = \text{Jason's age}$$
$$x + x - 5 = 21$$
$$2x - 5 = 21$$
$$2x - 5 + 5 = 21 + 5$$
$$2x = 26$$
$$x = 13$$
$$x - 5 = 8$$

Problem:

Jessica earns twice as much as Sara. Together they earn $51,000. How much does Jessica earn and how much does Sara earn.

Solution:

$$\text{Let } x = \text{Sara's earnings}$$
$$\text{Let } 2x = \text{Jessica's earnings}$$
$$x + 2x = \$51{,}000$$
$$3x = \$51{,}000$$
$$x = \$17{,}000$$
$$2x = \$34{,}000$$

Problem:

Stan pays twice as much in taxes as Michelle does. Michelle pays twice as much in taxes as Ellen does. The three of them pay a total of $70,000. How much tax does each of them pay?

Solution:

$$
\begin{aligned}
\text{Let } x &= \text{Ellen's taxes} \\
\text{Let } 2x &= \text{Michelle's taxes} \\
\text{Let } 4x &= \text{Stan's taxes} \\
x + 2x + 4x &= \$70{,}000 \\
7x &= \$70{,}000 \\
x &= \$10{,}000 \\
2x &= \$20{,}000 \\
4x &= \$40{,}000
\end{aligned}
$$

Are you checking your answers? Let's check the last problem:

$$
\begin{aligned}
x + 2x + 4x &= \$70{,}000 \\
\$10{,}000 + \$20{,}000 + \$40{,}000 &= \$70{,}000 \\
\$70{,}000 &= \$70{,}000
\end{aligned}
$$

Before we go on to somewhat different problems, do this set of problems:

1. Sales for the year were $245,000. In the first quarter they totalled $74,000; in the second, $82,000; in the third, $53,000. How much were sales in the fourth quarter?

2. Michael is twice as old as Diane and four times as old as Kyra. The sum of their ages is 56. How old is each?

3. Roger earns $50 a week more than Marsha. Eileen earns $40 more than Roger. And Beth earns $30 a week more than Eileen. The three of them earn a total of $1,060 a week. How much does each of them earn?

4. Max is two times as old as Wendy. Wendy is twice as old as Sue. If the sum of their ages is 140, how old is each?

Solutions:

1. Let x = sales in fourth quarter

$$
\begin{aligned}
\$74{,}000 + \$82{,}000 + \$53{,}000 + x &= \$245{,}000 \\
\$209{,}000 + x &= \$245{,}000 \\
x + \$209{,}000 - \$209{,}000 &= \$245{,}000 - \$209{,}000 \\
x &= \$36{,}000
\end{aligned}
$$

2.
$$
\begin{aligned}
\text{Let } x &= \text{Kyra's age} \\
\text{Let } 4x &= \text{Michael's age} \\
\text{Let } 2x &= \text{Diane's age} \\
x + 2x + 4x &= 56 \\
7x &= 56 \\
x &= 8 \\
2x &= 16 \\
4x &= 32
\end{aligned}
$$

3.

$$\text{Let } x = \text{Marsha's earnings}$$
$$\text{Let } x + \$50 = \text{Roger's earnings}$$
$$\text{Let } x + \$90 = \text{Eileen's earnings}$$
$$\text{Let } x + \$120 = \text{Beth's earnings}$$

$$x + x + 50 + x + \$90 + x + \$120 = \$1,060$$
$$4x + \$260 = \$1,060$$
$$4x + \$260 - \$260 = \$1,060 - \$260$$
$$4x = \$800$$
$$x = \$200$$
$$x + \$50 = \$250$$
$$x + \$90 = \$290$$
$$x + \$120 = \$320$$

4.

$$\text{Let Sue's age} = x$$
$$\text{Let Wendy's age} = 2x$$
$$\text{Let Max's age} = 4x$$
$$x + 2x + 4x = 140$$
$$7x = 140$$
$$x = 20$$
$$2x = 40$$
$$4x = 80$$

12 Advanced Problems Solving for *x*

The problems coming up are closely related to some of those we've been doing these last few pages. Your first move is to let $x = $ the unknown, and your second move is to set up an equation.

Problem:

The James Madison High School orchestra has 40 members. If one-eighth are in the percussion section, one quarter are in the woodwind section, one-quarter are in the string section, and the rest are in the brass section, how many orchestra members play brass instruments?

Solution:

$$\text{Let } x = \text{number of brass players}$$

$$x + \frac{1}{8} \times 40 + \frac{1}{4} \times 40 + \frac{1}{4} \times 40 = 40$$

$$x + \frac{40}{8} + \frac{40}{4} + \frac{40}{4} = 40$$

$$x + 5 + 10 + 10 = 40$$
$$x + 25 = 40$$
$$x + 25 - 25 = 40 - 25$$
$$x = 15$$

An alternate equation would be:
$$x = 40 - (\frac{1}{8} \times 40 + \frac{1}{4} \times 40 + \frac{1}{4} \times 40)$$

Solving, we'd obtain the same answer:
$$x = 40 - (\frac{40}{8} + \frac{40}{4} + \frac{40}{4})$$
$$x = 40 - (5 + 10 + 10)$$
$$x = 40 - 25$$
$$x = 15$$

Problem:

The First National Bank of Phoenix has twice as many loans in commercial real estate as in residential real estate. It has half as many business loans as residential real estate loans. If its loans total $700 million, how much of that total is in each category?

Solution:

Let x = residential real estate loans
Let $2x$ = commercial real estate loans

Let $\frac{x}{2}$ = business loans

$$x + 2x + \frac{x}{2} = \$700 \text{ million}$$

$$3x + \frac{x}{2} = \$700 \text{ million}$$

$$\frac{2}{1} \times \frac{3x}{1} + \frac{\cancel{2}^{1}}{1} \times \frac{x}{\cancel{2}_{1}} = 2 \times \$700 \text{ million}$$

$$6x + x = \$1{,}400 \text{ million}$$
$$7x = \$1{,}400 \text{ million}$$
$$x = \$200 \text{ million}$$
$$2x = \$400 \text{ million}$$

$$\frac{x}{2} = \$100 \text{ million}$$

Another way to represent the categories of loans avoids dealing with any fractions. This simplifies our calculations:

Let x = business loans
Let $2x$ = residential real estate loans
Let $4x$ = commercial real estate loans
$$x + 2x + 4x = \$700 \text{ million}$$
$$7x = \$700 \text{ million}$$
$$x = \$100 \text{ million}$$
$$2x = \$200 \text{ million}$$
$$4x = \$400 \text{ million}$$

With experience, you'll learn to set up problems in ways that will minimize your calculations. Incidentally, the more calculations you do, the greater the chance of making a mistake. How long does it take to acquire the experience needed? Let me put it this way: The more you do, the better you get. Even *I'm* getting better, and I've been at this since Grover Cleveland was President.

Problem:

At Abraham Lincoln High School, $\frac{3}{10}$ of the seniors receive a general diploma, $\frac{2}{10}$ receive a commercial diploma, $\frac{4}{10}$ receive an academic diploma, and 300 don't graduate. How many students are in the senior class and how many receive each type of diploma?

Solution:

$$\text{Let } x = \text{the number of students in the senior class}$$
$$\text{Let } .3x = \text{students receiving a general diploma}$$
$$\text{Let } .2x = \text{students receiving a commercial diploma}$$
$$\text{Let } .4x = \text{students receiving an academic diploma}$$

$$.3x + .2x + .4x + 300 = x$$
$$3x + 2x + 4x + 3000 = 10x$$
$$9x + 3000 = 10x$$
$$3000 = 10x - 9x$$
$$3000 = x$$
$$.2x = 600$$
$$.3x = 900$$
$$.4x = 1,200$$

Here's another group of problems:

1. There are five teams at Camp Delaware: the red team, with $\frac{5}{10}$ of the campers; the blue team, with $\frac{1}{10}$ of the campers; the gray team, with $\frac{3}{10}$ of the campers; the yellow team, with $\frac{1}{10}$ of the campers; and the green team, with the rest of the campers. If 300 children attend Camp Delaware, how many are on each team?

2. Jerry is four times as old as Mark. Mark is three times as old as Marie. If their combined age is 32, how old is each?

3. In the Presidential election held in the year 2000, 10 percent of the votes Ross Perot received came from the Northeast, 20 percent came from the Midwest, 25 percent came from the Far West, and a total of 9 million votes came from the South. How many votes did Perot receive in each region, and what was his total vote?

4. Millard Fabian obtained $\frac{1}{10}$ of his caloric intake from carbohydrates, $\frac{1}{10}$ from fat, $\frac{1}{5}$ from vegetables, and the rest from fruit. If he obtained 1,000 calories from fruit, how much did he receive from each of the other food sources, and how much was his total caloric intake?

Solutions:

1. Red team = $\dfrac{300}{5}$ = 60   Blue team = $\dfrac{300}{10}$ = 30

    Gray team = $\dfrac{3}{10}$ × 300 = 90   Yellow team = $\dfrac{300}{10}$ = 30

    Green team = 300 − (60 + 30 + 90 + 30)
    Green team = 300 − 210
    Green team = 90

2. Let Marie's age = x
    Let Mark's age = $3x$
    Let Jerry's age = $12x$
    $x + 3x + 12x = 32$
    $16x = 32$
    $x = 2$
    $3x = 6$
    $12x = 24$

3.   Votes in South = 100% − (10% + 20% + 25%)
                       = 100% − 55%
                       = 45%
    45% of the vote = 9 million
    Let total vote = x
    $.45x$ = 9 million
    $\dfrac{.45x}{.45} = \dfrac{9,000,000}{.45}$
    $x = 20,000,000$
    Votes in Northeast = 20,000,000 × .10 = 2,000,000
    Votes in Midwest = 20,000,000 × .20 = 4,000,000
    Votes in Far West = 20,000,000 × .25 = 5,000,000

4. Let total caloric intake = x
    Let carbohydrates = $.1x$
    Let fat = $.1x$
    Let vegetables = $.2x$
    Fruit = $x − (.1x + .1x + .2x)$
          = $x − .4x$
          = $.6x$
    $.6x$ = 1,000 calories
    $\dfrac{.6x}{.6} = \dfrac{1,000}{.6}$
    $x = 1,667$
    Carbohydrates = $.1x = .1 × 1,667 = 167$
    Fat = $.1x = 167$
    Vegetables = $.2x = .2 × 1,667 = 333$

13

So far I've refrained from trying to place any type of problem into a category, but a good name for the next type would be combination problems. You may want to call them complicated problems. But whatever we call them, they can be solved the same way that we solved the previous problems in this chapter: letting x = the unknown and then setting up an equation.

Problem:

Roxanne is two years younger than Darlene. Darlene is three times Philip's age. The sum of their ages is 26. How old is each?

Solution:

$$\text{Let } x = \text{Philip's age}$$
$$\text{Let } 3x = \text{Darlene's age}$$
$$\text{Let } 3x - 2 = \text{Roxanne's age}$$
$$x + 3x + 3x - 2 = 26$$
$$7x - 2 = 26$$
$$7x - 2 + 2 = 26 + 2$$
$$7x = 28$$
$$x = 4$$
$$3x = 12$$
$$3x - 2 = 10$$

Are you still checking your work? Let's check *this* one:

Check:

$$x + 3x + 3x - 2 = 26$$
$$4 + 12 + 10 = 26$$
$$26 = 26$$

Problem:

Henry earns twice as much as Jane. Mary earns $2,000 more than Henry. If they earn a total of $102,000, how much does each person earn?

Solution:

$$\text{Let } x = \text{Jane's earnings}$$
$$\text{Let } 2x = \text{Henry's earnings}$$
$$\text{Let } 2x + \$2,000 = \text{Mary's earnings}$$
$$x + 2x + 2x + \$2,000 = \$102,000$$
$$5x + \$2,000 = \$102,000$$
$$5x + \$2,000 - \$2,000 = \$102,000 - \$2,000$$
$$5x = \$100,000$$
$$x = \$20,000$$
$$2x = \$40,000$$
$$2x + \$2,000 = \$42,000$$

Problem:

Peter has $5 more than Gloria. Gloria has twice as much money as Irene. Irene has twice as much money as Wendy. Together they have $93. How much money does each person have?

Solution:

$$\text{Let } x = \text{Wendy's money}$$
$$\text{Let } 2x = \text{Irene's money}$$
$$\text{Let } 4x = \text{Gloria's money}$$
$$\text{Let } 4x + \$5 = \text{Peter's money}$$
$$x + 2x + 4x + 4x + \$5 = \$93$$
$$11x + \$5 = \$93$$
$$11x + \$5 - \$5 = \$93 - \$5$$
$$11x = \$88$$
$$x = \$8$$
$$2x = \$16$$
$$4x = \$32$$
$$4x + \$5 = \$37$$

I think we've made these problems complicated enough, so let's do one last problem set.

1. Bob is three years older than Harvey. Harvey is twice George's age. Mel is four years younger than George. The sum of their ages is 29. How old is each?

2. North Carolina has three times the population of Utah and twice the population of Oregon. Arkansas has one million people less than Oregon. If the total population of these four states is 27 million, how many people live in each state?

3. The XYZ Corporation is owned by four people, who hold a total of 3,500 shares. Mike holds 100 more than Sue and 200 less than Joe. Stu holds twice as many shares as Joe. How many shares does each person hold?

4. In September Sally earned twice as much in commissions as Alice. Alice earned $100 more than Joan. Joan earned $300 less than Robin. These four people earned a total of $4,600 in commissions. How much did each person earn?

Solutions:

1.
$$\text{Let George's age} = x$$
$$\text{Let Harvey's age} = 2x$$
$$\text{Let Bob's age} = 2x + 3$$
$$\text{Let Mel's age} = x - 4$$
$$x + 2x + 2x + 3 + x - 4 = 29$$
$$6x - 1 = 29$$

$$6x - 1 + 1 = 29 + 1$$
$$6x = 30$$
$$x = 5$$
$$2x = 10$$
$$2x + 3 = 13$$
$$x - 4 = 1$$

2. Let North Carolina's population = $3x$
   Let Utah's population = x

   Let Oregon's population = $\dfrac{3x}{2}$

   Let Arkansas' population = $\dfrac{3x}{2} - 1$

$$3x + x + \dfrac{3x}{2} + \dfrac{3x}{2} - 1 = 27$$
$$6x + 2x + 3x + 3x - 2 = 54$$
$$14x - 2 = 54$$
$$14x - 2 + 2 = 54 + 2$$
$$14x = 56$$
$$x = 4$$
$$3x = 12$$
$$\dfrac{3x}{2} = 6$$
$$\dfrac{3x}{2} - 1 = 5$$

3.   Let Sue's share = x
      Let Mike's shares = $x + 100$
      Let Joe's shares = $x + 300$
      Let Stu's shares = $2(x + 300)$
$$x + x + 100 + x + 300 + 2(x + 300) = 3,500$$
$$3x + 400 + 2x + 600 = 3,500$$
$$5x + 1,000 = 3,500$$
$$5x + 1,000 - 1,000 = 3,500 - 1,000$$
$$5x = 500$$
$$x = 100$$
$$x + 100 = 600$$
$$x + 300 = 800$$
$$2(x + 300) = 1,600$$

4.   Let x = Joan's earnings
      Let $x + \$300$ = Robin's earnings
      Let $x + \$100$ = Alice's earnings
      Let $2(x + \$100$ = Sally's earnings
$$x + x + \$300 + x + \$100 + 2(x + \$100) = \$4,600$$
$$3x + \$400 + 2x + \$200 = \$4,600$$

$$5x + \$600 = \$4{,}600$$
$$5x + \$600 - \$600 = \$4{,}600 - \$600$$
$$5x = \$4{,}000$$
$$x = \$800$$
$$x + \$300 = \$1{,}100$$
$$x + \$100 = \$900$$
$$2\,(x + \$100) = \$1{,}800$$

SELF-TEST

1. In each problem, solve for x:

   a. $x - 4 = 7$ b. $x + 8 = 5$

   c. $x + 6 = -8$ d. $7x = 56$

   e. $\dfrac{x}{5} = 35$ f. $\dfrac{9x}{4} = 72$

   g. $\dfrac{7x}{2} + 5 = 19$

2. Find x in each problem:

   a. $1.2x = 132$ b. $.8x = 4$

3. Rico owns 10 percent of the Bangor Trading Corporation, Astrid owns 15 percent, Pei owns 35 percent, and Nils owns the rest. If each shares the profits in proportion to his or her percentage of the ownership, how would they split $400,000 profits?

4. Mr. Wong earns twice as much as Ms. Kerenski and five times as much as Mr. Mostelli. If their combined incomes total $340,000, how much does each person earn?

5. The First National Bank of Akron had deposits $100 million greater than those of the First National Bank of Toledo. The First National Bank of Toledo had deposits $200 million greater than those of the First National Bank of Canton. The First National Bank of Canton had deposits that were half as large as those of the First National Bank of Dayton. If the deposits of these four banks totalled $1 billion (one thousand million), what were the deposits of each bank?

ANSWERS

1. a. $x - 4 = 7$ b. $x + 8 = 5$
       $x = 11$ $x = 5 - 8$
                                      $x = -3$

   c. $x + 6 = -8$ d. $7x = 56$
       $x = -8 - 6$ $x = 8$
       $x = -14$

e. $\dfrac{x}{5} = 35$

$x = 175$

f. $\dfrac{9x}{4} = 72$

$9x = 288$

$x = 32$

g. $\dfrac{7x}{2} + 5 = 19$

$\dfrac{7x}{2} = 14$

$7x = 28$

$x = 4$

2. a. $1.2x = 132$

$12x = 1320$

$x = 110$

b. $.8x = 4$

$8x = 40$

$x = 5$

3. Let x = total profit

$.1x$ = Rico's share

$.15x$ = Astrid's share

$.35x$ = Pei's share

$.4x$ = Nils' share

$x = \$400,000$

$.1x = \$40,000$ = Rico's share

$.15x = \$60,000$ = Astrid's share

$.35x = \$140,000$ = Pei's share

$.4x = \$160,000$ = Nils' share

4.

Let x = Mr. Mostelli's earnings

Let $5x$ = Mr. Wong's earnings

Let $\dfrac{5x}{2}$ = Ms. Kerenski's earnings

$x + 5x + \dfrac{5x}{2} = \$340,000$

$2x + 10x + 5x = \$680,000$

$17x = \$680,000$

$x = \$40,000$ = Mr. Mostelli's earnings

$5x = \$200,000$ = Mr. Wong's earnings

$\dfrac{5x}{2} = \$100,000$ = Ms. Kerenski's earnings

5.

Let x = Canton Bank's deposits

Let $2x$ = Dayton Bank's deposits

Let $x + \$200$ million = Toledo Bank's deposits

Let $x + \$300$ million = Akron Bank's deposits

$x + 2x + x + \$200$ million $+ x + \$300$ million $= \$1,000$ million

$5x = \$500$ million

Canton Bank $= x = \$100$ million

Dayton Bank $= 2x = \$200$ million

Toledo Bank $= x + \$200$ million $= \$300$ million

Akron Bank $= x + \$300$ million $= \$400$ million

Before we go any further, I want you to be brutally frank with yourself. If you did reasonably well in each of the pretests and in the self-test, then your algebra background is certainly good enough to do the business math in this book. But if you need to do some extra work in algebra, a couple of books could help you. *Practical Algebra* and *Quick Algebra Review* (both from John Wiley & Sons, Inc.), which I wrote with Peter Selby, would help you relearn most of the algebra you had back in high school.

3 Percentages

In my many years of teaching, I've answered a lot of questions. The one I have been asked the most is "Do we have to know this?"

Of all the mathematical concepts covered in this book, which one do you have to know most? Percentages. Much of the business math we'll cover in the rest of this book requires a thorough understanding of percentages. And believe me, when you've completed this chapter, you'll definitely know your percentages.

1 Changing Decimals into Percents

Back in the first chapter, we talked about fractions and decimals. We know that the same number can be expressed as a fraction or as a decimal. For example, $\frac{1}{4}$ = .25. Think of these numbers as money—one quarter equals 25 cents.

We know that a quarter is a quarter of a dollar. Now guess what *percent* of a dollar is a quarter.

Did you guess 25 percent, or 25%?

Here's how to figure it out. Start with the decimal, .25. Convert it into a percent. What we do is move the decimal point two places to the right and add a percent sign:

.25 = .25.% = 25%

When we have a whole number like 25, we don't bother with the decimal point. If we wanted to, we could of course write 25% like this: 25.0%.

Now you try converting a few decimals into percents:

1. .32   2. .835   3. 1.29   4. .03   5. .41

Solutions:

1. 32%   2. 83.5%   3. 129%   4. 3%   5. 41%

Did you get each of these right? If you did, please go directly to frame 2.

If not, let's go over each problem:

1. .32 becomes 32.0% or 32%. We moved the decimal point two places to the right, tacked on a percentage sign, and then got rid of the decimal point since it wasn't needed.

2. .835 = 83.5%. Again, we moved the decimal point two places to the right and add a percentage sign.

3. 1.29 = 129.0% = 129%. Once again, we moved the decimal point two places to the right, and added a percentage sign. And we got rid of the decimal point because it wasn't needed.

4. .03 = 3.% = 3%

5. 0.41 = 41.% = 41%

2

Now we'll add a wrinkle. Convert the number 1.2 into a percent.

What did you get? Was it 120%? What we do is add a zero to 1.2 to make it 1.20, and then move the decimal two places to the right and add the percent sign. What gives us the right to add a zero? Well, it's OK to do this as long as it doesn't change the value of the number, 1.2. Because 1.2 = 1.20, we can do this. Can we add a zero to the number 30 without changing its value? If we add a zero, we get 300. Does 30 = 300? If you think it does, then I'd like to trade my $30 for your $300.

Ready for another problem set? All right, then, convert these numbers into percents:

1. 2.6   2. 1.0   3. 17.3   4. 200.1   5. 45.4

Solutions:

1. 260%   2. 100%   3. 1,730%   4. 20,010%   5. 4,540%

3

If you got those right, then you're ready for another wrinkle. Convert the number 5 into a percent.

What did you get? 500%. Here's how we did it. We started with 5, added a decimal point and a couple of zeros: 5 = 5.00. Then we converted 5.00 into a percent by moving the decimal point two places to the right and adding a percent sign: 5.00 = 5.00.% = 500%.

Here's another group of problems for you. Change each number into a percent:

1. 1   2. 82   3. 90   4. 22   5. 10

Solutions:

1. 100%   2. 8,200%   3. 9,000%   4. 2,200% 5. 1,000%

Did you get everything right? If so, please go directly to frame 4. If you need a little help, let's do these one at a time.

1. The number 1 is the same as the number 1.00 because you can always place a decimal after a whole number and then tack on as many zeros as you want after the decimal. Once we have 1.00, just move the decimal two places to the right and add a percentage sign: 1.00 = 100.%, or 100%.

2. 82 is equal to 82.00. Then just move the decimal point two places to the right and add a percentage sign: 82.00 = 8,200%.

    The rest of the problems are just as easy:

3. 90 = 90.00 = 9,000%

4. 22 = 22.00 = 2,200%

5. 10 = 10.00 = 1,000%

4 | Changing Fractions Into Percents

Just a few minutes ago I said that a number could be expressed as a fraction, as a decimal, or as a percent. I said that $\frac{1}{4}$ = .25 = 25%.

You may remember that in Chapter 1, we converted fractions into decimals. So $\frac{1}{4}$ is converted into .25 by dividing 4 into 1:

$$\frac{.2\ 5}{4)\overline{1.0^20}}$$

Now let's try another way of getting from $\frac{1}{4}$ to 25%. We're going to use an old trick, actually a law of arithmetic. The law says that whatever you do to the bottom of a fraction, you must do to the top. In other words, if you multiply the denominator by a certain number, you must multiply the numerator by that same number.

We'll start with the fraction, $\frac{1}{4}$:

$$\frac{1 \times 25}{4 \times 25} = \frac{25}{100}$$

What did we do? We multiplied the numerator and the denominator by 25. Why 25? Because we wanted to get the denominator equal to 100. Having 100 on the bottom of a fraction makes it very easy to convert that fraction into a percent.

All right, we have $\frac{25}{100}$—which comes out to 25%. How did we do that? We removed the 100, or mathematically, we multiplied the fraction by 100, then added a percent sign. In other words,

$$\frac{25}{100} \times \frac{100}{1} = \frac{25}{\cancel{100}_1} \times \frac{\cancel{100}^1}{1} = 25\%$$

This is exactly the same process as converting a decimal into a percent. The decimal .25 becomes 25% when we move the decimal point two places to the right and add a percent sign. Moving a decimal two places to the right is the same as multiplying by 100. Similarly, when we changed the fraction $\frac{25}{100}$ into a percent, we also multiplied by 100 and added a percent sign.

Now you do this one. Read $\frac{34}{100}$ as a percent.

What did you get? I'll bet you got 34%. So what you did was multiply $\frac{34}{100}$ by 100 and add a percent sign.

How would you convert $\frac{9}{50}$ into a percent? Try it right here:

I hope you did it like this:

$$\frac{9 \times 2}{50 \times 2} \qquad \frac{18}{100} = 18\%$$

Do you follow what I did? I multiplied the top (or numerator) by 2 and the bottom (or denominator) of the fraction by 2. Am I allowed to do that? Yes! You are allowed to multiply the numerator and denominator of a fraction by the same number because it does not change that fraction's value.

Why did I multiply the numerator and denominator by 2? Because I wanted to make the denominator 100 so that I could easily convert this fraction into a percent. So whenever you get the chance, convert the denominator into 100. It can make your life a lot easier.

Now try this group of problems. In each case, convert the fraction into a percent.

1. $\dfrac{6}{50} =$ 2. $\dfrac{7}{20} =$ 3. $\dfrac{8}{10} =$

4. $\dfrac{2}{25} =$ 5. $\dfrac{1}{5} =$

Solutions:

1. $\dfrac{6 \times 2}{50 \times 2} = \dfrac{12}{100} = 12\%$ 2. $\dfrac{7 \times 5}{20 \times 5} = \dfrac{35}{100} = 35\%$

3. $\dfrac{8 \times 10}{10 \times 10} = \dfrac{80}{100} = 80\%$ 4. $\dfrac{2 \times 4}{25 \times 4} = \dfrac{8}{100} = 8\%$

5. $\dfrac{1 \times 20}{5 \times 20} = \dfrac{20}{100} = 20\%$

5

So far every fraction has been quite easy to convert into hundredths, then, the number written over 100 is read as a percentage. For instance, $\frac{17}{100} = 17\%$ and $\frac{89}{100} = 89\%$. But what if we had a fraction that could not easily be converted into hundredths? Like $\frac{3}{8}$. How do we change $\frac{3}{8}$ into a percent?

We do it in two steps. First we change $\frac{3}{8}$ into a decimal:

$$8\overline{)3.0^60^40}$$
$$.3\,7\,5$$

Then we move the decimal point two places to the right and add a percent sign: .375 = 37.5%

I did that one. Now you do this one. Change $\frac{17}{40}$ into a percent. Use the space right here:

Solution:

I showed you a trick near the end of Chapter 1 when we did some fast division. Dividing 40 into 17 must be done by long division, which is what I'll bet you did. Here's my trick:

$$\frac{17}{40} = \frac{1.7}{4.0}$$

What did we do? We divided the numerator, 17, by 10, and then we divided the denominator, 40, by 10. (You can easily divide a number by 10 by simply moving its decimal point one space to the left.) But why did we bother to divide 17 and 40 by 10? Why would we rather have

$\frac{1.7}{4.0}$ than $\frac{17}{40}$? Because then we can do short division instead of long division. (Of course, if you happen to be using a calculator, there is no difference between long and short division.)

$$\underset{4\overline{)1.7^10^20}}{.4\ 2\ 5} = 42.5\%$$

In general, when you need to divide the denominator of a fraction into a numerator, first reduce the fraction to the lowest possible terms, and then, if possible, divide the numerator and denominator by 10 or even 100 if that can get you from long division to short division.

Well, it's time for another problem set. Change each fraction into percents:

1. $\dfrac{19}{200}$ 2. $\dfrac{10}{27}$ 3. $\dfrac{1}{12}$ 4. $\dfrac{37}{60}$ 5. $\dfrac{13}{18}$

Solutions:

1. $200\overline{)19} = \underset{2\overline{).19^10}}{.09\ 5} = 9.5\%$

2. $\underset{27\overline{)10.00}}{.37} = 37\%$
    $\phantom{27\overline{)}}\underline{-8.1x}$
    $\phantom{27\overline{)}}1\ 90$
    $\phantom{27\overline{)}}\underline{-1\ 89}$

3. $\underset{12\overline{)1.000}}{.083} = 8.3\%$
    $\phantom{12\overline{)}}\underline{-96x}$
    $\phantom{12\overline{)}}40$
    $\phantom{12\overline{)}}\underline{-36}$

4. $60\overline{)37} = \underset{6\overline{)3.7^10^40^40}}{.6\ 1\ 6\ 6} = 61.7\%$

5. $\underset{18\overline{)13.000}}{.722} = 72.2\%$
    $\phantom{18\overline{)}}\underline{-12\,6xx}$
    $\phantom{18\overline{)}}40$
    $\phantom{18\overline{)}}\underline{-36}$
    $\phantom{18\overline{)}}40$
    $\phantom{18\overline{)}}\underline{-36}$

By convention we usually round to one decimal. So if you rounded to a whole number or to two or three decimals, then your answers may have differed just a bit from mine.

So how did you do? Did you get everything right? If you did, then you can pass GO, collect $200 (if you can find someone willing to give it to you), go directly to the section called "Percentages as Numbers," and then skip Quick Quiz 3.1. But if you didn't get all of these right, then stay right here and work out the next set of problems. You've heard the saying, "practice makes perfect"? Now we'll prove it.

Change these fractions into percents.

1. $\dfrac{3}{15}$ 2. $\dfrac{1}{8}$ 3. $\dfrac{13}{22}$ 4. $\dfrac{19}{30}$ 5. $\dfrac{123}{600}$

Solutions:

1. $15\overline{)3} = 5\overline{)1.00}^{\,.20} = 20\%$

2. $8\overline{)1.0^20^40}^{\,.1\,2\,5} = 12.5\%$

3. $22\overline{)13.000}^{\,.5909} = 59.1\%$
   $\begin{array}{r} -11\,0\,xx \\ \hline 2\,00 \\ -1\,98 \\ \hline 20 \\ -0 \\ \hline 200 \end{array}$

4. $30\overline{)19} = 3\overline{)1.9^10^10^10}^{\,.6\,3\,3\,3} = 63.3\%$

5. $600\overline{)123} = 6\overline{)1.230}^{\,.205} = 20.5\%$

How did you do this time? If you want more practice, just copy each of the problems from the last two sets on another sheet of paper and work them out again. If you got them right, please read the box called "Percentages as Numbers" and then take Quick Quiz 3.1.

Percentages as Numbers

Let's take a closer look at the relationship among decimals, fractions, and percentages. We'll begin with the fraction $\frac{1}{100}$. How much is $\frac{1}{100}$ as a percent? It's 1 percent. And how much is the decimal, .01, as a percent? Also 1%.

We've seen, then, that $\frac{1}{100} = .01 = 1\%$. How about .10 and $\frac{10}{100}$? As a percent, they're both equal to 10%.

Now we're going to throw you a curve ball. How much is the number 1 as a decimal, a fraction, and as a percent? Write your answers here:

One may be written as 1.0, or $\frac{1}{1}$ (or $\frac{100}{100}$), or as 100%.

It's easy to go from fractions and decimals to percents if you follow the procedures we've outlined in this chapter. It doesn't matter that much whether you can verbalize these procedures. In math our bottom line is always the same—coming up with the right answer.

---

1. Convert these decimals into percents:
    a. .84   b. .906   c. .02

2. Convert these numbers into percents:
    a. 1.1   b. 25.8   c. 115.4

3. Convert these numbers into percents:
    a. 261   b. 99   c. 5

4. Convert these fractions into percents:
    a. $\dfrac{13}{50}$ b. $\dfrac{9}{20}$ c. $\dfrac{4}{25}$

5. Convert these fractions into percents:
    a. $\dfrac{4}{17}$ b. $\dfrac{1}{12}$ c. $\dfrac{29}{53}$

Answers to Quick Quiz 3.1

1. a. .84 = 84%   b. .906 = 90.6%   c. .02 = 2%

2. a. 1.1 = 1.10 = 110%   b. 25.8 = 25.80 = 2,580%   c. 115.4 = 115.40 = 11,540%

3. a. 261 = 261.00 = 26,100%   b. 99 = 99.00 = 9,900%   c. 5 = 5.00 = 500%

4. a. $\dfrac{13}{50} = \dfrac{26}{100} = 26\%$ b. $\dfrac{9}{20} = \dfrac{45}{100} = 45\%$ c. $\dfrac{4}{25} = \dfrac{16}{100} = 16\%$

5. a. $\dfrac{4}{17} = $
```
        .2352 = 23.5%
    17)4.0000
     -3 4xxx
        60
       -51
        90
       -85
        50
       -34
```

b. $\dfrac{1}{12} = $
```
        .0833 = 8.3%
    12)1.0000
     -96xx
        40
       -36
        40
       -36
```

c. $\dfrac{29}{53} = $
```
        .5471 = 54.7%
    53)29.0000
     -26 5xxx
        2 50
       -2 12
        380
       -371
         90
        -53
```

6 Finding Percentage Changes

You were earning $500 and got a $20 raise. By what percentage did your salary go up? Try to figure it out right here:

Solution:

Percentage change = $\dfrac{\text{change}}{\text{original number}}$

$$= \frac{\$20}{\$500} = \frac{2}{50} = \frac{4}{100} = 4\%$$

You'll notice that we have a nice formula to help us solve percentage change problems. Here's how it works: Your salary is $500, so that's the original number. You got a $20 raise; that's the change.

Next, we substitute these numbers into the formula. And then we solve. Once we have $\frac{20}{500}$, we could reduce it all the way down to $\frac{1}{25}$ by dividing both the numerator and the denominator by 20, and solve by using division:

$$\begin{array}{r} .04 = 4\% \\ 25\overline{)1.00} \\ -1.00 \end{array}$$

Next problem: On New Year's Eve you made a resolution to lose 30 pounds by the end of March. And sure enough, your weight dropped from 140 pounds to 110. By what percentage did your weight fall?

Solution:

Percentage change = $\dfrac{\text{change}}{\text{original number}}$

$$= \frac{30}{140} = \frac{3}{14}$$

$$\begin{array}{r} .2142 = 21.4\% \\ 14\overline{)3.0000} \\ -2\,8\text{xxx} \\ \hline 20 \\ -14 \\ \hline 60 \\ -56 \\ \hline 40 \\ -28 \end{array}$$

Time for another problem set:

1. What is the percentage change if we go from 150 to 180?

2. What is the percentage change if we start with 130 and end up with 200?

3. If Jessica Storey's real estate taxes rose from $6,000 to $8,500, by what percentage did they rise?

4. Harriet Gold's time for running a mile fell from 11 minutes to 8 minutes. By what percentage did her time fall?

Solutions:

1. Percentage change $= \dfrac{\text{change}}{\text{original number}} = \dfrac{30}{150} = \dfrac{1}{5} = \dfrac{20}{100} = 20\%$

2. Percentage change $= \dfrac{\text{change}}{\text{original number}} = \dfrac{70}{130} = \dfrac{7}{13}$

$$
\begin{array}{r}
.538 = 53.8\% \\
13\overline{)7.000} \\
-6\ 5\text{xx} \\
\hline
50 \\
-39 \\
\hline
110 \\
-104 \\
\hline
6
\end{array}
$$

3. Percentage change $= \dfrac{\text{change}}{\text{original number}} = \dfrac{\$2,500}{\$6,000} = \dfrac{25}{60} = \dfrac{5}{12}$

$$
\begin{array}{r}
.4166 = 41.7\% \\
12\overline{)5.0000} \\
-4\ 8\text{xxx} \\
\hline
20 \\
-12 \\
\hline
80 \\
-72 \\
\hline
80 \\
-72
\end{array}
$$

4. Percentage change $= \dfrac{\text{change}}{\text{original number}} = \dfrac{3}{11}$

$$
\begin{array}{r}
.2727 = 27.3\% \\
11\overline{)3.0000} \\
-2\ 2\text{xxx} \\
\hline
80 \\
-77 \\
\hline
30 \\
-22 \\
\hline
80 \\
-77
\end{array}
$$

7 | Fast Percentage Changes

Pick a number. Any number. Now triple it. By what percentage did your number increase? Take your time. Use this space to calculate the percentage:

What did you get? Three hundred percent? Nice try, but that's not the right answer.

As an example, let's take the number 100. Triple it in your head. Now use the percentage change formula to get the answer. (Incidentally, you may have gotten the right answer, so you may be wondering why I'm making such a big deal. But I know from sad experience that almost no one gets this right on their first try.)

So where were we? The formula. Write it down in this space, substitute numbers into it, and then solve:

Solution:

$$\text{Percentage change} = \frac{\text{change}}{\text{original number}} = \frac{200}{100} = 200\%$$

Let's go over this problem, step-by-step. We picked a number, 100. Next, we tripled it. Which gives us 300. Now we plug our numbers into the formula. Our original number is 100. And the change when we go from 100 to 300? It's 200. From there it's just arithmetic: $\frac{200}{100} = 200\%$.

This really isn't that hard. In fact you're going to get really good at just looking at a couple of numbers and figuring out percentage changes in your head.

Whenever you go from 100 to a higher number, the percentage increase is the difference between 100 and the new number. Suppose you were to quadruple a number. What's the percentage increase? It's 300 (400 – 100). When you double a number, what's the percentage increase? It's 100% (200 – 100).

Here's a set of problems for you to try. What's the percentage increase from 100 to

| 1. 150 | 2. 320 | 3. 275 | 4. 500 | 5. 425 |

Solutions:

| 1. 50% | 2. 220% | 3. 175% | 4. 400% | 5. 325% |

8

The number 100 is very easy to work with. Sometimes you can use it as a substitute for another number. For example, what's the percentage increase if we go from 3 to 6? Isn't it the same as if you went from 100 to 200? It is a 100% increase. What's the percentage increase from 5 to 20? It's the same as the one from 100 to 400. Which is a 300% increase.

What we've been doing here is just playing around with numbers, seeing if we can get them to work for us. As you get more comfortable with numbers, you can try to manipulate them the way we just did.

Now I'm going to throw you another curve ball. If a number—any number—were to decline by 100%, what number would you be left with? I'd really like you to think about this one.

What did you get? You should have gotten 0. That's right—no matter what number you started with, a 100% decline leaves you with 0.

9 | Percentage Change Applications

You'll find this section very easy. First question: You're driving at 40 MPH and increase your speed by 20%. How fast are you now going?

Solution:
$$40 + .2 \times 40 = 40 + 8 = 48$$

You'll notice that we converted 20% to .2 to work out the problem. Now do this set of problems.

1. You cut back on eating and your $50 weekly food bill falls by 30%. What is your new food bill?

2. Jason Jones was getting 20 miles per gallon. But when he slowed down to an average speed of 70 MPH, his gas mileage rose by 40 percent. What is his new gas mileage?

3. If you were making $20,000 and got a 15% pay increase, how much would you now be making?

4. A school that had 650 students had a 22% increase in enrollment. How much is its new enrollment?

Solutions:

1. $50 – (.3 × $50) = $50 – $15 = $35

2. 20 + .4 × 20 = 20 + 8 = 28

3. $20,000 + .15 × $20,000 = $20,000 + $3,000 = $23,000

4. 650 + .22 × 650 = 650 + 143 = 793

$$
\begin{array}{r}
650 \\
\times\ .22 \\
\hline
13\ 00 \\
130\ 0 \\
\hline
143.00
\end{array}
$$

QUICK QUIZ 3.2

1. What is the percentage change if we go from 210 to 250?

2. What is the percentage change if we start with 65 and end up with 85?

3. If Max Fine's salary fell from $31,000 to $27,500, by what percentage did it fall?

4. Pick a number. Double it. By what percentage did it increase?

5. What's the percentage increase from 100 to
   a. 290?
   b. 400?
   c. 340?

6. What's the percentage increase from 6 to 18?

7. If your real estate taxes were $12,200 and rose by 18%, how much would you now be paying?

8. If your sales, which had been $13,700, declined by 8%, how much would your new level of sales be?

Answers to Quick Quiz 3.2

1. $\frac{40}{210} = \frac{4}{21}$

$$\begin{array}{r} .1904 = 19.0\% \\ 21)\overline{4.0000} \\ -2.1\text{ xxx} \\ \hline 1\ 90 \\ -1\ 89 \\ \hline 100 \\ -84 \end{array}$$

2. $\frac{20}{65} = \frac{4}{13}$

$$\begin{array}{r} .3076 = 30.8\% \\ 13)\overline{4.0000} \\ -3\ 9\text{ xxx} \\ \hline 100 \\ -91 \\ \hline 90 \\ -78 \end{array}$$

3. $\frac{\$3,500}{\$31,000} = \frac{35}{310} = \frac{7}{62}$

$$\begin{array}{r} .1129 = 11.3\% \text{ (fell 11.3\%)} \\ 62)\overline{7.0000} \\ -6\ 2\text{ xxx} \\ \hline 80 \\ -62 \\ \hline 180 \\ -124 \\ \hline 560 \\ -558 \end{array}$$

4. 100%

5. a. 190%   b. 300%   c. 240%

6. $\frac{12}{6} = 2 = 200\%$

7. $12,200 + ($12,200 × .18) = $12,200 + $2,196 = $14,396

8. $13,700 − ($13,700 × .08) = $13,700 − $1,096 = $12,604

Let's stop for a minute to catch our breath. So how did you do? If you got more than one problem wrong, go back to frame 6 and work your way back to this point. Don't worry if you need to repeat—it's probably impossible to make it all the way through this book without ever repeating any parts of it. Besides, they say that the second time around is better.

10 Percentage Distribution

A class had half girls and half boys. What percentage of the class was girls and what percentage of the class was boys? The answers are obviously 50% and 50%. That's all there is to percentage distribution. Of course the problems do get a bit more complicated, but all percentage distribution problems start out with one simple fact: The distribution will always add up to 100%.

Here's another one. One quarter of the players on a baseball team are pitchers, one quarter are outfielders, and the rest are infielders. What is the team's percentage distribution of pitchers, infielders, and outfielders?

Solution: Pitchers are $\frac{1}{4}$, or 25%; outfielders are also $\frac{1}{4}$, or 25%. So infielders must be the remaining 50%.

Here's another question. If, over the course of a week, you obtained 250 grams of protein from red meat, 150 from fish, 100 from poultry, and 50 from other sources, what percentage of your protein intake came from red meat and what percentage came from each of the other sources?

red meat	250 grams
fish	150 grams
poultry	100 grams
other	50 grams
	550 grams

Try to work this out for yourself. Hint: 550 grams = 100%.

Solution:

$$\text{red meat} = \frac{250}{550} = \frac{25}{55} = \frac{5}{11} = 45.5\%$$

$$\begin{array}{r} .4\,5\,4\,5 \\ 11\overline{)5.0^60^50^60} \end{array}$$

$$\text{fish} = \frac{150}{550} = \frac{15}{55} = \frac{3}{11} = 27.3\%$$

$$\begin{array}{r} .2\,7\,2\,7 \\ 11\overline{)3.0^80^30^80} \end{array}$$

$$\text{poultry} = \frac{100}{550} = \frac{10}{55} = \frac{2}{11} = 18.2\%$$

$$\text{other} = \frac{50}{550} = \frac{5}{55} = \frac{1}{11} = 9.1\%$$

```
     .1 8 1 8
11)2.0⁹0²0⁹0

     .09 09
11)1.00¹00
```

Check:

```
 ³4¹5.5
  27.3
  18.2
   9.1
 100.1
```

When doing percentage distribution problems, it's always a good idea to check your work. If your percentages don't add up to 100, then you've definitely made a mistake, so you'll need to go back over all your calculations. Because of rounding, my percentages added up to 100.1. Occasionally, you'll end up with 100.1 or 99.9 when you check, which is fine.

Are you getting the knack? Take Quick Quiz 3.3 to be sure.

QUICK QUIZ 3.3

1. Denver has 550,000 whites, 150,000 Hispanics, 100,000 blacks, and 50,000 Asian-Americans. Calculate the percentage distribution of these groups. Be sure to check your work.

2. Eleni Zimiles has 8 red beads, 4 blue beads, 3 white beads, 2 yellow beads, and 1 green bead. What is the percentage distribution of Eleni's beads?

3. Georgia-Pacific ships 5,000 freight containers a week. Fifteen hundred are sent by air, 2,300 go by rail, and the rest by truck. What percentage is sent by air, rail, and truck, respectively?

Answers to Quick Quiz 3.3

```
1. 550      whites = 550/850 = 55/85 = 11/17        .647 = 64.7%
   150                                            17)11.000
   100                                             -10 2xx
    50                                                 8 0
   850                                               -6 8
                                                     1 20
                                                    -1 19
```

Hispanics $= \dfrac{150}{850} = \dfrac{15}{85} = \dfrac{3}{17}$

$$\begin{array}{r} .176 = 17.6\% \\ 17\overline{)3.000} \\ -1\,7xx \\ \hline 1\,30 \\ -1\,19 \\ \hline 110 \\ -102 \\ \hline 8 \end{array}$$

blacks $= \dfrac{100}{850} = \dfrac{10}{85} = \dfrac{2}{17}$

$$\begin{array}{r} .117 = 11.8\% \\ 17\overline{)2.000} \\ -1\,7xx \\ \hline 30 \\ -17 \\ \hline 130 \\ -119 \\ \hline 11 \end{array}$$

Asian-Americans $= \dfrac{50}{850} = \dfrac{5}{85} = \dfrac{1}{17}$

$$\begin{array}{r} .058 = 5.9\% \\ 17\overline{)1.000} \\ -85x \\ \hline 150 \\ -136 \\ \hline 14 \end{array}$$

Check:

$$\begin{array}{r} {}^{2}6{}^{3}4.7 \\ 1\,7.6 \\ 1\,1.8 \\ 5.9 \\ \hline 10\,0.0 \end{array}$$

2. 8
    4
    3
    2
    1
    ̄ ̄
    18

red $= \dfrac{8}{18} = \dfrac{4}{9}$ $\begin{array}{r}.4\,4\,4 = 44.4\%\\9\overline{)4.0^40^40}\end{array}$

blue $= \dfrac{4}{18} = \dfrac{2}{9}$ $\begin{array}{r}.2\,2\,2 = 22.2\%\\9\overline{)2.0^20^20}\end{array}$

white $= \dfrac{3}{18} = \dfrac{1}{6}$ $\begin{array}{r}.1\,6\,6\,6 = 16.7\%\\6\overline{)1.0^40^40^40}\end{array}$

yellow $= \dfrac{2}{18} = \dfrac{1}{9}$ $\begin{array}{r}.1\,1\,1 = 11.1\%\\9\overline{)1.0^10^10}\end{array}$

green $= \dfrac{1}{18}$ $$\begin{array}{r} .0555 = 5.6\% \\ 18\overline{)1.0000} \\ -90xx \\ \hline 100 \\ -90 \\ \hline 100 \\ -90 \\ \hline 10 \end{array}$$

Check:

$$^{2}4^{2}4.4$$
$$22.2$$
$$16.7$$
$$11.1$$
$$\underline{5.6}$$
$$100.0$$

3.   air $= \dfrac{1500}{5000} = \dfrac{15}{50} = \dfrac{30}{100} = 30\%$

rail $= \dfrac{2300}{5000} = \dfrac{23}{50} = \dfrac{46}{100} = 46\%$

truck $= \dfrac{1200}{5000} = \dfrac{12}{50} = \dfrac{24}{100} = 24\%$

Check:

$$30$$
$$46$$
$$\underline{24}$$
$$100$$

You must know how to do percentage distributions if you are going to succeed at business math. We'll close out this chapter with one more quick quiz and then a self-test. If you get everything right, go directly to Part II. But if you get just one wrong, you'll need to go back to frame 9.

QUICK QUIZ 3.4

1. The University of Wisconsin alumni association has 45,000 members. Women younger than 40 total 4,500; 12,800 are men younger than 40; 7,900 are women older than 40; the remainder are men older than 40. Find the percentage distribution of all four membership categories. Remember to check your work.

2. Mrs. Potts baked three apple pies, two blueberry pies, five cherry pies, and six key-lime pies for the town bake-off. What percentage of the pies were apple, blueberry, cherry, and key lime?

3. During the July 4th weekend, a video store rented 300 westerns, 450 martial arts movies, 100 musicals, 250 children's movies, and 50 foreign films. What percentage of the rentals was in each category?

Answers to Quick Quiz 3.4

1. women under 40 $= \dfrac{4,500}{45,000} = \dfrac{45}{450} = \dfrac{1}{10} = \dfrac{10}{100} = 10\%$

women over 40 $= \dfrac{7{,}900}{45{,}000} = \dfrac{79}{450} = \dfrac{7.9}{45}$

$$
\begin{array}{r}
.1755 = 17.6\% \\
45\overline{)7.9000} \\
-4\ 5\,\text{xxx} \\
\hline
3\ 40 \\
-3\ 15 \\
\hline
250 \\
-225 \\
\hline
250 \\
-225 \\
\hline
25
\end{array}
$$

men under 40 $= \dfrac{12{,}800}{45{,}000} = \dfrac{128}{450} = \dfrac{64}{225}$

$$
\begin{array}{r}
.284 = 28.4\% \\
225\overline{)64.000} \\
-45\ 0\,\text{xx} \\
\hline
19\ 00 \\
-18\ 00 \\
\hline
1\ 000 \\
-900 \\
\hline
100
\end{array}
$$

$$
\begin{array}{r}
4{,}500 \\
7{,}900 \\
12{,}800 \\
\hline
25{,}200
\end{array}
$$

$$
\begin{array}{r}
45{,}000 \\
-25{,}200 \\
\hline
19{,}800
\end{array}
$$

men over 40 $= \dfrac{19{,}800}{45{,}000} = \dfrac{198}{450} = \dfrac{99}{225} = \dfrac{33}{75} = \dfrac{11}{25}$

$$
\begin{array}{r}
.444 = 44\% \\
25\overline{)11.000} \\
-10\ 0\,\text{xx} \\
\hline
1\ 00 \\
-1\ 00
\end{array}
$$

Check:

$$
\begin{array}{r}
10.0 \\
17.6 \\
28.4 \\
44.0 \\
\hline
100.0
\end{array}
$$

2.   apple $= \dfrac{3}{16}$

$$
\begin{array}{r}
.1875 = 18.8\% \\
16\overline{)3.0000} \\
-1\ 6\,\text{xxx} \\
\hline
1\ 40 \\
-1\ 28 \\
\hline
120 \\
-112 \\
\hline
80
\end{array}
$$

blueberry $= \dfrac{2}{16} = \dfrac{1}{8}$

$$
\begin{array}{r}
.1\ 2\ 5 = 12.5\% \\
8\overline{)1.0^20^40}
\end{array}
$$

$$\text{cherry} = \frac{5}{16}$$

$$\begin{array}{r} .3125 = 31.3\% \\ 16\overline{)5.0000} \\ -4\,8\text{xxx} \\ \hline 20 \\ -16 \\ \hline 40 \\ -32 \\ \hline 80 \end{array}$$

$$\text{key lime} = \frac{6}{16} = \frac{3}{8}$$

$$\begin{array}{r} .3\ 7\ 5 = 37.5\% \\ 8\overline{)3.0^60^40} \end{array}$$

Check:

$$\begin{array}{r} 18.8 \\ 12.5 \\ 31.3 \\ 37.5 \\ \hline 100.1 \end{array}$$

3.
$$\begin{array}{r} 300 \\ 450 \\ 100 \\ 250 \\ 50 \\ \hline 1{,}150 \end{array}$$

$$\text{westerns} = \frac{300}{1{,}150} = \frac{30}{115} = \frac{6}{23}$$

$$\begin{array}{r} .260 = 26.1\% \\ 23\overline{)6.0000} \\ -4\,6\text{xxx} \\ \hline 1\,40 \\ -1\,38 \\ \hline 200 \end{array}$$

$$\text{martial arts} = \frac{450}{1{,}150} = \frac{45}{115} = \frac{9}{23}$$

$$\begin{array}{r} .391 = 39.1\% \\ 23\overline{)9.0000} \\ -6\,9\text{xxx} \\ \hline 2\,10 \\ -2\,07 \\ \hline 30 \\ -23 \\ \hline 70 \end{array}$$

$$\text{musicals} = \frac{100}{1{,}150} = \frac{10}{115} = \frac{2}{23}$$

$$\begin{array}{r} .086 = 8.7\% \\ 23\overline{)2.0000} \\ -1\,84\text{xx} \\ \hline 160 \\ -138 \\ \hline 220 \end{array}$$

$$\text{children's movies} = \frac{250}{1{,}150} = \frac{25}{115} = \frac{5}{23}$$

$$\begin{array}{r} .217 = 21.7\% \\ 23\overline{)5.000} \\ -4\,6\text{xx} \\ \hline 40 \\ -23 \\ \hline 170 \\ -161 \\ \hline 9 \end{array}$$

$$\text{foreign films} = \frac{50}{1,150} = \frac{5}{115} = \frac{1}{23}$$

$$\begin{array}{r} .043 = 4.3\% \\ 23\overline{)1.0000} \\ -92\text{xx} \\ \hline 80 \\ -69 \\ \hline 110 \end{array}$$

Check:

$$\begin{array}{r} 26.1 \\ 39.1 \\ 8.7 \\ 21.7 \\ 4.3 \\ \hline 99.9 \end{array}$$

Are you ready to do some more problems to test your knowledge of the entire chapter? If you are, then begin Chapter 3 Self-Test right now. If you'd like to go review some or all of the chapter before taking this test, take all the time you need.

SELF-TEST

Changing Decimals into Percents

1. Change these decimals into percents:
   a. 3.14
   b. 0.78
   c. 32

2. Change these decimals into percents:
   a. 167.4
   b. 0.9
   c. 17.3

3. Change these numbers into percents:
   a. 44
   b. 10
   c. 7

Changing Fractions into Percents

4. Change these fractions into percents:

   a. $\dfrac{8}{25}$

   b. $\dfrac{7}{10}$

   c. $\dfrac{3}{5}$

5. Change these fractions into percents:

   a. $\dfrac{5}{19}$

   b. $\dfrac{7}{8}$

   c. $\dfrac{18}{300}$

Finding Percentage Changes

6. What is the percentage change when we go from
   a. 240 to 300?
   b. 150 to 100?
   c. 80 to 100?

Fast Percentage Changes

7. What is the percentage change from 100 to
   a. 450?
   b. 162?
   c. 88?
   d. 330?

8. If we go from 2 to 10, what is the percentage increase?

Percentage Change Applications

9. On July 1, 1998, the Dow Jones Average stood at 4,100. Over the next three months it fell by 25%. What was the Dow Jones Average on October 1, 1998?

10. Bryant Christopher Thomas purchased a $1 million yacht on which he paid a luxury tax of 10%. What was the total cost of the yacht?

11. Monte Seewald was earning $44,000 and received a 20% pay increase. How much was his new pay?

Percentage Distribution

12. In Professor Patricia Lagleder's accounting class, 2 students received A's, 3 received B's, 5 received C's, 4 received D's, 5 received F's, and 6 students withdrew from the course with a grade of W. What is the percentage distribution of grades in Professor Lagleder's class?

Changing Decimals into Percents

1. a. $3.14 = 314\%$ b. $0.78 = 78\%$ c. $.32 = 32\%$

2. a. $167.4 = 16,740\%$ b. $0.9 = 90\%$ c. $17.3 = 1,730\%$

3. a. $44 = 4,400\%$ b. $10 = 1,000\%$ c. $7 = 700\%$

Changing Fractions into Percents

4. a. $\dfrac{8}{25}$ $.32 = 32\%$

$$25\overline{)8.00}$$
$$-7\ 5x$$
$$50$$

b. $\dfrac{7}{10} = 70\%$

c. $\dfrac{3}{5} = 60\%$ $.60$

$$5\overline{)3.00}$$

5. a. $\dfrac{5}{19}$ $.263 = 26.3\%$

$$19\overline{)5.000}$$
$$-3\ 8xx$$
$$1\ 20$$
$$-1\ 14$$
$$60$$
$$-57$$

b. $\dfrac{7}{8}$ $.875 = 87.5\%$ $8\overline{)7.0^60^40}$

c. $\dfrac{18}{300}$ $.06 = 6\%$

$$300\overline{)18.00}$$
$$-18\ 00$$

Finding Percentage Changes

6. a. 240 to 300? % change $= \dfrac{\text{change}}{\text{original number}} = \dfrac{60}{240} = \dfrac{1}{4} = 25\%$

b. 150 to 100? $\dfrac{50}{150} = \dfrac{1}{3} = 33\frac{1}{3}\%$ or 33.3%

c. 80 to 100? $20 = \dfrac{20}{80} = 25\%$

Fast Percentage Changes

7. a. $450 = 350\%$

b. $162 = 62\%$

c. $88 = -12\%$

d. $330 = 230\%$

8. $\dfrac{8}{2} = \dfrac{4}{1} = 400\%$

Percentage Change Applications

9.
```
    4100
   ×.75
  205 00
 2870 00
 3075.00
```

10. $1,000,000 + $100,000 = $1,100,000

11. $44,000 + $8,800 = $52,800

Percentage Distribution

12.
```
 2
 3
 5
 4
 5
 6
25
```

A: $\dfrac{2}{25} = \dfrac{8}{100} = 8\%$

B: $\dfrac{3}{25} = \dfrac{12}{100} = 12\%$

C: $\dfrac{5}{25} = \dfrac{12}{100} = 20\%$

D: $\dfrac{4}{25} = \dfrac{16}{100} = 16\%$

F: $\dfrac{5}{25} = \dfrac{20}{100} = 20\%$

W: $\dfrac{6}{25} = \dfrac{24}{100} = 24\%$

Part II   Retailing Applications

__4__ Markup and Markdown

Almost no one can resist a bargain. When a store has marked *down* sale items by 40%, 50%, or even more, these low prices are often considered bargains. Sometimes the stores even claim to be selling some things for less than cost. One might wonder how these stores can stay in business.

On the other hand, we hear about merchandise being marked up 100%, 150%, 200%, or even more. And we feel we're being ripped off by these markups.

We need to realize that stores have many other costs besides paying for the merchandise they sell. They also have to cover rent, salaries, taxes, advertising, utilities, insurance, and depreciation, as well as myriad other costs that come with running a business.

And so, it is within that context that we should view mark*ups* and mark*downs*. Are we really being ripped off or are we actually getting bargains? Most often the truth lies somewhere in between.

In general, retailing is extremely competitive, so few stores can make huge profits by overpricing. In the late 1980s, B. Altmans, Macy's, Korvettes, and Federated Department Stores, as well as several other chains went through bankruptcy. Perhaps this apocryphal story best typifies the problems that retailers must deal with.

A woman had been repeatedly shoplifting at Kleins (a New York department store that went bankrupt in the 1970s). One day, as she got caught for maybe the two-hundredth time, a guard said to her, "Mary, why do you keep coming in here? Why don't you go across the street to Mays (another department store that went belly up) and steal a little from them?"

"Are you kidding?" she replied. "And pass up these bargains!"

1 Markup Based on Cost

A storeowner must charge a price high enough not only to cover cost, but also to make a profit as well. After all, she's not in business for her health.

So if you owned a business, you would mark up what you sold well above cost so that you could cover your operating costs. For instance, if you purchased inventory for $100,000, you might need to sell it for $150,000 just to cover the $50,000 it cost you to run your store for a few months. After all, you must pay rent, salaries, utilities, and other operating costs.

In frames 1 through 3 we'll concentrate on markup based on cost, which is really the more widely used form of markup. Markup can also be based on selling price, a subject we'll cover in frames 4 through 8.

Let's start with this basic equation:

$$\text{cost} + \text{markup} = \text{selling price}$$

Think of cost as being 100%, markup as being, say, 50%, and selling price being 150%. Or, if markup were 40%, then selling price would be 140%. Now if selling price were 140%, it would be 140% of cost. And if selling price happened to be 150%, then it would be 150% of cost.

Problem:

Mark Anthony sold military equipment. He received a shipment of swords, which cost him $120 each. If he marked them up by 50%, what was their selling price?

Solution:

$$\text{cost} + \text{markup} = \text{selling price}$$
$$\$120 + \$120 \times .5 = \text{selling price}$$
$$\$120 + \$60 = \text{selling price}$$
$$\$180 = \text{selling price}$$

2

There are actually three types of problems we can do using this equation. In the first type, we knew the cost and the markup and had to find the selling price. Now we'll try a second type of problem.

Problem:

Joe's hotdog stand buys hotdogs with buns for 40 cents and sells them for a dollar. How much is his markup?

Solution:

$$\text{cost} + \text{markup} = \text{selling price}$$
$$\$.40 + \text{markup} = \$1.00$$
$$\text{markup} = \$.60$$

In terms of percentages:

$$\text{cost} + \text{markup} = \text{selling price}$$
$$100\% + \text{markup} = 250\%$$
$$\text{markup} = 150\%$$

3

So far we found selling price and we found markup. What's left? Finding cost.

Problem:

Janet Lowrey is a florist. She marks up her tulips 50% and sells them for $20 a dozen. How much do they cost her?

Solution:

$$\text{cost} + \text{markup} = \text{selling price}$$
$$\text{cost} + 50\% \text{ (of cost)} = \$20$$
$$150\% \text{ of cost} = \$20$$
$$1.5 \times \text{cost} = \$20$$
$$\text{cost} = \$20 \div 1.5$$
$$\text{cost} = \$13.33$$

Now let's try a whole group of problems. In some we'll be finding cost, in some we'll find markup, and in the rest we'll be finding selling price.

QUICK QUIZ 4.1

1. Betty Lou Dorr has a boutique. She marks up her clothing by 120%. How much do the dresses she sells for $100 cost her?

2. Alice Blythe marks up the stereo equipment she sells by 60%. If a set of speakers cost her $140, what does she charge for them?

3. Gomez Appliances buys lawn mowers for $120 and sells them for $199. What is their dollar markup, and what is their markup as a percent of selling price?

4. Johnson and Johnson sells aspirin to drug wholesalers at a 500% markup. If Johnson and Johnson receives $1 per bottle, how much does it cost the company to produce a bottle of aspirin?

5. Susie Wong sells world atlases. If she marks them up by 40% and they cost her $22, how much does she charge for them?

6. Chuck Stickney has a sandwich shop. If it costs him 80 cents to make a tuna sub and he sells it for $2.25, what percentage is his markup?

Answers to Quick Quiz 4.1

1. cost + markup = selling price
    cost + 120% cost = $100
    220% cost = $100
    cost = $100 ÷ 2.2
    cost = $45.45

2. cost + markup = selling price
    $140 + 60% cost = selling price
    $140 + .6 × $140 = selling price
    $140 + $84 = selling price
    $224 = selling price

3. cost + markup = selling price
    $120 + markup = $199
    markup = $79
    markup % = markup ÷ cost
    markup % = 79 ÷ 120
    markup % = 65.8%

4. cost + markup = selling price
    cost + 500% cost = $1
    6 × cost = $1
    cost = $1 ÷ 6
    cost = $.17

5. cost + markup = selling price
    $22 + 40% cost = selling price
    $22 + .4 × $22 = selling price
    $22 + $8.80 = selling price
    $30.80 = selling price

6. cost + markup = selling price
    $.80 + markup = $2.25
    markup = $1.45
    markup % = $1.45 ÷ $.80
    markup % = 181.3%

To calculate markups, you need to know how to calculate percentage changes. If you got all the problems right in Quick Quiz 4.1, please go directly to frame 4. But if you got one or more problems wrong, I want you to ask yourself if you really understand percentage changes. If the answer happens to be no, then you must reread Chapter 3. Markups and markdowns *are* percentage changes. Once you've got them down, this chapter will be a piece of cake.

---

4 Markup Based on Selling Price

Until recently nearly all retail businesses based their markup on cost, but today almost as many companies now base their markup on a percent of selling price. How does that affect us? It means we have to learn a whole new set of calculations.

In the last section, when we knew cost and markup, we could find selling price. When we knew markup and selling price, we could find cost. And when we knew cost and selling price, we could find markup.

Well, there's some *good* news and some *bad* news. The good news is that when we know two of these three variables, we can easily find the third. The bad news is that we must learn three different equations in order to find them.

Let's say we know the markup in dollars, we know the selling price, and we want to find the markup percentage. Here's the formula we use

dollar markup ÷ selling price = markup percent

Suppose that dollar markup is $3 and the selling price is $4. How much is the markup percent?

Solution:

dollar markup ÷ selling price = markup percent
$3 ÷ $4 = markup percent
.75 = 75% = markup percent

5

What if we knew the cost and selling price and wanted to calculate the markup based on selling price? We could still use the same formula, but first we would have to find the dollar markup.

Problem:

The cost is $50, and the selling price is $75. How much is the markup percent?

Solution:

markup = selling price – cost
markup = $75 – $50
markup = $25
dollar markup ÷ selling price = markup percent
$25 ÷ $75 = markup percent
333 = 33.3% = markup percent

6

Now we'll do the second type of problem, when we know both the selling price and the markup percent and need to find the dollar markup. The formula is

selling price × markup percent = dollar markup

Let's say that the selling price is $50 and the markup is 20%. Find the dollar markup.

Solution:

selling price × markup percent = dollar markup
$50 × .2 = dollar markup
$10 = dollar markup

7

Two down, one to go. This time we know the selling price and the dollar markup and need to find the cost. This one is simple subtraction.

selling price – dollar markup = cost

Problem:

If the selling price is $170 and the dollar markup is $40, how much is the cost?

Solution:

$$\text{selling price} - \text{dollar markup} = \text{cost}$$
$$\$170 - \$40 = \text{cost}$$
$$\$130 = \text{cost}$$

8

We've saved our best for last. What is the cost of a suit if the markup is 80% of the selling price and if the selling price is $200?

Do you have a formula? Yes! Use selling price – dollar markup = cost. The trick is to find dollar markup. Give it a try.

Solution:

$$\text{selling price} - \text{dollar markup} = \text{cost}$$
$$\$200 - .8 \times \$200 = \text{cost}$$
$$\$200 - \$160 = \text{cost}$$
$$\$40 = \text{cost}$$

Well, it looks as though you're ready to try Quick Quiz 4.2

QUICK QUIZ 4.2

1. If the selling price is $20 and the dollar markup is $8, how much is the markup percentage?

2. The selling price is $130 and the dollar markup is $35. How much is the cost?

3. What is the cost if the markup is 60% of the selling price and if the selling price is $150?

4. If the selling price is $2,000 and the markup is 35%, find the dollar markup.

5. If the selling price is $195 and the dollar markup is $53, how much is the cost?

6. If the selling price is $65 and the dollar markup is $12, how much is the markup percentage?

7. If the selling price is $550 and the markup is 40%, find the dollar markup.

8. What is the cost if the markup is 40% of the selling price, and if the selling price is $240?

Answers to Quick Quiz 4.2

1. markup percent $= \dfrac{\text{dollar markup}}{\text{selling price}}$

    $= \dfrac{\$8}{\$20}$

    $= \dfrac{4}{10}$

    $= 40\%$

2. selling price – dollar markup = cost
    $$\$130 - \$35 = \text{cost}$$
    $$\$95 = \text{cost}$$

3. selling price – markup = cost
    $$\$150 - .6 \times \$150 = \text{cost}$$
    $$\$150 - \$90 = \text{cost}$$
    $$\$60 = \text{cost}$$

4. dollar markup = selling price × % markup
    dollar markup $= \$2,000 \times .35$
    dollar markup $= \$700$

5. selling price – markup = cost
    $$\$195 - \$53 = \text{cost}$$
    $$\$142 = \text{cost}$$

6. markup % $= \dfrac{\text{markup}}{\text{selling price}}$

    markup % $= \dfrac{\$12}{\$65}$

    markup % $= 18.5\%$

7. dollar markup = selling price × % markup
    $$= \$550 \times .40$$
    $$= \$220$$

8. cost = selling price – dollar markup
    $$= \$240 - (\$240 \times .40)$$
    $$= \$240 - \$96$$
    $$= \$144$$

If you got everything right, then you're definitely ready for frame 9. If you got more than one wrong, then please go back to frame 4 and give it another shot.

9   Markup Based on Cost vs. Markup Based on Selling Price

So far, I've been going on and on about markups based on cost and markups based on selling price. Are these markups the same? If they were, I can assure you that I would not have bothered to write two separate sections.

OK, if they're not the same, then how are they different? That's a good question. Which is larger, a 20% markup on cost, or a 20% markup on selling price?

One would think that a 20% markup on selling price is larger. Now let's prove it. A new Honda Accord cost a dealer $10,000. How much is a 20% markup on cost?

It's $2,000. So then how much is the car's selling price? It's $12,000.

How much is a 20% markup on selling price if selling price is $12,000?

It's $2,400. So for a Honda Accord that sells for $12,000, a 20% markup on cost would be $2,000, but a 20% markup on selling price comes to $2,400.

This leads to a very important question. You go to your friendly automobile dealer. "What's your markup?" you ask her. And she replies, "It's 20%." What's your follow-up question?

"Is that a 20% markup on cost or on selling price?" See if you can get a straight answer.

So a Honda that cost a dealer $10,000 and is marked up by 20% has a selling price of $12,000. The markup is $2,000.

But what if the markup were based on *price* instead of *cost*? How much would that 20% markup be if the price were $12,000?

It would be $12,000 × .2 = $2,400.

To summarize: You have a car selling for $12,000 that has been marked up by 20%. If that markup was based on cost, the markup is $2,000. But if that markup is based on selling price, the markup is $2,400.

We've done a lot of problems so far in this chapter, but here's one we haven't seen. A shoe store buys a pair of shoes for $50. How much will it charge if it uses a selling-price–based markup of 40%?

This is a little complicated, so I'll work it out for you.

$$\text{Selling price} - .4 \times \text{selling price} = \$50$$
$$.6 \times \text{selling price} = \$50$$
$$\text{selling price} = \frac{\$50}{.6}$$
$$\text{selling price} = \$83.33$$

Problem:

A microwave cost Sears $160. How much will Sears charge if it uses a selling-price–based markup of 50%?

Solution:

$$\text{selling price} - \text{markup based on selling price} = \text{cost}$$
$$\text{selling price} - .5 \times \text{selling price} = \$160$$
$$.5 \times \text{selling price} = \$160$$
$$\text{selling price} = \frac{\$160}{.5}$$
$$\text{selling price} = \$320$$

Now let's turn it up a notch:

Problem:

A pair of sneakers cost a sneaker store $60.
   a. How much would the sneakers sell for if the store used a cost-based markup of 40%?
   b. How much would the store charge if it had a 40% selling-price–based markup?

Solution:

a. cost + markup = selling price
$60 + .4 × $60 = selling price
$60 + $24 = selling price
$84 = selling price

b. selling price – markup based on selling price = cost
selling price – .4 × selling price = $60
.6 × selling price = $60

$$selling\ price = \frac{\$60}{.6}$$

selling price = $100

Now it's time for another quiz.

QUICK QUIZ 4.3

1. Mel Tong sells kitchen sets that cost him $350. How much does he charge if he uses a selling-price–based markup of 70%

2. The Gap sets a 60% selling-price–based markup on its jeans. If a pair of jeans costs the Gap $19, how much does it charge?

3. A TV cost the TSS appliance store $140.
    a. How much would it sell for if TSS used a cost-based markup of 80%?
    b. How much would the store charge if it had an 80% selling-price–based markup?

4. Mary Rae's Pet Store pays $100 for collie pups.
    a. How much do the pups sell for if the store had a 75% markup based on cost?
    b. What would the store charge if it had a selling price-based markup of 75%?

Answers to Quick Quiz 4.3

1. selling price – markup based on selling price = cost
selling price – .7 × selling price = $350
.3 × selling price = $350

$$selling\ price = \frac{\$350}{.3}$$

selling price = $1,166.67

2. selling price – markup based on selling price = cost
selling price – .6 × selling price = $19
.4 × selling price = $19

$$selling\ price = \frac{\$19}{.4}$$

selling price = $47.50

3. a.   cost + markup = selling price
$140 + .8 × $140 = selling price
$140 + $112 = selling price
$252 = selling price

    b.   selling price – markup based on selling price = cost
selling price – .8 × selling price = $140
.2 × selling price = $140

$$\text{selling price} = \frac{\$140}{.2}$$

selling price = $700

4. a.   cost + markup = selling price
$100 + .75 × $100 = selling price
$100 + $75 = selling price
$175 = selling price

    b.   selling price – markup based on selling price = cost
selling price – .75 × selling price = $100
.25 selling price = $100

$$\text{selling price} = \frac{\$100}{.25}$$

selling price = $400

10 Markdown

Who can resist a bargain? Imagine a store offering markdowns of 50, 60, or even 70%. Some markdowns!

Of course we might ask why they're offering such great bargains. Often they'll tell us: "Lost our lease," "Going out of business," "Must make room for new stock," or "Must raise cash."

I remember a cartoon I saw many years ago. A man and his young son were sitting in front of a store. A big sign in the window said: GOING OUT OF BUSINESS. The caption read, "Some day, son, this store will be yours."

It's not legal to advertise that you're going out of business if you're really not—no matter how much you've marked down your merchandise. But let's ask the *real* reasons why these stores might be offering such great bargains. Maybe what they're selling—mainly clothing—is going out of style. Maybe they're getting rid of the stuff that hasn't sold. Maybe what they're selling—mainly food—is perishable: If they don't sell it right away, they won't be able to sell it at all. This is not to say that the reasons they're giving are untrue. It's just that there may be other reasons for offering large markdowns that they'd rather not advertise.

Sometimes stores offer special promotions just to get you into the store. When they say they are selling before cost, this may well be true. In which case the goods they are selling are called loss leaders. The owners are betting that if they can just lure you into their stores, you'll buy not just the marked down items, but some other things as well.

Suppose that Roxanne's Dress Shop is having a sale. Everything is marked down by 40%. If you bought a dress for $40, what was its price before the sale?

Solution:

$$\text{sale price} + \text{markdown} = \text{original price}$$
$$\$40 + .4 \times \text{original price} = \text{original price}$$
$$\$40 = .6 \times \text{original price}$$
$$\frac{\$40}{.6} = \text{original price}$$
$$\$66.67 = \text{original price}$$

11

You may have noticed that the markdown is found the same way we found the markup on selling price in the last two sections. Now we'll try something new. A dress is marked down from $50 to $35. How much is the markdown amount and the markdown percentage?

Solution:

$$\text{markdown amount} = \$50 - \$35 = \$15$$
$$\text{markdown \%} = \frac{\text{markdown}}{\text{original price}} = \frac{\$15}{\$50} = 30\%$$

12

Finally, there are multiple markdowns. An air conditioner was selling for $400. The store marked it down by 20%, and when no one bought it, it was marked down an additional 20% (from its last price). How much is it selling for now?

Solution:

$$\text{original price} - \text{markdown} = \text{intermediate price}$$
$$\$400 - .2 \times \$400 = \text{intermediate price}$$
$$\$400 - \$80 = \text{intermediate price}$$
$$\$320 = \text{intermediate price}$$
$$\text{intermediate price} - \text{markdown} = \text{current price}$$
$$\$320 - .2 \times \$320 = \text{intermediate price}$$
$$\$320 - \$64 = \text{intermediate price}$$
$$\$256 = \text{intermediate price}$$

Here's another one. A store marks down an item by 25% from its original price of $1,000. The item is then marked down two more times, by 25%, and then by another 10%. What is the current price?

Solution:

original price – markdown = first intermediate price
$1,000 – .25 × $1,000 = first intermediate price
$1,000 – $250 = first intermediate price
$750 = first intermediate price
first intermediate price – markdown = second intermediate price
$750 – .25 × $750 = second intermediate price
$750 – $187.50 = second intermediate price
$562.50 = second intermediate price
second intermediate price – markdown = current price
$562.50 – .1 × $562.50 = current price
$562.50 – $56.25 = current price
$506.25 = current price

We've covered so much material that it's already time for another self-quiz.

QUICK QUIZ 4.4

1. The Main Street Gift Shop has marked down its stuffed animals by 30%. If you bought a stuffed bear for $14, what was its price before the sale?

2. A lawn mower is marked down from $259 to $199. How much is the markdown amount and the markdown percent?

3. A beach chair is marked down from $39.99 by 20% and then by another 15%. How much is its current price?

4. A sport jacket is marked down from $119.95 by 25%, then 20%, then another 20%. What is its current price?

Answers to Quick Quiz 4.4

1. sale price + markdown = original price
$14 + .3 × original price = original price
$14 = .7 × original price

$$\frac{\$14}{.7} = \text{original price}$$

$20 = original price

2. original price – sale price = markdown
$259 – $199 = markdown
$60 = markdown

$$\text{markdown \%} = \frac{\$60}{\$259}$$

$$= 23.2\%$$

3. original price – markdown = intermediate price
$39.99 – $39.99 × .2 = intermediate price
$39.99 – $8 = intermediate price
$31.99 = intermediate price
intermediate price – markdown = current price
$31.99 – $31.99 × .15 = current price
$31.99 – $4.80 = current price
$27.19 = current price

4.
$$\text{original price} - \text{first markdown} = \text{first intermediate price}$$
$$\$119.95 - \$119.95 \times .25 = \text{first intermediate price}$$
$$\$119.95 - \$29.99 = \text{first intermediate price}$$
$$\$89.96 = \text{first intermediate price}$$
$$\text{first intermediate price} - \text{markdown} = \text{second intermediate price}$$
$$\$89.96 - \$89.96 \times .2 = \text{second intermediate price}$$
$$\$89.96 - \$17.99 = \text{second intermediate price}$$
$$\$71.97 = \text{second intermediate price}$$
$$\text{second intermediate price} - \text{markdown} = \text{current price}$$
$$\$71.97 - \$71.97 \times .2 = \text{current price}$$
$$\$71.97 - \$14.39 = \text{current price}$$
$$\$57.58 = \text{current price}$$

SELF-TEST

Markup based on cost

1. Sylvia Cranston owns an auto supply store and marks up her stock by 75%. How much do the seat covers that she sells for $24.99 cost her?

2. Ted Burns sells carpeting, which he marks up by 45%. If a square yard costs him $6.25, what does he charge?

3. The Ethical Pharmacy receives $6.99 for a bottle of vitamins. If there's a 120% markup, how much does the bottle of vitamins cost the pharmacy?

4. Maris Preen has a coffee shop. If it costs her 8 cents to make a cup of coffee and she charges 75 cents, what percentage is her markup?

Markup based on selling price

5. If the selling price is $50 and the dollar markup is $11, what is the markup percentage?

6. If the selling price is $175 and the dollar markup is $56, what is the cost?

7. What is the cost if the markup is 60% of the selling price and if the selling price is $120?

8. If the selling price is $1,500 and the markup is 35%, find the dollar markup.

Markup based on cost vs. markup based on selling price

9. Sue Ann Rodriguez sells living room sets that cost her $475. How much does she charge if she uses a selling-price–based markup of 55%?

10. The Limited sets a 70% selling-price–based markup on its jeans. If a pair of jeans costs the Limited $21, how much does it charge?

11. An air conditioner cost Nick's Appliances $175.
    a. How much would it sell for if Nick used a cost-based markup of 60%?
    b. How much would the store charge if it had a 75% selling-price–based markup?

Markdown

12. Cheryl's Beauty Supply has marked down its shampoos by 35%. If you bought a bottle of shampoo for $3.25, what was its price before the sale?

13. A Sony Walkman was marked down from $59.95 to $39.95. How much is the markdown amount and the markdown percent?

14. A blouse is marked down from $69.95 by 20%, then an additional 20%, and then 15% more. What is its current price?

ANSWERS

Markup based on cost

1. cost + markup = selling price
   cost + .75 × cost = $24.99
   1.75 cost = $24.99
   $$cost = \frac{\$24.99}{1.75}$$
   cost = $14.28

2. cost + markup = selling price
   $6.25 + .45 × $6.25 = selling price
   $6.25 + $2.81 = selling price
   $9.06 = selling price

3. cost + markup = selling price
   cost + 1.2 × cost = $6.99
   2.2 cost = $6.99
   $$cost = \frac{\$6.99}{2.2}$$
   cost = $3.18

4. cost + markup = selling price
   $.08 + markup = $.75
   markup = $.67
   $$markup \% = \frac{markup}{cost}$$
   $$= \frac{\$.67}{\$.08}$$
   $$= 8.375$$
   $$= 837.5\%$$

Markup based on selling price

5. $$markup \% = \frac{markup}{selling\ price}$$
   $$= \frac{\$11}{\$50}$$
   $$= 22\%$$

6. selling price – markup = cost
   $175 – $56 = $119

7. selling price – markup = cost
   $120 – .6 × $120 = cost
   $120 – 72 = cost
   $48 = cost

8. selling price × % markup = dollar markup
   $1,500 × .35 = dollar markup
   $525 = dollar markup

Markup based on cost vs. markup based on selling price

9. cost + markup = selling price
   $475 + .55 × selling price = selling price
   $475 = .45 selling price
   $$\frac{\$475}{.45} = selling\ price$$
   $1,055.56 = selling price

10. cost + markup = selling price
    $21 + .7 × selling price = selling price
    $21 = .3 selling price
    $$\frac{\$21}{.3} = selling\ price$$
    $70 = selling price

11. a. cost + markup = selling price
     $175 + .6 × $175 = selling price
     $175 + $105 = selling price
     $280 = selling price

    b.   cost + markup = selling price
     $175 + .75 × selling price = selling price
     $175 = .25 selling price
$$\frac{\$175}{.25} = \text{selling price}$$
     $700 = selling price

Markdown

12. selling price + markdown = original price
    $3.25 + .35 × original price = original price
    $3.25 = .65 original price
$$\frac{\$3.25}{.65} = \text{original price}$$
    $5 = original price

13. original price – sale price = markdown
    $59.95 – $39.95 = markdown
    $20 = markdown
$$\text{markdown \%} = \frac{\text{markdown}}{\text{original price}}$$
$$\text{markdown \%} = \frac{\$20}{\$59.95}$$
    markdown % = 33.4%

14. original price – first markdown = first intermediate price
    $69.95 – .2 × $69.95 = first intermediate price
    $69.95 – $13.99 = first intermediate price
    $55.96 = first intermediate price

    first intermediate price – second markdown = second intermediate price
    $55.96 – .2 × $55.96 = second intermediate price
    $55.96 – $11.19 = second intermediate price
    $44.77 = second intermediate price

    second intermediate price – third markdown = current price
    $44.77 – .15 × $44.77 = current price
    $44.77 – $6.72 = current price
    $38.05 = current price

5 Trade and Cash Discounts

In the last chapter you employed your skills with percentages to find retail markups and markdowns. Now we'll use those same skills to calculate trade and cash discounts.

Recently I called a pen manufacturer and attempted to place an order for 2,000 pens. I thought they'd give me a nice quantity discount on such a big order. But the manufacturer wouldn't even talk to me. They dealt only with distributors and retailers, but never with the general public. But I wanted to buy *2,000* pens, I protested. Two thousand is not a large quantity, I was told.

Had I been a retailer or a distributor, I might have received a quantity discount, although the manufacturer more commonly filled much larger orders. Stationery stores that charge 98 cents for pens might be paying the manufacturer less than 49 cents.

Retailers get quantity discounts and regular trade discounts, as well as a variety of other discounts. Then, after receiving all those discounts, they turn around and mark up those goods by 50 or 100% or sometimes even more.

1 Discount from List Price

If you buy from a retailer, you pay retail, or list price. Sometimes that price is actually printed right on the item. For example, a paperback novel might have the price $6.95 printed right on the cover.

Manufacturers and wholesalers always offer retailers a discount off list price, or suggested retail price. Think about it. If the retailers had to pay full price, how could they possibly meet their expenses, let alone make a profit?

How much does the retailer pay for goods? Sometimes 20% less than list, sometimes 30%, sometimes 40%, and sometimes even less. Regular bookstores (called trade bookstores), for example, get a 50% discount off list for most books. But college bookstores generally get only 20% discount on textbooks. You might ask why?

Well, there may be two reasons. First, the college bookstores are shipped several cartons of books for each course, and within two weeks, the books are either sold or shipped back to the publisher. But for run-away bestsellers, most trade bookstores order only 5 or 10 copies of most books, and the books sit on the shelves for months taking up valuable space. So to entice the bookstores to carry their books, the publishers offer a higher discount off list price.

There's another reason why publishers offer college bookstores only a 20% discount for textbooks. These same stores almost always buy back used books at only a fraction of what the students paid, and then turn around and resell them for about three-quarters of the price of a new book. In fact, selling used books is a lot more profitable than selling new books. So it's my guess that if college bookstores stopped buying back used books, the publishers would offer them larger discounts. But because that will probably never happen, we won't have to worry about it.

Speaking of books, one of my textbooks has a list price of $43.95. How much do college bookstores pay for it if my publisher offers them a 20% discount?

Solution:

$$\text{Net price} = \text{list price} - \text{discount}$$
$$= \$43.95 - .2 \times \$43.95$$
$$= \$43.95 - \$8.79$$
$$= \$35.16$$

Problem:

Say you worked at a car dealership that gets its cars at 18% off list. If a certain car lists for $15,000, how much does the dealer pay?

Solution:

$$\text{Net price} = \text{list price} - \text{discount}$$
$$= \$15,000 - .18 \times \$15,000$$
$$= \$15,000 - \$2,700$$
$$= \$12,300$$

Are you ready for the first quick-quiz? All right, then, here it comes:

QUICK QUIZ 5.1

1. Goodyear gives a 27% discount off list on its tires. If Joe's Garage ordered 200 tires that listed at $45.99 each, how much would it have to pay?

2. The Smithtown Stationery Shop ordered 10 boxes of Expresso fine-point pens. If these pens list at $.99 and there are 10 pens in a box, how much did the store have to pay if it received a 35% discount off list?

3. The Friendly Food Center gets a 23% discount off list on all boxes of cereals it receives from a wholesaler. If a box of Quaker Oats retails for $2.49, how much does the store pay for two dozen boxes?

Answers to Quick Quiz 5.1

1. Net price = list price − discount
   = $45.99 − .27 × $45.99
   = $45.99 − $12.42
   = $33.57
   $33.57 × 200 = $6,714

2. Net price = list price − discount
   = $.99 − .35 × $.99
   = $.99 − $.3465
   = $.6435
   $.6435 × 100 = $64.35

3. Net price = list price − discount
   = $2.49 − .23 × $2.49
   = $2.49 − $.5727
   = $1.9173
   24 × $1.9173 = $46.02

You may have noticed that discounts from list price are a lot like markdowns in the last chapter. The only difference is that markdowns are offered to the final consumers, or the public, and discounts from list, or trade discounts, are offered to retailers. The names are different, but the math is exactly the same.

2 Quantity Discounts

Did you hear about the panhandler who asked passersby for 8 cents for a cup of coffee? Finally someone stopped and asked where he could buy a cup of coffee for 8 cents. "So who buys retail?" the panhandler replied.

The whole point of this story is to impress upon you the importance of quantity discounts. Because of shipping and handling costs, most suppliers offer such discounts.

Suppose you had a soft drink delivery route. You made 20 stops, delivering 5 cases at each stop. Imagine if instead you had to make just one stop to drop off 100 cases. Wouldn't you be happy to offer a quantity discount to the customer who buys 100?

Problem:

Your company offers a quantity discount on deliveries of at least 20 cases. You sell a case of soda to stores for $9, but offer a 10% discount to stores accepting delivery of 20 cases or more. How much do you charge a store that orders 25 cases?

Solution:

$$\begin{aligned}
\text{Net price} &= \text{regular price} - \text{discount} \\
&= \$9 - .1 \times \$9 \\
&= \$9 - \$.90 \\
&= \$8.10
\end{aligned}$$
$$\$8.10 \times 25 = \$202.50$$

Problem:

If Philip Morris offers an 8% discount on deliveries of at least 20 cartons of cigarettes and 12% on deliveries of at least 100 cartons, how much would your store pay for 20 cartons if the regular price were $12 a carton (for orders of under 20 cartons)?

Solution:

$$\begin{aligned}
\text{Net price} &= \text{regular price} - \text{discount} \\
&= \$12 - .08 \times \$12 \\
&= \$12 - \$.96 \\
&= \$11.04
\end{aligned}$$
$$\$11.04 \times 20 = \$220.80$$

Problem:

How much would a store pay on an order of 140 cartons?

Solution:

$$\begin{aligned}
\text{Net price} &= \text{regular price} - \text{discount} \\
&= \$12 - .12 \times \$12 \\
&= \$12 - \$1.44 \\
&= \$10.56
\end{aligned}$$
$$\$10.56 \times 140 = \$1,478.40$$

Now we're ready for another set of problems:

QUICK QUIZ 5.2

1. Wellbilt Beds offers retail stores a 10% discount on all orders greater than $3,000. Sam's Furniture places an order for $3,800. How much does the store have to pay?

2. Airtemp offers retailers a 15% discount off the $300 regular price for air conditioners if more than 40 are delivered at one time. Greenwich Appliances orders 50. How much does it pay?

3. Seagram's offers a discount of 5% off all orders of $1,000 or more and 8% off all orders of more than $2,000.

a. If Buy-Rite Liquor Store places an order for $1,549, how much does it pay?

b. If Al's Liquors places an order for $3,712, how much does it have to pay?

4. Grandma's Soup offers a quantity discount of 7% on all deliveries of over 20 cartons. If the Fairmont Grocery orders 30 cartons, how much does this order cost if the regular price is $12.50 per carton?

5. Poland Spring Water gives a 10% discount on deliveries of at least 50 gallons and a 15% discount on deliveries of at least 100 gallons. The regular price the stores pay for deliveries of less than 50 gallons is 40 cents per gallon.

a. How much would a store have to pay for 75 gallons?

b. How much would a store have to pay for 120 gallons?

Answers to Quick Quiz 5.2

1. Net price = regular price – discount
   = $3,800 – .1 × $3,800
   = $3,800 – $380
   = $3,420

2. Net price = regular price – discount
   = $300 – .15 × $300
   = $300 – $45
   = $255
   $255 × 50 = $12,750

3. a. Net price = regular price – discount
   = $1,549 – .05 × $1,549
   = $1,549 – $77.45
   = $1,471.55

   b. Net price = regular price – discount
   = $3,712 – .08 × $3,712
   = $3,712 – $296.96
   = $3,415.04

4. 30 × $12.50 × .93 = $348.75

5. a. 75 × .40 × .90 = $27
   b. 120 × .40 × .85 = $40.80

I'm sure you noticed that I took a couple of shortcuts doing problems 4 and 5. Shortcuts are fine if you continue getting the right answers. Speaking of right answers, how did you do? If you got everything right, then proceed to frame 3. If you got more than one wrong answer, then you need to go back to frame 4 so that you can review quantity discounts. Don't get discouraged. Doing business math is a lot like some country and western dances. You take two steps forward and one step back. And in no time at all, you'll have danced your way through the entire book.

3 ■ Cash Discounts

Trade suppliers really love to be paid on time. In fact they're so anxious to see their money that they often offer their customer discounts—usually about 2% off the bill—if they pay within ten days.

This is very attractive to companies that have the funds available, but every supplier has stories about some of their deadbeat customers. The first job I got after college was writing credit reports on very small businesses for Dun & Bradstreet. My job was to find out about the financial condition of these companies and how quickly they paid their bills. Some kept their suppliers waiting 180 days, 270 days, and even a full year.

Why didn't they pay promptly and take the 2% discount? Some simply didn't have the money. But others would rather hold on to the money for as long as a year because that was worth more to them than a 2% discount. So for these companies, not paying their bills was, in effect, getting a no-interest loan from their suppliers. And from the suppliers' perspective, the question was no longer *when* they were going to get paid, but *if* they were going to get paid at all.

We're now going to consider three very common cash discounts, each of which encourages the customer to pay promptly. The most common is the ordinary dating method discount. Then we'll talk about the end of month discount and the receipt of goods discount.

4 ■ Ordinary Dating Method Discount

Suppliers very commonly offer their customers a 2% discount if they pay within ten days of the invoice, or billing date. If customers don't take advantage of this discount, then they have to pay the full amount within 30 days. These terms are written, 2/10, n/30, and read "two ten, net thirty."

Suppose the invoice is dated May 3. If you pay by May 13, you get a 2% discount. But if you don't take advantage of this discount, then the full amount must be paid within 30 days. It's n/30 or net thirty, because the buyer will also receive a trade discount, or discount off list, and possibly a quantity discount as well. The buyer is entitled to these discounts whether or not she takes advantage of the 2/10 discount.

Problem:

Jason's Health Foods received a bill dated July 9, with terms 2/10, n/30. The bill, which was for $538.75, was paid on July 15. How much did Jason's Health Foods pay?

Solution:

Cash discount = $538.75 × .02 = $10.78
Amount due = $538.75 − $10.78 = $527.97

5

Although 2/10, net/30 is the most common cash discount offered, sometimes suppliers offer more complex cash discounts. How would you read this one: 3/10, 1/20, net/45?

Read it as, "Three ten (or three percent off if you pay within ten days), one twenty (or one percent off if you pay within 20 days), net forty-five (or full amount must be paid within 45 days)."

Problem:

Allied Display Company receives an invoice dated September 1 for $9,164.87, terms 2/10, 1/20, n/30. How much does Allied Display pay if the bill is paid on September 19th?

Solution:

Cash discount = $9,164.87 × .01 = $91.65
Amount due = $9,164.87 − $91.65 = $9,073.22

Problem:

Caesar's Carpet Discount Center received an invoice dated November 3 for $3,954.13, terms 4/10, 2/20, n/45. How much does Caesar's pay if the bill is paid November 8?

Solution:

Cash discount = $3,954.13 × .04 = $158.17
Amount due = $3,954.13 − $158.17 = $3,795.96

6   End of Month (EOM) Discount

Suppose your company received a bill for $3,000, with sales terms 2/10 EOM. The bill was dated April 18. This means that you're entitled to a 2% discount if you pay this bill on or before the tenth day of the month *after* the date of the bill. In other words, you get the discount if you pay on or before May 10.

There *is* an exception to this rule, when the invoice is dated on or after the 26th of the month. In that case the discount is allowed if the bill is paid within the first ten days of the *second* month after the month in the date on the invoice.

This is a lot easier than it sounds. An invoice dated April 18 is payable by May 10. And how about an invoice dated April 28? That's payable on or before June 10.

Problem:

The Aspen Tree Specialists receive an order for $2,873.14. The invoice is dated March 27, with sales terms 3/10 EOM. How much does Aspen pay if the bill is paid on May 5?

Solution:

$$\$2,873.14 \times .03 = \$86.19$$
$$\$2,873.14 - \$86.19 = \$2,786.95$$

Problem:

Ajax Guard Dogs received a $3,000 invoice dated July 6, with sales terms 2/10 EOM. How much does Ajax pay if the bill is paid on August 2?

Solution:

$$\$3,000 \times .98 = \$2,940$$

We performed a mathematical sleight of hand by multiplying $3,000 by .98, instead of multiplying $3,000 by .02 to get the discount of $60 and subtracting that from $3,000 to get the amount paid. Doing it this way saves us a step, so we'll do it from here on.

Problem:

Minnie's Music gets a $1,397.63 bill, sales terms 2/10 EOM, that is dated March 23. If it is paid on April 8, how much is due?

Solution:

$$\$1,397.63 \times .98 = \$1,369.68$$

---

7 **Receipt of Goods (ROG) Discount**

Two down, one to go. I have a question for you: How long does it take from the time an order is shipped until it's actually received? Have you ever gotten something the next day? Have you ever had to wait a week? Suppose your business received an order on February 15 with an invoice dated February 4, and sales terms 2/10, n/30? You would not even have a *chance* to take advantage of that discount. A supplier can easily avoid that problem by offering 2/10 ROG, or 2% off if you pay within 10 days after your receipt of goods.

Problem:

The Majestic Dry Cleaners gets a $1,247.83 bill on January 8, dated January 3, with sales terms 2/10 ROG, net/30. If the bill is paid on January 15, how much is the amount due?

Solution:

$$\$1,247.83 \times .98 = \$1,222.87$$

Problem:

Nationwide Auto Insurance took delivery on a $19,875 shipment on May 20. The invoice was dated May 15 and sales terms were 3/10 ROG. If the bill was paid on May 30, how much was the amount due?

Solution:

$$\$19,985 \times .97 = \$19,278.75$$

Problem:

Alamo Rent A Car gets a bill for $16,958.07 dated January 14. The order is received January 20, and sales terms are 2/10 ROG, net/30. If Alamo pays on January 28, how much is due?

Solution:

$$\$16,958.07 \times .98 = \$16,618.91$$

Now we're going to do a little mix and match. I'll provide the mix of problems, and you'll match them. We'll be doing the ordinary dating method discount, the end of the month (EOM) discount, and the receipt of goods (ROG) discount. You don't have to memorize the names of these discounts, but you *do* need to be able to use them.

QUICK QUIZ 5.3

1. Laurelton Electric gets a bill for $7,582.25 dated March 12. The order is received March 16 and sales terms are 3/10 ROG, net/30. If the company pays on March 24, how much is due?

2. An order dated August 8 for $953.72 was received on August 12 by City Barn Antiques. Sales terms were 3/10, 1/15, net/30. If the bill was paid on August 20, how much was the amount due?

3. An order for $7,408.39 dated November 4 was received on November 7. Sale terms were 2/10/EOM. The bill was paid on December 8. How much was the amount due?

4. Big Yellow Moving Company received a $1,477.53 order dated February 12 on February 17. If the terms of sale were 3/10 ROG, how much was the amount due if the bill was paid on February 25?

5. The Rockdale Drug Company received an order on July 9 for $6,935.38. The invoice was dated July 5 and the terms of sale were 3/10, 2/20, 1/30, net/45.
   a. If Rockdale paid on July 14, how much was the amount due?
   b. If Rockdale paid on July 17, how much was the amount due?

6. Parkway Instant Printing received a $4,052.61 order on May 7. The invoice was dated May 3 and the sales terms were 3/10 EOM. How much is the amount due if the bill is paid on June 8?

Answers to Quick Quiz 5.3

1. $7,582.25 × .97 = $7,354.78
2. $953.72 × .99 = $944.18
3. $7,408.39 × .98 = $7,260.22
4. $1,477.53 × .97 = $1,433.20
5. a. $6,935.38 × .97 = $6,727.32
   b. $6,935.38 × .98 = $6,796.67
6. $4,052.61 × .97 = $3,931.03

It's pretty easy to get these three cash discounts mixed up. If you got each of these right, then proceed directly to frame 8. If you got one or more wrong, I've got a deal for you. Go back to frame 3 and work your way through the entire section on cash discounts. Then take Quick Quiz 5.3 again. I'll bet you'll do a lot better. So what's the deal I'm offering you? I can't give a discount, but the deal is that after you've gone through cash discounts a second time, you may go on to frame 8 even if you don't get everything right in Quick Quiz 5.3.

If you're in business and get bills that specify cash discounts, you can always refer back to frames 3 to 7 of this chapter. So you won't have to go around for the rest of your life with terms like ROG and EOM fixed in your memory, because you've got this book as a reference.

8 Chain Discounts

Sometimes manufacturers, wholesalers, and other suppliers are feeling particularly generous. Not only will they offer retailers the regular trade discount, but on top of that a quantity discount, and even a discount for early payment. But that's not all, folks! Sometimes manufacturers will give advertising discounts to retailers who feature particular items in their newspaper ads.

For example, if Bloomingdales advertises colognes and perfumes, it's likely that the store received an advertising discount from the manufacturer. Similarly, if Krogers Supermarkets set up large displays of breakfast cereals, the stores would get a display discount.

Problem:

Let us suppose that a store received a trade discount of 60%, a quantity discount of 15%, an early payment discount of 3%, an advertising discount of 15%, and a display discount of 10%. If we were to add up all these discounts, how much would that come to?

Solution:

$$60\% + 15\% + 3\% + 15\% + 10\% = 103\%.$$

How could that be? If a retailer received discounts totalling more than 100%, that would mean that the wholesaler or manufacturer would have to pay the retailer just to take the goods off his hands. Which would be absurd.

So we don't add up these discounts. Do you remember what we did in the earlier problems in this chapter? If the list price was $100 and the trade discount was 45%, we just multiplied $100 by .55 to find how much the retailer had to pay. If we have two or three or four discounts, we can work out each discount individually, but I've got a great shortcut. It's called the net decimal equivalent, and it's found by multiplying what the retailer pays after taking the trade discount by what he pays after each of the other discounts he takes.

Let's work out a simple problem. A retailer is entitled to a trade discount of 60%, a quantity discount of 15%, and an early payment of 3%. First we convert each percentage into a decimal: .6, .15, and .03. Then we subtract each decimal from 1: .4, .85, and .97. To find the net decimal equivalent we multiply $.4 \times .85 \times .97$ and get .3298. If the list price were $100, the retailer would have to pay $32.98.

You'll get the hang of this with a few more problems under your belt. Here's one:

Guild Sewing Machines received a shipment of sewing machines that list for $300. If Guild is entitled to a trade discount of 45%, a quantity discount of 5%, and an advertising discount of 10%, how much does it pay for each machine?

Solution:

$$\text{Net decimal equivalent} = .55 \times .95 \times .9 = .47025$$
$$\$300 \times .47025 = \$141.08$$

As you can see, you don't want to round off the net decimal equivalent. By convention, we express these chain discounts in declining order: 45/10/5. Now let's try this one:

Problem:

Ace Cycles is entitled to 30/10/2 chain discount. If Ace purchased 60 mountain bikes that listed at $235, how much did it have to pay?

Solution:

Net decimal equivalent = .7 × .9 × .98 = .6174
60 × $235 × .6174 = $8,705.34

Are you ready for one last set of problems? I hope so, because here it comes.

<table><tr><td>**QUICK QUIZ 5.4**</td><td>

1. The Skydive Parachute Center received a bill for 100 pairs of jumping boots that list at $99.99. If the supplier provided a 40/15/10/5 discount, how much did Skydive have to pay?

2. Lennox Heating Systems received a bill for equipment that listed at $35,400. It was entitled to a chain discount of 30/15/5. How much did it have to pay?

3. Sahadi Importing Company purchased 100 five-pound bags of pistachio nuts that retail at $13.50 a piece. If Sahadi received a chain discount of 50/10/5, how much did it have to pay?

4. Lord & Taylor received a shipment of 400 pairs of Jordache jeans that list at $49.95. How much did the store pay if it was entitled to a chain discount of 55/15/10/2?

</td></tr></table>

Answers to Quick Quiz 5.4

1. Net decimal equivalent = .6 × .85 × .9 × .95 = .43605
100 × $99.99 = $9,999
$9,999 × .43605 = $4,360.06

2. Net decimal equivalent = .70 × .85 × .95 = .56525
$35,400 × .56525 = $20,009.85

3. Net decimal equivalent = .5 × .9 × .95 = .4275
100 × $13.50 = $1,350
$1,350 × .4275 = $577.13

4. Net decimal equivalent = .45 × .85 × .9 × .98 = .337365
400 × $49.95 = $19,980
$19,980 × .337365 = $6,740.55

SELF-TEST

We've covered a lot of different discounts in this chapter. Now we're going to see how well you can use them. But I'm going to give you a break. When you do these problems, if you need to refer back to the chapter text,

I won't say anything. The most important thing about discount problems is not to memorize their solutions, but just to be able to get the right answers.

Discounts from List Price

1. Sony provides retailers with a 35% discount off list on all new VCRs. If Macy's orders 3,500 VCRs that list for $325 each, how much will Macy's pay for the order?

2. Liz Claiborne sells dresses to retailers for 55% off list. If Ann's Dress Shop orders 24 dresses that list for $69.95, how much does the store have to pay?

3. The Bass Shoe Company offers retailers a 42% discount off list. If Treadeasy Shoes orders 40 pairs of shoes that list for $79.95 each, how much does Treadeasy pay?

Quantity Discounts

4. Campbell's Soup offers a quantity discount of 7% on all deliveries of more than 20 cartons. The price per carton is $12.50. If the Fairmont Grocery orders 30 cartons, how much does this order cost?

5. Poland Spring Water gives a 10% discount on deliveries of at least 50 gallons and a 15% discount on deliveries of at least 100 gallons. The regular price the stores pay for deliveries of less than 50 gallons is 40 cents per gallon.
   a. How much would a store have to pay for 75 gallons?
   b. How much would a store have to pay for 120 gallons?

6. Pepsi gives a 9% discount on deliveries of at least 25 cases and a 13% discount on deliveries of at least 50 cases. The regular price is $7 per case.
   a. How much would a store have to pay for 20 cases?
   b. How much would a store have to pay for 90 cases?

Cash Discounts

7. Alamo Rent A Car gets a bill for $16,958.07 dated January 14. The order is received January 20 and sales terms are 2/10 ROG, n/30. If Alamo pays on January 28, how much is due?

8. An order for $3,704.56 dated April 27 was received on May 1. Sale terms were 3/10 EOM. The bill was paid on June 9. How much was due?

9. The Buono Flooring Company received a $9,748.17 order on November 16. The invoice was dated November 12 and the terms of sale were 2/10, 1/20, n/30.
   a. If Buono paid on November 20, what was the amount due?
   b. If Buono paid on November 29, how much was due?

10. Century 21 Realty received an invoice for $27,633.48 dated October 22, sales terms 2/10 EOM. If the bill was paid on November 26, what was the amount due?

11. Nationwide Auto Insurance took delivery on a $19,875 shipment on May 20. The invoice was dated May 15 and sales terms were 3/10 ROG. If the bill was paid on May 30, how much was due?

12. Allsafe Ladder and Scaffolding Company received an invoice dated January 17 for $12,315.62. The shipment arrived on January 28 and the sales terms were 3/10, 2/20, 1/30, n/45.
     a. How much was due if the bill was paid on January 27?
     b. How much was due if the bill was paid on February 1?

Chain Discounts

13. Gravesend Flag Company received a bill for 4,000 flags that list at $19.49 each. If the manufacturer provided a 60/20/2 discount, how much did Gravesend have to pay?

14. Adam Auto School received a bill of $12,437.12. The company was entitled to a chain discount of 45/10/5. How much did the company have to pay?

15. Three Star Mason Supplies purchased 1,000 100-pound bags of cement that retail for $16.85 each. If the company received a chain discount of 40/15/10/3, how much did it have to pay?

16. Nieman-Marcus received a shipment of 700 blouses that list for $69.99 each. How much did the company pay if it was entitled to a chain discount of 60/20/15/10?

ANSWERS

Discounts for List Price

1. $325 × 0.65 = $211.25 for each VCR
    $211.25 × 3,500 = $739,375

2. $69.95 × 0.45 = $31.4775
    $31.4775 × 24 = $755.46

3. $79.95 × 0.58 = $46.371 per pair
    $46.371 × 40 = $1,854.84 for 40 pairs

Quantity Discounts

4. $12.50 × 0.93 = $11.625 per carton
    $11.625 × 30 = $348.75 for 30 cartons

5. a. 0.40 × 0.90 = $0.36 per gallon
        $0.36 × 75 = $27 for 75 gallons

    b. 0.40 × 0.85 = $0.34 per gallon
       $0.34 × 120 = $40.80 for 120 gallons

6. a. $7 × 20 = $140 (no discount)

    b. $7 × 0.87 = $6.09 per case
       $6.09 × 90 = $548.10

Cash Discounts

7. $16,958.07 × 0.98 = $16,618.91

8. $3,704.56 × 0.97 = $3,593.42

9. a. $9,748.17 × 0.98 = $9,553.21
    b. $9,748.17 × 0.99 = $9,650.69

10. $27,633.48 (no discount)

11. $19,875 × 0.97 = $19,278.75

12. a. $12,315.62 × 0.97 = $11,946.15
     b. $12,315.62 × 0.98 = $12,069.31

Chain Discounts

13. Net decimal equivalent = 0.40 × 0.80 × 0.98 = 0.3136
       $19.49 × 0.3136 = $6.112064 for 1 flag
      $6.112064 × 4,000 = $24,448.26

14.   0.55 × 0.90 × 0.95 = 0.47025
    $12,437.12 × 0.47025 = $5,848.56

15. 0.60 × 0.85 × 0.90 × 0.97 = 0.44523
       $16.85 × 0.44523 = $7.5021255
     $7.5021255 × 1,000 = $7,502.13

16. 0.40 × 0.80 × 0.85 × 0.90 = 0.2448
       $69.99 × 0.2448 = $17.133552 per blouse
     17.133552 × 700 = $11,993.49

6 Taking Inventory

Almost every retail business carries a stock of inventory on its shelves. If your shelves were bare, or if you carried only a limited selection of goods, your sales would suffer.

But the more inventory you carry, the more it will cost you. You might have tens or even hundreds of thousands of dollars tied up in inventory, not to mention all that valuable shelf space that is being used.

We are going to focus on three aspects of inventory: (1) methods of inventory evaluation; (2) estimating the amount of inventory; and (3) measuring inventory turnover. We'll discuss three methods of inventory evaluation—the weighted average, FIFO, and LIFO methods.

When it comes to estimating a store's inventory, you can always take a physical inventory, but that involves counting every item individually, which can be extremely expensive and time consuming. We'll look at the most widely used way of estimating inventory—the retail method.

And finally, we'll measure inventory turnover, introducing the two basic measures—inventory turnover at retail and inventory turnover at cost.

1 Weighted Average Inventory Method

When business firms sell off their inventory, they know exactly how much they charged for each unit. But they may have been holding some

TABLE 6.1

Date	Units	Cost	Total Cost
1/1	100	$2.50	_____
5/4	200	2.60	_____
8/23	50	2.65	_____

TABLE 6.1A

ANSWERS TO TABLE 6.1

Date	Units	Cost	Total Cost
1/1	100	$2.50	$250.00
5/4	200	2.60	520.00
8/23	50	2.65	132.50
	350		$902.50

$$\text{Average cost} = \frac{\$902.50}{350} = \$2.58$$

of their inventory for months before selling it. So, for instance, some of the inventory sold in September may have been purchased in August, some in May, and some in January.

So what's the problem? The problem is that the inventory the firm bought in January, May, and August may have cost three different prices. This would be especially true if this were a period of high inflation or if the inventory had been purchased from different suppliers.

Why does the firm need to know how much its inventory cost in the first place? The owners of a firm always need to know how well they're doing. Or how large their profits are. Or whether the firm losing money. Not only do they need this information for themselves, but they must keep accurate records for tax purposes.

The weighted average method of inventory valuation is very much like figuring a grade point average in college. Suppose you took a four-credit course and two three-credit courses. You would multiply your grade in the four-credit course by four, and your grades in each of the three-credit courses by three. Then, after adding up these three products, you would divide that number by ten, or the total number of credits. Using the weighted average method of inventory valuation, we multiply the cost of the inventory that we purchased times the number of units we purchased on that date. We then add the total cost of our inventory purchases and divide that sum by the total number of units we purchased. This process sounds a lot more complicated than it actually is.

The weighted average method of inventory valuation is the first of the three methods we shall consider. Let's continue the problem we started at

TABLE 6.2

Date of Purchase	Units	Cost	Total Cost
6/15	8	$8,365	_____
6/29	11	8,433	_____
7/3	9	8,509	_____
7/29	15	8,531	_____

TABLE 6.2A

ANSWERS TO TABLE 6.2

Date of Purchase	Units	Cost	Total Cost
6/15	8	$8,365	$66,920
6/29	11	8,433	92,763
7/3	9	8,509	76,581
7/29	15	8,531	127,965
	43		$364,229

$$\text{Average cost} = \frac{\$364,229}{43} = \$8,470.44$$

the beginning of this section. A firm sold off some inventory in September that had been purchased in January, May, and August. Suppose that it bought 100 units on January 1, 200 units on May 4, and 50 units on August 23, and that it had sold these 350 units on September 6. Given the information in Table 6.1, see if you can figure out the average cost (or, technically, the weighted average cost) per unit. See Table 6.1A for the solution.

Once you have completed Table 6.1, find the average cost of inventory based on the information in Table 6.2. See Table 6.2A for the solution.

QUICK QUIZ 6.1

Find average cost of inventory for these problems.

1.

Date	Units	Cost	Total Cost
8/9	10	$215	_____
8/24	14	217	_____
9/3	7	213	_____
10/15	12	214	_____

2.

Date of Purchase	Units	Cost	Total Cost
10/5	73	$10.17	_____
11/21	96	10.18	_____
12/4	81	10.13	_____
12/30	55	10.11	_____

3. Date of Purchase	Units	Cost	Total Cost
4/5	143	$198.06	_____
6/3	122	199.34	_____
9/12	260	199.87	_____
11/22	208	200.12	_____

Answers to Quick Quiz 6.1

1. Date	Units	Cost	Total Cost
8/9	10	$215	$2,150
8/24	14	217	3,038
9/3	7	213	1,491
10/15	12	214	2,568
	43		$9,249

$$\text{Average cost} = \frac{\$9,249}{43} = \$215.09$$

2. Date of Purchase	Units	Cost	Total Cost
10/5	73	$10.17	$ 742.41
11/21	96	10.18	977.28
12/4	81	10.13	820.53
12/30	55	10.11	556.05
	305		$3,096.27

$$\text{Average cost} = \frac{\$3,096.27}{305} = \$10.152.$$

3. Date of Purchase	Units	Cost	Total Cost
4/5	143	$198.06	$ 28,322.58
6/3	122	199.34	24,319.48
9/12	260	199.87	51,966.20
11/22	208	200.12	41,624.96
	733		$146,233.22

$$\text{Average cost} = \frac{\$146,233.22}{733} = \$199.503.$$

If you got each of these right, then you're ready to go on to frame 2. If you had one or more wrong answers, then you should review frame 1 and retake Quick Quiz 6.1.

2 FIFO Inventory Method

The first-in, first-out inventory evaluation method makes two basic assumptions: (1) the oldest inventory is sold first; and (2) the current inventory is what was acquired most recently.

TABLE 6.3

Date of Purchase	Units Purchased	Cost per Unit	Total Cost
Beginning Inventory	36	$10	$360
3/6	17	8	136
4/26	19	7	133
5/19	23	9	207
	95		$836

Goods available for sale	95
Units sold	–52
Ending inventory	43

When you buy milk, don't you check the date stamped on the carton? If today were October 17, you might be a little nervous about buying milk stamped with that date. You'd look for a carton that was stamped October 21 or perhaps an even later date.

Often the people who stack the supermarket shelves will place the newer items in the back and move the older items to the front. You may have no way of knowing this, except when you buy items that have date stamps. The next time you're shopping, check to see if newer milk is in the back of the case and the older milk is placed in the front. If you find the milk is arranged that way, you'll know that they're using the FIFO inventory method.

Remember that we're really dealing with an accounting concept of inventory evaluation, so we're *saying* that the first items in are the first sold. Even if the actual physical flow of goods does not always follow the pattern of first in, first out, the Internal Revenue Service still allows companies to use the FIFO method. Now let's get down to actual cases.

Use the information in Table 6.3 to find the cost of goods sold using FIFO. I'm going to do this problem with you step-by-step. The first step is to study the table.

Step 2: Find which items at which prices are in the ending inventory at the bottom of the table. There are 43 items in the ending inventory, and these were the most recently purchased items.

Did you find which items were purchased most recently? The 23 items that were purchased on May 19 and the 19 that were purchased on April 26 add up to just 42, so we need to take one more item that was purchased on March 6.

Step 3: We're going to calculate the cost of the ending inventory. To do that we multiply the cost per item times the number of items, and then add the sums to get the cost of the ending inventory:

5/19	23 items	×	$9	=	$207
4/26	19 items	×	7	=	133
3/6	1 item	×	8	=	8
	43 items				$348

TABLE 6.4

Date of Purchase	Units Purchased	Cost per Unit	Total Cost
Beginning Inventory	78	$12	$936
7/15	50	11	550
8/1	32	10	320
9/22	41	13	533
	201		$2,339

Goods available for sale	201
Units sold	−142
Ending inventory	59

Solution:

9/22	41 items	×	$13	=	$533
8/1	18 items	×	10	=	180
	59 items				$713

Cost of goods sold = cost of goods available for sale − ending inventory
= $2,339   − $713
= $1,626

Step 4: We're finally ready to find the cost of goods sold:

Cost of goods sold = cost of goods available for sale − ending inventory
= $836   − $348
= $488

Now it's your turn. Find the cost of goods sold using the data from Table 6.4 using FIFO. The solution is provided with the table, but try not to look until you've tried on your own.

QUICK QUIZ 6.2

Using these tables, find the cost of goods sold, using FIFO.

1. Date of Purchase	Units Purchased	Cost per Unit	Total Cost
Beginning Inventory	216	$190	$41,040
5/10	173	177	30,621
7/1	156	173	26,988
9/29	180	181	32,580
	725		$131,229

Goods available for sale	725
Units sold	−519
Ending inventory	206

2.

Date of Purchase	Units Purchased	Cost per Unit	Total Cost
Beginning Inventory	1,014	$19	$19,266
11/28	531	20	10,620
12/15	659	22	14,498
1/2	527	23	12,121
2/6	670	24	16,080
	3,401		$72,585

Goods available for sale	3,401
Units sold	−2,200
Ending inventory	1,201

3.

Date of Purchase	Units Purchased	Cost per Unit	Total Cost
Beginning Inventory	1,257	$1.97	$2,476.29
3/17	461	1.99	917.39
4/6	596	2.04	1,215.88
5/30	342	2.10	718.20
	2,656		$5,327.72

Goods available for sale	2,656
Units sold	−1,588
Ending inventory	1,068

Answers to Quick Quiz 6.2

1. 9/29 180 items × 181 = $32,580
   7/1   26 items × 173 = 4,498
                          $37,078

   Cost of goods sold = cost of goods available for sale – ending inventory
                      = $131,229   – $37,078
                      = $ 94,151

2. 2/6 670 items × 24 = $16,080
        527 items × 23 = 12,121
          4 items × 22 =   88
                         $28,289

   Cost of goods sold = cost of goods available for sale – ending inventory
                      = $72,585   – $28,289
                      = $44,296

3. 5/30 342 items × $2.10 = $ 718.20
   4/6   596 items × 2.04 =   1,215.84
   3/17 130 items × 1.99 =   258.70
                            $2,192.74

   Cost of goods sold = cost of goods available for sale – ending inventory
                      = $5,327.72   – $2,192.74
                      = $3,134.98

TABLE 6.5

Date of Purchase	Units Purchased	Cost per Unit	Total Cost
Beginning inventory	36	$10	$360
3/6	17	8	136
4/26	19	7	133
5/19	23	9	207
	95		$836

Goods available for sale	95
Units sold	−52
Ending inventory	43

Solution:

$$36 \text{ items} \times \$10 = \$360$$
$$7 \text{ items} \times \$\ 8 = \underline{\ \ 56}$$
$$\$416$$

Cost of goods sold = cost of goods available for sale − ending inventory
= $836   − $416
= $420

---

3 LIFO Inventory Method

The last-in, first-out inventory evaluation method makes the opposite assumptions from those made in the FIFO method. The two basic assumptions of LIFO are (1) the newest inventory is sold first; and (2) the current inventory is what was acquired earliest.

So the cost of the ending inventory is based on the cost of the oldest stock. There is a great tax advantage to LIFO. Assuming that the newer, higher costing inventory is sold first raises the costs of the firm. The higher the costs, the lower the profits. And the lower the profits, the lower the taxes that the firm will have to pay.

Using the data in Table 6.5, I'm going to find the cost of goods sold using the LIFO method of inventory evaluation.

Once you've read Table 6.5, it's your turn. Using the data in Table 6.6, find the cost of goods sold using the LIFO method of inventory evaluation.

Table 6.7 gives you one more LIFO problem in which to find the cost of goods sold.

TABLE 6.6

Date of Purchase	Units Purchased	Cost per Unit	Total Cost
Beginning inventory	78	$12	$936
7/15/96	50	11	550
8/1/96	32	10	320
9/22/96	41	13	533
	201		$2,339

Goods available for sale	201
Units sold	−142
Ending inventory	59

Solution:

59 items × $ 12 = $708

Cost of goods sold = cost of goods available for sale − ending inventory

= $2,339   − $708

= $1,631

TABLE 6.7

Date of Purchase	Units Purchased	Cost per Unit	Total Cost
Beginning inventory	216	$190	$41,040
5/10	173	177	30,621
7/1	156	173	26,988
9/29	180	181	32,580
	725		$131,229

Goods available for sale	725
Units sold	519
Ending inventory	206

Solution:

206 items × $190 = $39,140

Cost of goods sold = cost of goods available for sale − ending inventory

= $131,229   − $39,140

= $ 92,089

QUICK QUIZ 6.3 For each of these, use LIFO to find the cost of goods sold.

1.

Date of Purchase	Units Purchased	Cost per Unit	Total Cost
Beginning inventory	1,014	$19	$19,266
9/28	531	20	10,620
10/15	659	22	14,498
11/2	527	23	12,121
12/6	670	24	16,080
	3,401		$72,585

Goods available for sale 3,401
Units sold   −2,227
Ending inventory   1,174

2.

Date of Purchase	Units Purchased	Cost per Unit	Total Cost
Beginning inventory	1,257	$1.97	$2,476.29
3/17	461	1.99	917.39
4/6	596	2.04	1,215.84
5/30	342	2.10	718.20
	2,656		$5,327.72

Goods available for sale 2,656
Units sold   −1,588
Ending inventory   1,068

3.

Date of Purchase	Units Purchased	Cost per Unit	Total Cost
Beginning inventory	63	$177	$11,151
7/31	46	179	8,234
9/14	29	183	5,307
11/23	37	186	6,882
	175		$31,574

Goods available for sale 175
Units sold   −88
Ending inventory   87

Answers to Quick Quiz 6.3

1.   1,014 items × $19 = $19,266
         160 items × 20 =   3,200
                     $22,466

Cost of goods sold = cost of goods available for sale − ending inventory
                = $72,585   − 22,466
                = $50,119

2.   1,068 items × $1.97 = $2,103.96

Cost of goods sold = cost of goods available for sale – ending inventory
= $5,327.72   – $2,103.96
= $3,223.76

3.   63 items × $177 = $11,151
24 items × $179 =   4,296
$15,447

Cost of goods sold = cost of goods available for sale – ending inventory
= $31,574   – $15,447
= $16,130

4   Retail Method of Estimating Inventory

How do you take the inventory of your store? You can take a physical inventory by counting everything on your shelves. But as we said earlier in the chapter, that would be extremely expensive and time-consuming. You can do an eyeball estimate, which, of course, sacrifices accuracy, but definitely saves time and money. Some stores, especially supermarkets, have electronic scanners at their checkout counters, which have the capability of keeping track of inventory. But few retail stores can afford this system. And finally, a growing number of stores are entering every sale into their computer system, to keep a running total of all items in their inventory.

What we're going to do here is called the retail method of estimating inventory. Although it's not as precise as the other methods we just described, it can be done very quickly, using figures that most firms have available. We're about to estimate our inventory by using the figures in Table 6.8.

I've got a couple of very easy addition problems for you to do. First find cost of goods available for sale at cost. And then find cost of goods available at retail. Do your work right on Table 6.8.

Did you get $19,500 for cost of goods available for sale at cost? And did you get $31,300 for cost of goods available for sale at retail? Good! Now take cost of goods available for sale at retail and subtract ending inventory at retail.

TABLE 6.8

	Cost	Retail
Beginning inventory	$12,100	$19,500
Net purchases during month	7,400	11,800
Cost of goods available for sale	_____	
Net sales for month		6,400
Ending inventory at retail		_____
Cost ratio		_____
Ending inventory at cost		_____

TABLE 6.8A

ANSWERS TO TABLE 6.8

	Cost	Retail
Beginning inventory	$12,100	$19,500
Net purchases during month	7,400	11,800
Cost of goods available for sale	$19,500	$31,300
Net sales for month		6,400
Ending inventory at retail		$24,900
Cost ratio		
Ending inventory at cost		

TABLE 6.8B

ANSWERS TO TABLE 6.8

	Cost	Retail
Beginning inventory	$12,100	$19,500
Net purchases during month	7,400	11,800
Cost of goods available for sale	$19,500	$31,300
Net sales for month		6,400
Ending inventory at retail		$24,900
Cost ratio		0.62
Ending inventory at cost		$15,438

TABLE 6.9

	Cost	Retail
Beginning inventory	$188,200	$301,600
Net purchases during month	171,400	274,000
Cost of goods available for sale	_____	_____
Net sales for month		289,700
Ending inventory at retail		_____
Cost ratio		_____
Ending inventory at cost		_____

TABLE 6.9A

ANSWERS TO TABLE 6.9

	Cost	Retail
Beginning inventory	$188,200	$301,600
Net purchases during month	171,400	274,000
Cost of goods available for sale	$359,600	$575,600
Net sales for month		289,700
Ending inventory at retail		$285,900
Cost ratio		0.62
Ending inventory at cost		$177,258

You should have gotten $24,900. So right now Table 6.8 looks just like Table 6.8A.

Two more calculations and we're finished. The formula for the cost ratio is:

$$\text{Cost ratio} = \frac{\text{cost of goods available for sale at cost}}{\text{cost of goods available for sale at retail}}$$

Calculate the cost ratio to the nearest hundredth (that is, round to two decimal places).

Solution:

$$\text{Cost ratio} = \frac{\$19,500}{\$31,300} = 0.62$$

And now we're finally ready to find our ending inventory at cost. All we need to do is multiply ending inventory at retail by the cost ratio. So do that and then write your cost ratio and your ending inventory at cost right on Table 6.8. Then check to see if all of your figures match mine in Table 6.8B.

The retail method of estimating inventory can be done by just filling in a table. So fill in Table 6.9 and check your work with mine in Table 6.9A.

QUICK QUIZ 6.4

In these problems, fill in the table to find the ending inventory at cost.

1.

	Cost	Retail
Beginning inventory	$91,600	$137,300
Net purchases during month	47,000	70,400
Cost of goods available for sale	_____	_____
Net sales for month		86,900
Ending inventory at retail		_____
Cost ratio		_____
Ending inventory at cost		_____

2.

	Cost	Retail
Beginning inventory	$19,500	$33,200
Net purchases during month	9,800	16,700
Cost of goods available for sale	_____	_____
Net sales for month		21,400
Ending inventory at retail		_____
Cost ratio		_____
Ending inventory at cost		_____

3.

	Cost	Retail
Beginning inventory	$107,100	$203,000
Net purchases during month	89,500	70,100
Cost of goods available for sale	_____	
Net sales for month		188,600
Ending inventory at retail		_____
Cost ratio		_____
Ending inventory at cost		_____

Answers to Quick Quiz 6.4

1.

	Cost	Retail
Beginning inventory	$91,600	$137,300
Net purchases during month	47,000	70,400
Cost of goods available for sale	$138,600	$207,700
Net sales for month		86,900
Ending inventory at retail		$120,800
Cost ratio		0.67
Ending inventory at cost		$80,936

2.

	Cost	Retail
Beginning inventory	$19,500	$33,200
Net purchases during month	9,800	16,700
Cost of goods available for sale	$29,300	$49,900
Net sales for month		21,400
Ending inventory at retail		$28,500
Cost ratio		0.59
Ending inventory at cost		$16,815

3.

	Cost	Retail
Beginning inventory	$107,100	$203,000
Net purchases during month	89,500	107,100
Cost of goods available for sale	$196,600	$373,100
Net sales for month		188,600
Ending inventory at retail		$184,500
Cost ratio		0.53
Ending inventory at cost		$97,785

5   Measuring Inventory Turnover

Carrying inventory is a major business expense. A medium-size grocery, sporting goods, furniture, or clothing store has tens of thousands of dollars tied up in inventory. And this inventory, of course, also takes up valuable shelf space. So the faster you can move your inventory, the more money you make.

TABLE 6.10

Net sales	$117,400
Beginning inventory at retail	62,600
Ending inventory at retail	53,900
Cost of goods sold	66,500
Beginning inventory at cost	35,400
Ending inventory at cost	30,500

$$\text{Average inventory at retail} = \frac{\text{beginning inventory} + \text{ending inventory}}{2}$$

$$= \frac{\$62,600 + 53,900}{2} = \frac{116,500}{2} = \$58,250$$

$$\text{Inventory turnover at retail} = \frac{\text{net sales}}{\text{average inventory at retail}}$$

$$= \frac{\$117,400}{58,250} = 2.02$$

Food stores usually have very high rates of inventory turnover, while stores that sell appliances, furniture, consumer electronics, hardware and home furnishings all have relatively low turnover rates. In the problems that follow, we haven't specified the period of inventory turnover, but it is most commonly one month.

Inventory turnover is the number of times that a business firm replaces its inventory over a specific period of time. Two different rates can be calculated: (1) inventory turnover at retail and (2) inventory turnover at cost.

6

First we'll find inventory turnover at retail. We'll use this formula:

$$\text{Inventory turnover at retail} = \frac{\text{net sales}}{\text{average inventory at retail}}$$

We'll need some numbers to plug into this formula. You'll find them in Table 6.10. Net sales can be plugged right in, but we'll need to do a little work to find average inventory at retail.

7

Now we'll use information from Table 6.10 to find inventory turnover at cost. First, we'll find average inventory at cost:

$$\text{Average inventory at cost} = \frac{\text{beginning inventory} + \text{ending inventory}}{2}$$

$$= \frac{\$35,400 + \$30,500}{2} = \frac{65,900}{2}$$

$$= \$32,950$$

TABLE 6.11

Net sales	$60,600
Beginning inventory at retail	53,400
Ending inventory at retail	58,700
Cost of goods sold	41,600
Beginning inventory at cost	36,800
Ending inventory at cost	40,000

$$\text{Average inventory at retail} = \frac{\text{beginning inventory} + \text{ending inventory}}{2}$$

$$= \frac{\$53,400 + \$58,700}{2} = \frac{\$112,100}{2} = \$56,050$$

$$\text{Inventory turnover at retail} = \frac{\text{net sales}}{\text{average inventory at retail}}$$

$$= \frac{\$60,600}{\$56,050} = 1.08$$

$$\text{Average inventory at cost} = \frac{\text{beginning inventory} + \text{ending inventory}}{2}$$

$$= \frac{\$36,800 + \$40,000}{2} = \frac{\$76,800}{2} = \$38,400$$

$$\text{Inventory turnover at cost} = \frac{\text{net sales}}{\text{average inventory at cost}}$$

$$= \frac{\$60,600}{\$38,400} = 1.58$$

$$\text{Inventory turnover at cost} = \frac{\text{net sales}}{\text{average inventory at cost}}$$

$$= \frac{\$117,400}{32,950} = 3.56$$

Let's work out one more problem before we complete the final quick quiz of this chapter. Using the information in Table 6.11, find (a) inventory turnover at retail and (b) inventory turnover at cost.

QUICK QUIZ 6.5

For each of these problems, find (a) inventory turnover at retail, and (b) inventory turnover at cost.

1. Net sales	$17,300
Beginning inventory at retail	12,500
Ending inventory at retail	13,000
Cost of goods sold	9,100
Beginning inventory at cost	6,900
Ending inventory at cost	7,300

2. Net sales $175,600
   Beginning inventory at retail   214,700
   Ending inventory at retail   202,400
   Cost of goods sold   101,900
   Beginning inventory at cost   122,800
   Ending inventory at cost   113,700

3. Net sales $88,200
   Beginning inventory at retail   113,000
   Ending inventory at retail   117,900
   Cost of goods sold   46,900
   Beginning inventory at cost   59,100
   Ending inventory at cost   61,400

Answers to Quick Quiz 6.5

1. Average inventory at retail = $\dfrac{\text{beginning inventory} + \text{ending inventory}}{2}$

$$= \frac{\$12,500 + \$13,000}{2} = \frac{\$25,500}{2} = \$12,750$$

Inventory turnover at retail = $\dfrac{\text{net sales}}{\text{average inventory at retail}}$

$$= \frac{\$17,300}{\$12,750} = 1.36$$

Average inventory at cost = $\dfrac{\text{beginning inventory} + \text{ending inventory}}{2}$

$$= \frac{\$6,900 + \$7,300}{2} = \frac{\$14,200}{2} = \$7,100$$

Inventory turnover at cost = $\dfrac{\text{net sales}}{\text{average inventory at cost}}$

$$= \frac{\$17,300}{\$7,100} = 2.44$$

2. Average inventory at retail = $\dfrac{\text{beginning inventory} + \text{ending inventory}}{2}$

$$= \$214,700 + \frac{\$202,400}{2} = \frac{\$417,100}{2} = \$208,550$$

Inventory turnover at retail = $\dfrac{\text{net sales}}{\text{average inventory at retail}}$

$$= \frac{\$175,600}{\$208,550} = 0.84$$

$$\text{Average inventory at cost} = \frac{\text{beginning inventory} + \text{ending inventory}}{2}$$

$$= \frac{\$122,800 + \$113,700}{2} = \frac{\$236,500}{2} = \$118,250$$

$$\text{Inventory turnover at cost} = \frac{\text{net sales}}{\text{average inventory at cost}}$$

$$= \frac{\$175,600}{\$118,250} = 1.48$$

3. $$\text{Average inventory at retail} = \frac{\text{beginning inventory} + \text{ending inventory}}{2}$$

$$= \frac{\$113,000 + \$117,900}{2} = \frac{\$230,900}{2} = \$115,450$$

$$\text{Inventory turnover at retail} = \frac{\text{net sales}}{\text{average inventory at retail}}$$

$$= \frac{\$88,200}{\$115,450} = 0.76$$

$$\text{Average inventory at cost} = \frac{\text{beginning inventory} + \text{ending inventory}}{2}$$

$$= \frac{\$59,100 + \$61,400}{2} = \frac{\$120,500}{2} = \$60,250$$

$$\text{Inventory turnover at cost} = \frac{\text{net sales}}{\text{average inventory at cost}}$$

$$= \frac{\$88,200}{\$60,250} = 1.46$$

SELF-TEST

Weighted Average Inventory Method

1. Find the weighted cost of inventory using the table.

Date	Units	Cost	Total Cost
7/19	12	$306	_____
7/31	15	304	_____
8/5	17	301	_____
8/28	14	302	_____

2. Find the weighted cost of inventory using the table.

Date	Units	Cost	Total Cost
2/6	115	$15.60	_____
3/1	104	15.53	_____
3/21	98	15.59	_____
4/18	111	15.55	_____

FIFO Inventory Method

3. Find the cost of goods sold with the FIFO using the data from the table.

Date of Purchase	Units Purchased	Cost per Unit	Total Cost
Beginning inventory	30	$10	$300
8/3	22	$12	264
8/26	19	$11	209
9/15	25	$13	325
	96		$1,098

Goods available for sale	96	
Units sold	−71	
Ending inventory	25	

4. Find the cost of goods sold with the FIFO using the data from the table.

Date of Purchase	Units Purchased	Cost per Unit	Total Cost
Beginning inventory	181	$12.96	$2,345.76
3/29	75	$13.03	977.25
4/12	63	$13.12	826.56
5/3	70	$13.09	916.30
	389		$5,065.87

Goods available for sale	389	
Units sold	−201	
Ending inventory	188	

LIFO Inventory Method

5. Find the cost of goods sold with the LIFO using the data from the table.

Date of Purchase	Units Purchased	Cost per Unit	Total Cost
Beginning Inventory	30	$10	$300
8/3	22	$12	264
8/26	19	$11	209
9/15	25	$13	325
	96		$1,098

Goods available for sale	96	
Units sold	−71	
Ending inventory	25	

6. Find the cost of goods sold with the LIFO using the data from the table.

Date of Purchase	Units Purchased	Cost per Unit	Total Cost
Beginning Inventory	181	$12.96	$2,345.76
3/29	75	$13.03	977.25
4/12	63	$13.12	826.56
5/3	70	$13.09	916.30
	389		$5,065.87

Goods available for sale	389	
Units sold	−201	
Ending inventory	188	

Retail Method of Estimating Inventory

7. Fill in the table to find the ending inventory at cost.

	Cost	Retail
Beginning Inventory	$15,200	$26,500
Net purchases during month	12,600	21,900
Cost of goods available for sale	_____	
Net sales for month		$20,200
Ending inventory at retail		_____
Cost ratio		_____
Ending inventory at cost		_____

8. Fill in the table to find the ending inventory at cost.

	Cost	Retail
Beginning Inventory	$48,700	$77,900
Net purchases during month	30,500	49,900
Cost of goods available for sale	___	___
Net sales for month		$52,100
Ending inventory at retail		___
Cost ratio		___
Ending inventory at cost		___

Measuring Inventory Turnover

9. Find (a) inventory turnover at retail, and (b) inventory turnover at cost.

Net sales	$140,000
Beginning inventory at retail	74,900
Ending inventory at retail	71,600
Cost of goods sold	82,100
Beginning inventory at cost	43,900
Ending inventory at cost	42,000

10. Find (a) inventory turnover at retail, and (b) inventory turnover at cost.

Net sales	$317,400
Beginning inventory at retail	195,800
Ending inventory at retail	199,300
Cost of goods sold	153,600
Beginning inventory at cost	94,800
Ending inventory at cost	96,500

ANSWERS

Weighted Average Inventory Method

1.
Date	Units	Cost	Total Cost
7/19	12	$306	$3,672
7/31	15	304	4,560
8/5	17	301	5,117
8/28	14	302	4,228
	58		$17,577

$$\frac{\$17,577}{58} = \$303.05$$

2. Date	Units	Cost	Total Cost
2/6	115	$15.60	$1,794.00
3/1	104	15.53	1,615.12
3/21	98	15.59	1,527.82
4/18	111	15.55	1,726.05
	428		$6,662.99

$$\frac{\$6,662.99}{428} = \$15.57$$

FIFO Inventory Method

3. Cost of goods sold = cost of goods available for sale – ending inventory
   = $1,098   – $325
   = $ 773

4. 5/3/95   70 items × $13.09 = $ 916.30
   4/12/95   63 items × 13.12 =   826.56
   3/29/95   55 items × 13.03 =   716.65
            188 items $2,459.51

   Cost of goods sold = cost of goods available for sale – ending inventory
   = $5,065.87   – $2,459.51
   = $2,606.36

LIFO Inventory Method

5. 25 items × $10 = $250

   Cost of goods sold = cost of goods available for sale – ending inventory
   = $1,098   – $250
   = $ 848

6. 181 items × $12.96 = $2,345.76
      7 items × $13.03 =   91.21
                    $2,436.97

   Cost of goods sold = cost of goods available for sale – ending inventory
   = $5,065.87   –2,436.97
   = $2,628.90

Retail Method of Estimating Inventory

7.

	Cost	Retail
Beginning Inventory	$15,200	$26,500
Net purchases during month	12,600	21,900
Cost of goods available for sale	$27,800	$48,400
Net sales for month		$20,200
Ending inventory at retail		$28,200
Cost ratio		0.57
Ending inventory at cost		$16,074*

$$\text{Cost ratio} = \frac{\$27,800}{\$48,400} = 0.57$$

Ending inventory at cost = *$28,200 × 0.57 = $16,074

8.

	Cost	Retail
Beginning Inventory	$48,700	$77,000
Net purchases during month	30,500	49,900
Cost of goods available for sale	$79,200	$126,900
Net sales for month		$52,100
Ending inventory at retail		$74,800
Cost ratio		0.62
Ending inventory at cost		$46,376*

$$\text{Cost ratio} = \frac{\$79,200}{\$126,900} = 0.62$$

$$\text{Ending inventory at cost} = *\$74,800 \times 0.62 = \$46,376$$

Measuring Inventory Turnover

9. (a) $\text{Average inventory at retail} = \dfrac{\text{beginning inventory} + \text{ending inventory}}{2}$

$$= \frac{\$74,900 + \$71,600}{2} = \frac{\$146,500}{2} = \$73,250$$

$\text{Inventory turnover at retail} = \dfrac{\text{net sales}}{\text{average inventory at retail}}$

$$= \frac{\$140,000}{\$73,250} = 1.91$$

(b) $\text{Average inventory at cost} = \dfrac{\text{beginning inventory} + \text{ending inventory}}{2}$

$$= \frac{\$43,900 + \$42,000}{2} = \frac{\$85,900}{2} = \$42,950$$

$\text{Inventory turnover at cost} = \dfrac{\text{net sales}}{\text{average inventory at cost}}$

$$= \frac{\$140,000}{\$42,950} = 3.26$$

10. (a) $\text{Average inventory at retail} = \dfrac{\text{beginning inventory} + \text{ending inventory}}{2}$

$$= \frac{\$195,800 + \$199,300}{2} = \frac{\$395,100}{2} = \$197,550$$

$\text{Inventory turnover at retail} = \dfrac{\text{net sales}}{\text{average inventory at retail}}$

$$= \frac{\$317,400}{\$197,550} = 1.61$$

(b) Average inventory at cost = $\dfrac{\text{beginning inventory} + \text{ending inventory}}{2}$

$\quad\quad = \dfrac{\$94,800 + \$96,500}{2} = \dfrac{\$191,300}{2} = \$95,650$

Inventory turnover at cost = $\dfrac{\text{net sales}}{\text{average inventory at cost}}$

$\quad\quad = \dfrac{\$317,400}{\$\,95,650} = 3.32$

Part III General Business Applications

7 Simple Interest

When we talk about simple interest, you might wonder: Is there any other kind? The answer is yes. There is also compound interest, which we'll be taking up in the next chapter.

OK, so what *is* simple interest? Suppose you put $100 in the bank for one year, and that bank paid 4% simple interest. At the end of a year, you would have $104 in your account—the $100 you started with and the $4 interest that you earned during the year.

We call the money that we put in the bank our principal. The interest that was earned was computed on the original principal and is called simple interest.

1 | The Simple Interest Formula

The formula for finding simple interest is: principal × rate × time. Principal is the money that is lent out (or borrowed). Rate is the rate of interest. And the time is expressed in years or as a fraction of a year.

How much interest is earned if $1,000 is lent out for two years at 6%?

Solution:

$$\text{Interest} = \text{principal} \times \text{rate} \times \text{time}$$
$$= \$1,000 \times .06 \times 2$$
$$= \$1,000 \times .12$$
$$= \$120$$

As Ross Perot has said so many times, "It's that simple."

Problem:

How much interest would be earned if $100 were lent out at 8% for six months?

Solution:

$$\text{Interest} = \text{principal} \times \text{rate} \times \text{time}$$
$$= \$100 \times .08 \times \frac{1}{2}$$
$$= \$100 \times .04$$
$$= \$4$$

QUICK QUIZ 7.1

1. How much interest would be earned if $500 were lent out at 7% for 2 years?

2. How much interest would be earned if $2,000 were lent out at 9% for 4 months?

3. How much interest would be earned if $10,000 were lent out at 5% for 3 years?

4. How much interest would be earned if $5,000 were lent out for 3 months at 6%

Answers to Quick Quiz 7.1

1. $500 \times .07 \times 2 = \$500 \times .14 = \$70$

2. $\$2,000 \times .09 \times \frac{4}{12} = \$2,000 \times .09 \times \frac{1}{3} = \$2,000 \times .03 = \$60$

3. $\$10,000 \times .05 \times 3 = \$10,000 \times .15 = \$1,500$

4. $\$5,000 \times .06 \times \frac{3}{12} = \$5,000 \times .06 \times \frac{1}{4}$
$$= \$5,000 \times .06 \times .25$$
$$= \$5,000 \times .015 = \$75$$

If you got each problem right, then go directly to frame 2. If you got just one wrong, you may be having a problem doing basic arithmetic. I think you should consider rereading frame 1 of Chapter 1 and possibly frame 1 of Chapter 3. After you've done that, then review frame 1 of this chapter and redo Quick Quiz 6.1.

2   Maturity Value

How much money do you get when a loan matures and you are repaid? You get back your principal plus some interest. The maturity value of a loan = principal + interest.

How much is the maturity value of a loan of $100 at 7% interest for one year?

Maturity value = principal plus interest
= $100 + interest

Interest = principal × rate × time
= $100 × .07 × 1
= $100 × .07
= $7

Maturity value = $100 + $7
= $107

That seems easy enough. Let's do some problems.

QUICK QUIZ 7.2

1. How much is the maturity value of $2,000 lent at 8% for 3 months?

2. How much is the maturity value of $5,000 lent at 6% for 4 months?

3. How much is the maturity value of $20,000 lent for 2 months at 6%?

Answers to Quick Quiz 7.2

1.   Interest = $2,000 × .08 × $\frac{3}{12}$

= $2,000 × .08 × .25
= $2,000 × .02 = $40
Maturity value = principal + interest
= $2,000 + $40
= $2,040

2.   Interest = $5,000 × .06 × $\frac{4}{12}$

= $5,000 × .06 × $\frac{1}{3}$
= $5,000 × .02 = $100
Maturity value = principal + interest
= $5,000 + $100
= $5,100

3.   Interest = $20,000 × .06 × $\frac{2}{12}$

= $20,000 × .06 × $\frac{1}{6}$
= $20,000 × .01 = $200
Maturity value = principal + interest
= $20,000 + $200
= $20,200

---

3 Solving for the Unknown

Do you remember how we spent all of Chapter 2 solving for *x*, the unknown? Now we're going to be solving for three more unknowns: *p*, *r*, and *t*. These three letters stand for *principal, rate,* and *time,* which appeared in the basic equation of this chapter:

$$\text{Interest} = \text{principal} \times \text{rate} \times \text{time}$$

Until now, we have been solving for interest. In general, when a relationship exists among four variables, if we already know three of them, we can solve for the fourth with simple arithmetic. And that's what we're going to be doing in this section.

4   Solving for the Principal

Let i = interest, p = principal, r = the rate of interest, and t = time. Suppose you happened to know i, r, and t, and wanted to find p. How would you do it?

The easiest way is to isolate p:

$$i = p \times r \times t$$

$$\frac{i}{r \times t} = p$$

To isolate p, we divided both sides of the equation by rt. What allows us to do that? The law of arithmetic that says what you do to one side of an equation, you must do to the other side as well.

If Gordon Park paid $85 interest on a one-year loan on which the rate of interest was 10%, how much did he borrow?

We're looking for p. How much are i, r, and t?

The variable i is $85, r is 10%, and t is 1 (time is expressed in terms of years).

Next, substitute these numbers into this equation for each of the letters:

$$p = \frac{i}{r \times t}$$

$$p = \frac{\$85}{.10 \times 1}$$

And finally, solve the equation for p, rounding to the nearest cent.

$$p = \frac{\$85}{.10}$$

$$p = \$850$$

All right, I did that one. Now you do this one: Jim Santangelo paid $117.40 interest on a six-month loan for which the rate of interest was 12%. How much money did he borrow?

Solution:

Let i = $117.40
Let r = .12

$$\text{Let } t = \frac{6}{12} = \frac{1}{2} = .5$$

$$p = \frac{i}{r \times t} = \frac{\$117.40}{.12 \times .5} = \frac{\$117.40}{.06}$$

$$= \$1,956.67$$

Here's one more. Sidney O'Toole paid $238.22 on a two-year loan. If the interest rate on the loan was 9.5%, how much money did he borrow?

Solution:

Let i = $238.22
Let r = .095
Let t = 2

$$p = \frac{i}{r \times t} = \frac{\$238.22}{.095 \times .2} = \frac{\$238.22}{.19}$$

$$= \$1,253.78$$

We'll have a few more of these after we take up two more unknowns, r and t.

5 | Solving for the Rate of Interest

Now we're going to be solving for r, the rate of interest. The analysis will be virtually the same as in the last section when we were solving for the principal, p. Once again, we'll go back to our basic equation:

$$i = p \times r \times t$$

This time, what are we looking for? Did you say we're looking for r? Good. Then see if you can isolate r right now:

Solution:

$$i = p \times r \times t$$

$$\frac{i}{p \times t} = r$$

Now we're ready to do business. If Helen Malone borrowed $4,000 for six months and paid $200 interest, what rate of interest did she pay?

Solution:

Let p = $4,000
Let $t = \frac{1}{2}$
Let i = $200

$$r = \frac{i}{p \times t} = \frac{\$200}{\$4,000 \times .5} = \frac{\$200}{\$2000} = .10 \text{ or } 10\%$$

Here's one more. Stephanie Kilgore paid $372.63 on a two-year, $7,500 loan. What interest rate was she charged?

Solution:

Let i = $372.63
Let p = $7,500
Let t = 2

$$r = \frac{i}{p \times t} = \frac{\$372.63}{\$7,500 \times 2} = \frac{\$372.63}{\$15,000} = 2.48\% = 2.5\%$$

We'll have a few more problems like these in just a couple of pages. But we have one more unknown to find: time.

6 Solving for the Time

So far we have solved for the principal, p, and the rate of interest, r. Now we'll solve for the time, t. To do that, we need to isolate t in our basic equation. See what you can do:

Solution:

$$i = p \times r \times t$$

$$\frac{i}{p \times r} = t$$

Now I'd like you to work out this problem: Dana Hale borrowed $10,000 at 7.5%. If she paid $375 in interest, for how long was the loan?

Solution:

Let i = $375
Let p = $10,000
Let r = .075

$$t = \frac{i}{p \times r} = \frac{\$375}{\$10,000 \times .075} = \frac{\$375}{\$750} = \frac{1}{2} = 6 \text{ months}$$

Here's another one. Alexandra Brooks borrowed $20,000 at 9%. If she paid $2,700 in interest, for how long was the loan?

Solution:

Let i = $2,700
Let p = $20,000
Let r = .09

$$t = \frac{i}{p \times r} = \frac{\$2,700}{\$20,000 \times .09} = \frac{\$2,700}{\$1,800} = 1.5 \text{ years} \\ \text{or 18 months}$$

7   Solving for Time, Rate, or Principal

In the course of the last few pages we have solved for each of three unknowns: the principal, the rate of interest, and the time of the loan. Each is solved by its own special formula. But as your instructors never tire of telling you, school is not the real world. In the real world, there are no ready-made formulas into which we can just plug in numbers and solve. Or perhaps, even more to the point, there are a bewildering array of formulas, so it's often unclear which formula is needed.

Well, welcome to the real world. We've just applied each of three formulas separately to solve for p, r, and t. Now we're going to continue finding these same variables—p, r, and t—but you're going to have to figure out which formula to use. It's really not all that hard. Just ask yourself as you're reading each problem: What am I solving for? Then use the appropriate formula. You'll get to do this in Quick Quiz 7.4.

QUICK QUIZ 7.4

1. If Clay Dobson borrowed $6,000 for three months and paid $150 interest, what rate of interest did he pay?

2. Kim Sung Rhee paid $259.36 interest on a six-month loan for which the rate of interest was 14%. How much money did she borrow?

3. Charlotte James paid $1,104.82 on a three-year $9,000 loan. What interest rate was she charged?

4. Walter Sochalski borrowed $50,000 at 8%. If he paid $1,000 in interest, for how long was the loan?

5. Kevin O'Malley borrowed $12,000 for nine months and paid $975 in interest. What rate of interest was he charged?

6. If Shari Lefkowitz paid $713.26 in interest on an 18-month loan for which the interest rate was 9%, how much money did she borrow?

7. If Louis Florio borrowed $15,000 at 12% and paid $450 in interest, for how long was the loan?

Answers to Quick Quiz 7.4

1. Let p = $6,000
    Let i = $150
    Let t = .25

$$r = \frac{i}{p \times t} = \frac{\$150}{\$6,000 \times .25} = \frac{\$150}{\$1,500} = .10 = 10\%$$

2. Let i = $259.36
    Let t = .5
    Let r = .14

$$p = \frac{i}{r \times t} = \frac{\$259.36}{.14 \times .5} = \frac{\$259.36}{.07} = \$3,705.14$$

3. Let i = $1,104.82
    Let p = $9,000
    Let t = 3

$$r = \frac{i}{p \times t} = \frac{\$1,104.82}{\$9,000 \times 3} = \frac{\$1,104.82}{\$27,000} = .0409 = 4.1\%$$

4. Let p = $50,000
    Let r = 8%
    Let i = $1,000

$$t = \frac{i}{p \times r} = \frac{\$1,000}{\$50,000 \times .08} = \frac{\$1,000}{\$4,000} = \frac{1}{4} = 3 \text{ months}$$

5. Let p = $12,000
    Let t = .75
    Let i = $975

$$r = \frac{i}{p \times t} = \frac{\$975}{\$12,000 \times .75} = \frac{\$975}{\$9,000} = .108 = 10.8\%$$

6. Let i = $713.26
    Let t = 1.5
    Let r = 9%

$$p = \frac{i}{r \times t} = \frac{\$713.26}{.09 \times 1.5} = \frac{\$713.26}{.135} = \$5,283.41$$

7. Let p = $15,000
    Let r = 12%
    Let i = $450

$$t = \frac{i}{p \times r} = \frac{\$450}{\$15,000 \times .12} = \frac{\$450}{\$1,800} = \frac{1}{4} = 3 \text{ months}$$

It's not hard to get mixed up with all these formulas. If you got each problem right, then you're definitely ready for frame 12. If you got two or more wrong, then you definitely should repeat frames 7 through 11, and retake Quick Quiz 7.4.

8. The Promissory Note

Promissory notes are IOUs. If I promised to pay you $1,000 three months from now, then the face value, or principal, of the note I'd give you would be $1,000. Let's assume that I will pay you 9% interest. What would my promissory note look like? It would look a lot like the one shown in Figure 7.1.

Most promissory notes are interest-bearing. So the sum of the face value (or principal) plus the interest (in dollars) is the maturity value of the note.

Why would someone ever write a promissory note that is non-interest bearing? Suppose you borrowed $3,000 from a friend or relative. Very often the borrower writes out a promissory note. You might promise to pay your Aunt Millie that $3,000 in six months. Aunt Millie is not requiring interest, so the maturity value of a noninterest-bearing note is the same as its face value.

______ BROOKLYN, NEW YORK ______

______ AFTER DATE ______ PROMISE TO PAY TO

THE ORDER OF ______

______ DOLLARS

PAYABLE AT ______

VALUE RECEIVED WITH INTEREST AT ______

NO. ______ DUE ______

______

FIGURE 7.1
Sample Promissory Note

$1,000 BROOKLYN, NEW YORK May 7, 1998

ninety days AFTER DATE I PROMISE TO PAY TO

THE ORDER OF Mary Lou Smith

one thousand 00/100 DOLLARS

PAYABLE AT Chemical Bank

VALUE RECEIVED WITH INTEREST AT 9%

NO. 136 DUE August 5, 1998

Stan Clair

FIGURE 7.2
Bank Loan

9 Simple Discount Note

If a bank gives you a \$10,000 loan, it may deduct the interest in advance. Suppose you signed the promissory note shown in Figure 7.2. At the end of one year, you would pay the bank \$10,000. If Bank of America deducted the interest in advance, it would actually be lending you only \$9,200 (\$10,000–\$800). We call the amount actually lent the proceeds. But because all the formulas in this chapter use the term principal, we'll stick with principal, rather than switch to proceeds in these formulas.

So you're really paying \$800 interest for a \$9,200 loan. Can you figure out the effective rate of interest that you're being charged to the nearest hundredth of a percent? Do your work right here:

Solution:

$$r = \frac{i}{p} = \frac{\$800}{\$9,200} = .08696 = 8.70\%$$

U.S. Treasury bills are a very popular form of discount note. They are denominated in amounts of at least $10,000, and have maturities of three months (91 days), six months (182 days), or one year.

Problem:

1. How much would you have to pay for a $10,000, 91-day Treasury bill paying 4% interest?

2. What is the effective interest rate you are receiving to the nearest hundredth of a percent?

Solution:

1. $i = \$10,000 \times .04 \times \dfrac{1}{4}$

$i = \$10,000 \times \dfrac{\overset{1}{\cancel{4}}}{100} \times \dfrac{1}{\underset{1}{\cancel{4}}}$

$i = \dfrac{\$10,\cancel{000}}{1\cancel{00}}$

$p = \$10,000 - \$100 = \$9,900$

2. $r = \dfrac{i}{p \times t} = \dfrac{\$100}{\$9,900 \times \frac{1}{4}} = \dfrac{\$100}{\$2,475} = 4.04\%$

Discounting is sometimes used by wholesalers and manufacturers, who have extended credit to retailers. It is also used by the Federal Reserve as a way of expanding credit. But as interesting as these forms of discounting may be, we'll stay with our straightforward problems using simple discount notes.

QUICK QUIZ 7.5

1. Tom Haley borrowed $5,000 on a simple discount note. The terms were $8\frac{1}{2}\%$, 60 days. Assume exact time, ordinary interest. How much were Haley's proceeds (the amount he actually borrowed), and what is the effective rate of interest that he paid to the nearest hundredth of a percent?

2. Roberto Santiago purchased a $100,000, six-month Treasury bill paying 9%.
   a. How much did he pay for this Treasury bill?
   b. What is his effective rate of interest to the nearest hundredth of a percent?

3. If you borrowed a sum of money for three months at 8% interest and signed a simple discount note promising to pay back $20,000,
   a. How much was the principal of your loan?
   b. What was your effective interest rate to the nearest hundredth of a percent?

Answers to Quick Quiz 7.5

1. $i = \$5,000 \times .085 \times \dfrac{60}{360}$

    $i = \$5,000 \times .085 \times .1667$

    $i = \$5,000 \times .0141695$

    $i = \$70.85$

    $p = \$5,000 - \$70.85 = \$4,929.15$

    $r = \dfrac{i}{p \times t} = \dfrac{\$70.85}{\$4,925.15 \times .1667} = \dfrac{\$70.85}{\$821.02} = 8.63\%$

2. $i = \$100,000 \times .09 \times .5$

    $i = \$100,000 \times .045$

    $i = \$4,500$

    $p = \$100,000 - \$4,500 = \$95,500$

    $r = \dfrac{i}{p \times t} = \dfrac{\$4,500}{\$95,500 \times .5} = \dfrac{\$4,500}{\$47,750} = 9.42\%$

3. $i = \$20,000 \times .08 \times .25$

    $i = \$20,000 \times .02$

    $i = \$400$

    $p = \$20,000 - \$400 = \$19,600$

    $r = \dfrac{i}{p \times t} = \dfrac{\$400}{\$19,600 \times .25} = \dfrac{\$400}{\$4,900} = 8.16\%$

10 Consumer Credit

You've probably seen signs like these, "No down payment; months to pay." "Buy now; pay later." What's the catch? The catch is that you'll probably end up paying a lot of interest.

First we'll calculate the APR, which is the annual percentage rate of interest that we are paying for the credit that is extended to us. Then we'll look at the cost of installment buying and of credit card debt.

11 The APR

All through this chapter we've been calculating interest rates. The formula that we're about to use to find the APR, or annual percentage rate, is a lot more complex than any formulas we have used so far, but when we deal with consumer credit, we're no longer talking about borrowing a fixed amount of money for a fixed amount of time.

Until now everything has been straightforward. You borrowed $1,000 for one year at 8% interest. You paid back the $1,000 at the end of the year, along with $80 interest. True, we added a wrinkle in the last section when we talked about the simple discount note, but there was still a fixed amount of money borrowed for a fixed time period. But installment buying and using credit cards involve paying off debt over a period of time. So the actual amount that you have borrowed declines as you make your monthly payments. That's why the APR formula is a lot more complex than the interest rate formulas we encountered earlier in the chapter.

$$\text{APR} = \frac{2 \times \text{number of payment periods in one year} \times \text{finance charge}}{\text{amount of loan} \times (\text{total number of payments} + 1)}$$

Now we're going to plug in some numbers. A total of $1,000 is borrowed at the stated interest rate of 10%. The loan is paid off in 12 monthly payments. Let's find the APR to the nearest tenth of a percent:

$$\text{Finance charge} = \$1,000 \times .10 = \$100$$

$$\frac{2 \times 12 \times \$100}{\$1,000 \times (12 + 1)} = \frac{24 \times \$100}{\$1,000 \times 13} = \frac{\$2,400}{\$13,000} = 18.5\%$$

As you can see, the APR is a lot higher than 10%. This is because you don't have the use of the $1,000 for a full year. As you pay off the loan, you have the use of a declining principal. We'll apply this formula now as we look at installment buying.

12   Installment Buying

Installment buying is just what it sounds like: You buy a good or service and pay it off over a period of months, or even years, one installment at a time. Installment buying came into vogue only 30 or 40 years ago. Before that, if you didn't have enough money to buy something, you could use a lay-away plan.

Under the lay-away plan, you also paid out what you owed in installments. When you made your last payment, you could take the product home. Installment buying is different in two basic ways. First, you get to take the good home right away; you don't have to wait until you've paid it off. And second, you may have to pay a lot of interest for this privilege.

I've got a great deal for you on a pickup truck. Just put a thousand down and pay $300 a month for the next three years. Of course, if you want to pay cash, the price is just $9,500.

Question:

If you pay it out over three years, how much the total interest is charged?

Solution:

If you paid cash, you would have paid $9,500. But if you paid it out over three years, you would have put $1,000 down, and then paid out $300 a month for 36 months, or $300 × 36. So your total payment would have come to $1,000 plus $10,800, or $11,800. So paying for the pickup in installments cost you $2,300 in interest ($11,800 − $9,500).

Question:

How much is the annual percentage rate of this loan (to the nearest tenth of a percent)? Use the APR formula to figure this out.

Solution:

$$APR = \frac{2 \times \text{number of payment periods in one year} \times \text{finance charge}}{\text{amount of loan} \times (\text{total number of payments} + 1)}$$

$$= \frac{2 \times 12 \times \$2,300}{\$10,800 \times (36 + 1)} = \frac{24 \times \$2,300}{\$10,800 \times 37} = \frac{\$55,200}{\$399,600} = 13.8\%$$

Question:

Now I'm going to sell you a bedroom set. Nothing down, two years to pay. The price is just $1,999, and the finance charge is an additional $374. If the payments are monthly, what is the APR to the nearest tenth of a percent?

Solution:

$$APR = \frac{2 \times 12 \times \$374}{\$1,999 \times (24 + 1)} = \frac{24 \times \$374}{\$1,999 \times 25} = \frac{\$8,976}{\$49,975} = 18.0\%$$

QUICK QUIZ 7.6

1. Tar Heel Furniture Outlet sells dining room sets for $6,000, on which there is a nominal interest rate of 8%. If quarterly payments are made over three years, how much is the APR to the nearest tenth of a percent?

2. Honest Jack offers 8.8% financing on all the cars in his lot. Terms are nothing down and four years to pay. If you bought a 1992 Chevy for $5,000, how much would your APR be to the nearest tenth of a percent if you made monthly payments?

3. How much would the APR be to the nearest tenth of a percent on a $2,000 loan if you made weekly payments for one year and the finance charges were $100?

4. Clara's Stereos offers 8% financing on all stereo equipment in the store. The terms are nothing down and two years to pay. If you bought a stereo system for $3,500, how much would your APR be to the nearest tenth of a percent if you made monthly payments?

Answers to Quick Quiz 7.6

1. Finance charge = $6,000 × .08 × 3 = $6,000 × .24 = $1,440

$$APR = \frac{2 \times 4 \times \$1,400}{\$6,000 \times (12 + 1)} = \frac{8 \times \$1,440}{\$6,000 \times 13} = \frac{\$11,520}{\$78,000} = 14.8\%$$

2. Finance charge = $5,000 × .088 × 4 = $5,000 × .352 = $1,760

$$\text{APR} = \frac{2 \times 12 \times \$1,760}{\$5,000 \times (48 + 1)} = \frac{24 \times \$1,760}{\$5,000 \times 49} = \frac{\$42,240}{\$245,000} = 17.2\%$$

3. $$\text{APR} = \frac{2 \times 52 \times \$100}{\$2,000 \times (52+1)} = \frac{104 \times \$100}{\$2,000 \times 53} = \frac{\$10,400}{\$106,000} = 9.8\%$$

4. Finance charge = $3,500 × .08 × 2 = $3,500 × .16 = $560

$$\text{APR} = \frac{2 \times 12 \times \$560}{\$3,500 \times (24 + 1)} = \frac{24 \times \$560}{\$3,500 \times 25} = \frac{\$13,440}{\$87,500} = 15.4\%$$

13 Credit Cards

Do you have any credit cards? The three most widely used are VISA, MasterCard, and American Express. There are also gasoline credit cards, department store credit cards, supermarket credit cards, as well as hundreds of others. All of them send out the same message as installment buying—buy now, pay later.

This is not to say that credit cards don't have other very important uses. When you travel, especially when you stay at a motel or rent a car, a credit card is a virtual necessity. When you buy a big-ticket item like a stereo, VCR, TV, or an expensive suit, it's a lot easier to pay by credit card than to carry around that much cash.

Credit cards also provide us with thousands of dollars worth of credit. And, of course, if you pay off your balance within a month after your purchases, you can avoid paying interest on the hundreds, or even thousands of dollars that had been lent to you. But if you don't pay off your entire balance each month, you can end up paying hundreds—or even thousands—of dollars in interest every year. Indeed, the banks that own the credit card companies prefer that you *don't* pay off everything you owe. Why? Because then they can charge you a whole lot of interest. In fact that's the main reason why they issue credit cards in the first place.

Although credit card interest rates vary widely, in the early 1990s, even though interest rates were at 20- and 30-year lows, nearly all credit cardholders were being charged APRs of more than 15%. So if you need to borrow money for any purpose, borrowing it on your credit card is not a very good idea, unless, of course, you don't have other alternatives.

Suppose, however, you have a hefty balance in your checking or savings account. Use that money to pay off as much of your credit card balance as you can. Or, if you're able to, you might even want to take out a home equity loan to pay off your credit card debt.

Think of it this way. If someone offered you 18 or 20% interest on your savings, you'd lend that person every penny you had. So it would make sense not to borrow at those high interest rates if there were any way to avoid it.

Your credit card interest is calculated by multiplying your average daily balance by the interest rate. For example, if your average daily balance during June were $1,000 and the monthly interest rate were 1.5%, then you would be charged $15 interest. But we're going to let you off the hook and not ask you to figure out your credit card interest. If you manage your money well, you won't have any credit card interest charges to worry about.

SELF-TEST

Calculating Simple Interest

1. How much interest would be earned if $5,000 were lent out at 6.5% for 3 years?

2. How much interest would be earned if $10,000 were lent out at 10% for three months?

3. How much interest would be earned if $50,000 were lent out at 5.5% interest for nine months?

Maturity Value

4. How much is the maturity value of a loan of $5,000 at 7% interest for two years?

5. How much is the maturity value of $15,000 lent out at 8.5% for six months?

6. How much is the maturity value of a loan of $25,000 at 10% interest for one year?

Solving for the Unknown

7. Katie McGee paid $596.24 interest on a nine-month loan for which the rate was 11%. How much money did she borrow?

8. Joyce A. Shaw borrowed $10,000 for three months. If she paid $225 in interest, what rate of interest did she pay?

9. Patricia J. Keller borrowed $12,000 at 10%. If she paid $600 in interest, for how long was the loan?

Simple Discount Note

10. Bryant Christopher Thomas takes out a $10,000 bank loan, from which the bank deducts the interest in advance. If the interest rate is 8% and the loan is for one year,
    a. How much was the principal of this loan?
    b. What was the effective interest rate he paid to the nearest hundredth of a percent?

11. Patricia Lagleder purchased a $50,000, six-month Treasury bill paying 5.5%.
    a. How much did she pay for this Treasury bill?
    b. What was her effective rate of interest to the nearest hundredth of a percent?

Consumer Credit

12. How much would the APR be to the nearest tenth of a percent on a $4,000 loan if you made weekly payments for one year and the finance charges were $250?

13. Staci Wolfram purchased some livingroom furniture with 11% financing, nothing down, and three years to pay. If she spent $3,000 on the furniture, how much was her APR to the nearest tenth of a percent if she made monthly payments?

ANSWERS

Calculating Simple Interest

1. Interest = principal × rate × time
   = $5,000 × .065 × 3
   = $5,000 × .195
   = $975

2. Interest = principal × rate × time
   = $10,000 × .10 × $\frac{1}{4}$
   = $10,000 × .025
   = $250

3. Interest = principal × rate × time
   = $50,000 × .055 × $\frac{3}{4}$
   = $50,000 × .04125
   = $2,062.50

Maturity Value

4. Interest = principal × rate × time
   = $5,000 × .07 × 2
   = $5,000 × .14
   = $700
   Maturity value = principal + interest
   = $5,000 + $700
   = $5,700

5. Interest = principal × rate × time
   = $15,000 × .085 × .5
   = $15,000 × .0425
   = $637.50
   Maturity value = principal + interest
   = $15,000 + $637.50
   = $15,637.50

6.   Interest = principal × rate × time

$$= \$25,000 \times .10 \times 1$$
$$= \$2,500$$

Maturity value = principal + interest

$$= \$25,000 + \$2,500$$
$$= \$27,500$$

Solving for the Unknown

7. Let i = \$596.24
   Let t = .75
   Let r = .11

$$p = \frac{i}{r \times t} = \frac{\$596.24}{.11 \times .75} = \frac{\$596.24}{.0825} = \$7,227.15$$

8. Let p = \$10,000
   Let t = .25
   Let i = \$225

$$r = \frac{i}{p \times t} = \frac{\$225}{\$10,000 \times .25} = \frac{\$225}{\$2,500} = \frac{9}{100} = .09$$

9. Let p = \$12,000
   Let i = \$600
   Let r = .10

$$p = \frac{i}{r \times t} = \frac{\$600}{\$12,000 \times .10} = \frac{\$600}{\$1,200} = \frac{1}{2} = 6 \text{ months}$$

Simple Discount Note

10. a. $i = \$10,000 \times .08 = \$800$
         $p = \$10,000 - \$800 = \$9,200$

    b. $r = \dfrac{i}{p \times t} = \dfrac{\$800}{\$9,200 \times 1} = \dfrac{\$800}{\$9,200} = 8.70\%$

11. a. $i = \$50,000 \times .055 \times .5 = \$50,000 \times .0275$
         $= \$1,375$
         $p = \$50,000 - \$1,375 = \$48,625$

    b. $r = \dfrac{i}{p \times t} = \dfrac{\$1,375}{\$48,625 \times .5} = \dfrac{\$1,375}{\$24,312.50} = 5.66\%$

Consumer Credit

12. $\text{APR} = \dfrac{2 \times 52 \times \$250}{\$4,000 \times (52 + 1)} = \dfrac{104 \times \$250}{\$4,000 \times 53} = \dfrac{\$26,000}{\$212,000} = 12.3\%$

13. Finance charge = $\$3,000 \times .11 \times 3 = \$3,000 \times .33$
                      $= \$990$

$$\text{APR} = \frac{2 \times 12 \times \$990}{\$3,000 \times (36 + 1)} = \frac{24 \times \$990}{\$3,000 \times 37} = \frac{\$23,760}{\$111,000}$$
$$= 21.4\%$$

8

Compound Interest and Present Value

Get ready to go back to the future and ahead to the past. We'll begin by relating simple interest to compound interest. And we'll finish by talking about the present value of future income.

Have you ever heard of the Rothschilds? They were an extremely wealthy European family that could have lived quite comfortably on the interest on their interest. Suppose you had *their* money. So you invested $1 billion and got a 5% return, or $25 million. And you reinvested that $25 million and got a 5% return, or $1,250,000. Now I think you could get by quite nicely on a million and a quarter a year, don't you?

1 The Difference Between Simple Interest and Compound Interest

Does your bank pay simple interest or compound interest? And what difference does it make anyway? Your bank definitely pays compound interest, and because it does, your money grows faster than it would if the bank paid just simple interest. Now I'm going to prove it.

If your bank paid 8% simple interest and you put $1,000 in your savings account today, how much money would be in your account one year from now? You can probably do it in your head, but here's how we did it in the first section of the preceding chapter:

$$\begin{aligned} \text{Interest} &= \text{principal} \times \text{rate} \times \text{time} \\ &= \$1{,}000 \times .08 \times 1 \\ &= \$80 \end{aligned}$$

$$\begin{aligned} \text{Maturity value} &= \text{principal} + \text{interest} \\ &= \$1{,}000 + \$80 \\ &= \$1{,}080 \end{aligned}$$

2

If your bank paid 8% simple interest, at the end of one year, your $1,000 balance would rise to $1,080. But what would happen to your $1,000 deposit if your bank compounds interest quarterly? Believe it or not, we can find out by using the simple interest formula.

We'll begin by calculating the simple interest for the first quarter (or three months):

$$\begin{aligned} \text{Interest} &= \text{principal} \times \text{rate} \times \text{time} \\ &= \$1{,}000 \times .08 \times .25 \\ &= \$1{,}000 \times .02 \\ &= \$20 \end{aligned}$$

$$\begin{aligned} \text{Maturity value} &= \text{principal} + \text{interest} \\ &= \$1{,}000 + \$20 \\ &= \$1{,}020 \end{aligned}$$

Next, we'll calculate the simple interest for the second quarter:

$$\begin{aligned} \text{Interest} &= \text{principal} \times \text{rate} \times \text{time} \\ &= \$1{,}020 \times .08 \times .25 \\ &= \$1{,}020 \times .02 \\ &= \$20.40 \end{aligned}$$

$$\begin{aligned} \text{Maturity value} &= \text{principal} + \text{interest} \\ &= \$1{,}020 + \$20.40 \\ &= \$1{,}040.40 \end{aligned}$$

Now let's calculate the simple interest for the third quarter:

$$\begin{aligned} \text{Interest} &= \text{principal} \times \text{rate} \times \text{time} \\ &= \$1{,}040.40 \times .08 \times .25 \\ &= \$1{,}040.40 \times .02 \\ &= \$20.81 \end{aligned}$$

$$\begin{aligned} \text{Maturity value} &= \text{principal} + \text{interest} \\ &= \$1{,}040.40 + \$20.81 \\ &= \$1{,}061.21 \end{aligned}$$

And finally, we'll compute the simple interest for the fourth quarter:

$$\begin{aligned} \text{Interest} &= \text{principal} \times \text{rate} \times \text{time} \\ &= \$1{,}061.21 \times .08 \times .25 \\ &= \$1{,}061.21 \times .02 \\ &= \$21.22 \end{aligned}$$

$$\begin{aligned} \text{Maturity value} &= \text{principal} + \text{interest} \\ &= \$1{,}061.21 + \$21.22 \\ &= \$1{,}082.43 \end{aligned}$$

If your bank paid 8% interest that was compounded quarterly, then your $1,000 deposit would have grown to $1,082.43 in one year. But if your bank had paid simple interest, then your $1,000 would have grown to just $1,080 in one year.

3

Most savings and loan associations and banks pay interest that is compounded daily. Question: Would your money grow faster if your interest were compounded *daily* or *quarterly?*

If you put $1,000 into a bank that paid simple interest of 6%, then at the end of a year you would have $1,060. But if that interest had been compounded quarterly, you would have had $1,061.36. And if it had been compounded daily, you would have had $1,062.70. So the more often your interest is compounded, the faster it grows.

4   The Compound Interest Tables

In the last frame we figured out the maturity value of $1,000 left in a bank savings account for one year if that bank paid 8% interest, compounded quarterly. It came to $1,082.43.

Question: If you deposited $1,000 in that same bank and left it there for 4 years, how much would its maturity value be? Could you just multiply that $82.43 in interest by 4 and tack it on to the $1,000? Close, but no cigar.

You could calculate the simple interest over the four-year period, quarter-by-quarter, for 16 quarters. Luckily there's a much better way. Just look up the answer in the compound interest tables. Someone was nice enough to compute these tables and save us all the time and trouble of calculating compound interest.

Our question was: If you deposited $1,000 and it was compounded quarterly for four years, how much would its maturity value be? If you were to glance at Table 8.1, you would see that it is arranged in terms of periods and that interest is compounded each period. In this problem, interest is compounded quarterly, so there are four periods each year.

Using the information we have, plug in the numbers that fit into this formula, and then find the rate per period.

$$\text{Rate per period} = \frac{\text{annual rate}}{\text{number of periods per year}}$$

Solution:

$$\frac{8\%}{4} = 2\%$$

This means that 8% compounded quarterly can be found in the compound interest tables under a rate of 2%. We need one more bit of information, then we can use the tables. How many periods are there?

TABLE 8.1

THE MATURITY VALUE OF $1 AT COMPOUND INTEREST RATES OF .5%, 1%, 1.5% AND 2%

Period	0.5%	1.0%	1.5%	2.0%
1	1.0050	1.0100	1.0150	1.0200
2	1.0100	1.0201	1.0302	1.0404
3	1.0151	1.0303	1.0457	1.0612
4	1.0202	1.0406	1.0614	1.0824
5	1.0253	1.0510	1.0773	1.1041
6	1.0304	1.0615	1.0934	1.1262
7	1.0355	1.0721	1.1098	1.1487
8	1.0407	1.0829	1.1265	1.1717
9	1.0459	1.0937	1.1434	1.1951
10	1.0511	1.1046	1.1605	1.2190
11	1.0564	1.1157	1.1780	1.2434
12	1.0617	1.1268	1.1960	1.2682
13	1.0670	1.1381	1.2135	1.2936
14	1.0723	1.1495	1.2318	1.3195
15	1.0777	1.1610	1.2502	1.3459
16	1.0831	1.1726	1.2690	1.3728
17	1.0885	1.1843	1.2880	1.4002
18	1.0939	1.1961	1.3073	1.4282
19	1.0994	1.2081	1.3270	1.4568
20	1.1049	1.2202	1.3469	1.4859
21	1.1104	1.2324	1.3671	1.5157
22	1.1160	1.2447	1.3876	1.5460
23	1.1216	1.2572	1.4084	1.5769
24	1.1272	1.2697	1.4295	1.6084
25	1.1328	1.2824	1.4510	1.6406
26	1.1385	1.2953	1.4727	1.6734
27	1.1442	1.3082	1.4948	1.7069
28	1.1499	1.3213	1.5172	1.7410
29	1.1556	1.3345	1.5400	1.7758
30	1.1614	1.3478	1.5631	1.8114
31	1.1672	1.3613	1.5865	1.8476
32	1.1730	1.3749	1.6103	1.8845
33	1.1789	1.3887	1.6345	1.9222
34	1.1848	1.4026	1.6590	1.9607
35	1.1907	1.4166	1.6839	1.9999
36	1.1967	1.4308	1.7091	2.0399
37	1.2027	1.4451	1.7348	2.0807
38	1.2087	1.4595	1.7608	2.1223
39	1.2147	1.4741	1.7872	2.1647
40	1.2208	1.4889	1.8140	2.2080

Well, we're looking at the interest compounded quarterly over four years. So how many quarters is that?

It's 16 quarters. Now if each quarter is a period, then we need to look up an interest rate of 2% for a period of 16 quarters. Another glance at Table 8.1 and you've got the answer.

Did you get 1.3728? Good, then we're in business. What you just found was the maturity value of one dollar left in the bank for four years at 8% interest compounded quarterly.

All right, now we're almost home. We just need to find the maturity value of $1,000 instead of one dollar. Figure it out right here:

Solution:

Just multiply $1.3728 by 1,000, which, of course, means moving the decimal point three places to the right. That gives us $1,372.80. Incidentally, if you've forgotten how to do that, you can quickly get back up to speed by reviewing fast multiplication in the first frame of Chapter 1.

Problem:

If $100 were left in a bank for five years in an account that paid 6% interest compounded quarterly, what would that $100 be worth at the end of five years?

Solution:

$$\text{Rate per period} = \frac{\text{annual rate}}{\text{number of periods per year}}$$

$$= \frac{6\%}{4} = 1.5\%$$

How many periods are there in five years? If each period is one quarter, there are four in one year, so there are 20 in five years. Looking up 1.5% interest in Table 8.1, we find that in period 20 the maturity value of $1 is $1.3469. Since we had deposited $100 in the bank, that $100 has grown to 100 × $1.3469 = $134.69.

Problem:

$100 is deposited for 10 years. If the annual rate of interest is 6%, compounded quarterly, what is the maturity value of that $100 at the end of 10 years?

Solution:

$$\text{Rate per period} = \frac{\text{annual rate}}{\text{number of periods per year}}$$

$$= \frac{6\%}{4} = 1.5\%$$

How many periods are there in 10 years? There are 40 (4 quarters in each year). Using Table 8.1, we find that in period 40 the maturity value of $1 is $1.8140. Because we deposited $100, we multiply $1.8140 by 100. Moving the decimal two places to the right, we get $181.40.

Problem:

$500 is deposited for 10 years. If the annual rate of interest is $3\frac{1}{2}$% and the interest is compounded *annually,* what is the maturity value of that $500 at the end of 10 years? Use the compound interest found in Table 8.2.

Solution:

First of all, do you need this formula?

$$\text{Rate per period} = \frac{\text{annual rate}}{\text{number of periods per year}}$$

The answer is no, because the interest is compounded annually. Can we still use Table 8.2? Certainly. The maturity of a dollar after 10 periods is $1.4106. We multiply that by 500 and get $705.30.

Problem:

Find the maturity value of $1,000 invested for two years at 6% interest compounded *monthly.* (Hint: Use Table 8.1.)

Solution:

$$\text{Rate per period} = \frac{\text{annual rate}}{\text{number of periods per year}} = \frac{6\%}{12} = \frac{1}{2}\%$$

Once we've figured out that 6% compounded monthly means 12 periods a year, we just look up $\frac{1}{2}$% for 24 periods in Table 8.1. (If there are 12 periods in one year, there are 24 in two years.) This comes to $1.1272. We multiply that by $1,000, and, moving the decimal point three places to the right, we get $1,127.20.

All right, no more Mr. Nice Guy. We've got a total of six—count 'em, six—compound interest tables in this chapter. I've been telling you which one to use for each problem, but from here on in, you're on your own. So good luck with the first quick quiz.

QUICK QUIZ 8.1

1. $2,000 is deposited for three years at 12% interest compounded quarterly. What is the maturity value of that deposit at the end of three years?

2. $5,000 is deposited for five years. The interest rate is 10% compounded semiannually. How much is the maturity value of the deposit after five years?

TABLE 8.2

THE MATURITY VALUE OF $1 AT COMPOUND INTEREST RATES OF 2.5%, 3%, 3.5%, AND 4%

Period	2.5%	3.0%	3.5%	4.0%
1	1.0250	1.0300	1.0350	1.0400
2	1.0506	1.0609	1.0712	1.0816
3	1.0769	1.0927	1.1087	1.1249
4	1.1038	1.1255	1.1475	1.1699
5	1.1314	1.1593	1.1877	1.2167
6	1.1597	1.1941	1.2293	1.2653
7	1.1887	1.2299	1.2723	1.3159
8	1.2184	1.2668	1.3168	1.3686
9	1.2489	1.3048	1.3629	1.4233
10	1.2801	1.3439	1.4106	1.4802
11	1.3121	1.3842	1.4600	1.5395
12	1.3449	1.4258	1.5111	1.6010
13	1.3785	1.4685	1.5640	1.6651
14	1.4130	1.5126	1.6187	1.7317
15	1.4483	1.5580	1.6753	1.8009
16	1.4845	1.6047	1.7340	1.8730
17	1.5216	1.6528	1.7947	1.9479
18	1.5597	1.7024	1.8575	2.0258
19	1.5986	1.7535	1.9225	2.1068
20	1.6386	1.8061	1.9898	2.1911
21	1.6796	1.8603	2.0594	2.2788
22	1.7216	1.9161	2.1315	2.3699
23	1.7646	1.9736	2.2061	2.4647
24	1.8087	2.0328	2.2833	2.5633
25	1.8539	2.0938	2.3632	2.6658
26	1.9003	2.1566	2.4460	2.7725
27	1.9478	2.2213	2.5316	2.8834
28	1.9965	2.2879	2.6202	2.9987
29	2.0464	2.3566	2.7119	3.1187
30	2.0976	2.4273	2.8068	3.2434
31	2.1500	2.5001	2.9050	3.3731
32	2.2038	2.5751	3.0067	3.5081
33	2.2588	2.6523	3.1119	3.6484
34	2.3153	2.7319	3.2209	3.7943
35	2.3732	2.8139	3.3336	3.9461
36	2.4325	2.8983	3.4503	4.1039
37	2.4933	2.9852	3.5710	4.2681
38	2.5557	3.0748	3.6960	4.4388
39	2.6196	3.1670	3.8254	4.6164
40	2.6851	3.2620	3.9593	4.8010

3. $3,000 is deposited for eight years. Interest is compounded annually at a rate of 11%. How much is the maturity value of the deposit after eight years?

4. If you were to deposit $7,000 for seven years and the bank paid 10% interest compounded quarterly, how much would the maturity value of your deposit be at the end of seven years?

Answers to Quick Quiz 8.1

1. Rate per period = $\dfrac{\text{annual rate}}{\text{number of periods per year}}$

   $= \dfrac{12\%}{4} = 3\%$ (12 periods)

   $\$1.4258 \times 2,000 = \$2,851.60$

2. Rate per period = $\dfrac{\text{annual rate}}{\text{number of periods per year}}$

   $= \dfrac{10\%}{2} = 5\%$ (10 periods)

   $\$1.6289 \times 5,000 = \$8,144.50$

3. 11% (8 periods)
   $\$2.3045 \times 3,000 = \$6,913.50$

4. $\dfrac{10\%}{4} = 2\frac{1}{2}\%$ (28 periods)

   $\$1.9965 \times 7,000 = \$13,975.50$

In the next frame, which talks about present value, we're going to loosen up again. We're going to go back to simple interest, so you won't be dealing with those compound interest tables. And you even have permission to use a calculator, although I personally believe that you're much better off working without one.

5 | Present Value

Economists are fond of saying that a dollar today is worth more than a dollar you will have in the future. Why? Because of inflation?

Maybe. But even if there were no inflation, a dollar today would *still* be worth more than a dollar you received some time in the future. How do we know this? Because even when there is no inflation, people are still willing to pay interest for the use of your money. And if *you* wanted to borrow money, you would be charged interest—inflation or no inflation.

OK, how much more is it worth? If the interest rate were 7%, how much would $100 today be worth in terms of dollars you will have one year from now?

Did you say $107? Then you're right! Naturally, we have a formula to figure these things out.

The present value of a dollar received one year from now is $\frac{1}{1+r}$, when r is the interest rate. Substitute .07 for r (remember 7% is equivalent to the decimal .07) in the formula and see what you get:

Did you divide 1.07 into 1? If you haven't, then do it now. All right, you should have gotten .9346 or 93.46 cents. So, a dollar one year from now would be worth only 93.46 cents today.

What if the interest rate were 5%? How much would a dollar received one year from now be worth today?

Solution:

$$\frac{1}{1+r} = \frac{1}{1.05} = 95.24 \text{ cents}$$

We'll do one more. What is the present value of a dollar when the interest rate is 12?

Solution:

$$\frac{1}{1+r} = \frac{1}{1.12} = 89.29 \text{ cents}$$

We can say, then, that when the interest rate rises, the present value of future dollars will decline, and when the interest rate falls, the present value of dollars held in the future will rise.

We can use a general formula for the present value of dollars held any numbers of years into the future:

Present value of a dollar received n years from now = $\frac{1}{(1+r)^n}$

If you're uncomfortable with algebra, you have nothing to worry about. Once you plug in the numbers for r and n, it's no longer algebra, but just arithmetic.

The letter n is an exponent. It tells us to multiply what's inside the parentheses by itself n times. I'm going to set up a simple problem by plugging in actual numbers into the formula:

Problem:

What is the present value of a dollar received two years from now if interest rate is 3%?

$$\frac{1}{(1+r)^n} = \frac{1}{(1.03)^2}$$

TABLE 8.3

THE MATURITY VALUE OF $1 AT COMPOUND INTEREST RATES OF 4.5%, 5%, 5.5%, AND 6%

Period	4.5%	5%	5.5%	6%
1	1.0450	1.0500	1.0550	1.0600
2	1.0920	1.1025	1.1130	1.1236
3	1.1412	1.1576	1.1742	1.1910
4	1.1925	1.2155	1.2388	1.2625
5	1.2462	1.2763	1.3070	1.3382
6	1.3023	1.3401	1.3788	1.4185
7	1.3609	1.4071	1.4547	1.5036
8	1.4221	1.4775	1.5347	1.5938
9	1.4861	1.5513	1.6191	1.6895
10	1.5530	1.6289	1.7081	1.7908
11	1.6229	1.7103	1.8021	1.8983
12	1.6959	1.7959	1.9012	2.0122
13	1.7722	1.8856	2.0058	2.1329
14	1.8519	1.9799	2.1161	2.2609
15	1.9353	2.0789	2.2325	2.3966
16	2.0224	2.1829	2.3553	2.5404
17	2.1134	2.2920	2.4828	2.6928
18	2.2085	2.4066	2.6215	2.8543
19	2.3079	2.5270	2.7656	3.0256
20	2.4117	2.6533	2.9178	3.2071
21	2.5202	2.7860	3.0782	3.3996
22	2.6337	2.9253	3.2475	3.6035
23	2.7522	3.0715	3.4261	3.8197
24	2.8760	3.2251	3.6146	4.0489
25	3.0054	3.3864	3.8134	4.2919
26	3.1407	3.5557	4.0231	4.5494
27	3.2820	3.7335	4.2444	4.8223
28	3.4297	3.9201	4.4778	5.1117
29	3.5840	4.1161	4.7241	5.4184
30	3.7453	4.3219	4.9839	5.7435
31	3.9139	4.5380	5.2581	6.0881
32	4.0900	4.7649	5.5472	6.4534
33	4.2740	5.0032	5.8523	6.8406
34	4.4664	5.2533	6.1742	7.2510
35	4.6673	5.5160	6.5138	7.6861
36	4.8774	5.7918	6.8721	8.1472
37	5.0969	6.0814	7.2500	8.6361
38	5.3262	6.3855	7.6488	9.1542
39	5.5659	6.7047	8.0695	9.7035
40	5.8164	7.0400	8.5133	10.2857

TABLE 8.4

THE MATURITY VALUE OF $1 AT COMPOUND INTEREST RATES OF 6.5%, 7%, 7.5%, AND 8%

Period	6.5%	7%	7.5%	8%
1	1.0650	1.0700	1.0750	1.0800
2	1.1342	1.1449	1.1556	1.1664
3	1.2079	1.2250	1.2423	1.2597
4	1.2865	1.3108	1.3355	1.3605
5	1.3701	1.4026	1.4356	1.4693
6	1.4591	1.5007	1.5433	1.5869
7	1.5540	1.6058	1.6590	1.7138
8	1.6550	1.7182	1.7835	1.8509
9	1.7626	1.8385	1.9172	1.9990
10	1.8771	1.9672	2.0610	2.1589
11	1.9992	2.1049	2.2156	2.3316
12	2.1291	2.2522	2.3818	2.5182
13	2.2675	2.4098	2.5604	2.7196
14	2.4149	2.5785	2.7524	2.9372
15	2.5718	2.7590	2.9589	3.1722
16	2.7390	2.9522	3.1808	3.4259
17	2.9170	3.1588	3.4194	3.7000
18	3.1067	3.3799	3.6758	3.9960
19	3.3086	3.6165	3.9515	4.3157
20	3.5236	3.8697	4.2479	4.6610
21	3.7527	4.1406	4.5664	5.0338
22	3.9966	4.4304	4.9089	5.4365
23	4.2564	4.7405	5.2771	5.8715
24	4.5330	5.0724	5.6729	6.3412
25	4.8277	5.4274	6.0983	6.8485
26	5.1415	5.8074	6.5557	7.3964
27	5.4757	6.2139	7.0474	7.9881
28	5.8316	6.6488	7.5760	8.6271
29	6.2107	7.1143	8.1442	9.3173
30	6.6144	7.6123	8.7550	10.0627
31	7.0443	8.1451	9.4116	10.8677
32	7.5022	8.7153	10.1175	11.7371
33	7.9898	9.3253	10.8763	12.6761
34	8.5091	9.9781	11.6920	13.6901
35	9.0622	10.6766	12.5689	14.7854
36	9.6513	11.4239	13.5116	15.9682
37	10.2786	12.2236	14.5249	17.2456
38	10.9467	13.0792	15.6143	18.6253
39	11.6583	13.9948	16.7854	20.1153
40	12.4161	14.9744	18.0443	21.7245

TABLE 8.5

THE MATURITY VALUE OF $1 AT COMPOUND INTEREST RATES OF 8.5%, 9%, 9.5%, AND 10%

Period	8.5%	9%	9.5%	10%
1	1.0850	1.0900	1.0950	1.1000
2	1.1772	1.1881	1.1990	1.2100
3	1.2773	1.2950	1.3129	1.3310
4	1.3859	1.4116	1.4377	1.4641
5	1.5037	1.5386	1.5742	1.6105
6	1.6315	1.6771	1.7238	1.7716
7	1.7701	1.8280	1.8876	1.9487
8	1.9206	1.9926	2.0669	2.1436
9	2.0839	2.1719	2.2632	2.3579
10	2.2610	2.3674	2.4782	2.5937
11	2.4532	2.5804	2.7137	2.8531
12	2.6617	2.8127	2.9715	3.1384
13	2.8879	3.0658	3.2537	3.4523
14	3.1334	3.3417	3.5629	3.7975
15	3.3997	3.6425	3.9013	4.1772
16	3.6887	3.9703	4.2719	4.5950
17	4.0023	4.3276	4.6778	5.0545
18	4.3425	4.7171	5.1222	5.5599
19	4.7116	5.1417	5.6088	6.1159
20	5.1121	5.6044	6.1416	6.7275
21	5.5466	6.1088	6.7251	7.4002
22	6.0180	6.6586	7.3639	8.1403
23	6.5296	7.2579	8.0635	8.9543
24	7.0846	7.9111	8.8296	9.8497
25	7.6868	8.6231	9.6684	10.8347
26	8.3401	9.3992	10.5869	11.9182
27	9.0491	10.2451	11.5926	13.1100
28	9.8182	11.1672	12.6939	14.4210
29	10.6528	12.1722	13.8998	15.8631
30	11.5583	13.2677	15.2203	17.4494
31	12.5407	14.4618	16.6663	19.1944
32	13.6067	15.7634	18.2495	21.1138
33	14.7633	17.1821	19.9833	23.2252
34	16.0181	18.7284	21.8817	25.5477
35	17.3797	20.4140	23.9604	28.1025
36	18.8569	22.2513	26.2367	30.9127
37	20.4598	24.2539	28.7291	34.0040
38	22.1989	26.4367	31.4584	37.4044
39	24.0858	28.8160	34.4470	41.1448
40	26.1331	31.4095	37.7194	45.2593

TABLE 8.6

THE MATURITY VALUE OF $1 AT COMPOUND INTEREST RATES OF 10.5%, 11%, 11.5%, AND 12%

Period	10.5%	11%	11.5%	12%
1	1.1050	1.1100	1.1150	1.1200
2	1.2210	1.2321	1.2432	1.2544
3	1.3492	1.3676	1.3862	1.4049
4	1.4909	1.5181	1.5456	1.5735
5	1.6474	1.6851	1.7234	1.7623
6	1.8204	1.8704	1.9215	1.9738
7	2.0116	2.0762	2.1425	2.2107
8	2.2228	2.3045	2.3889	2.4760
9	2.4562	2.5580	2.6636	2.7731
10	2.7141	2.8394	2.9699	3.1058
11	2.9991	3.1518	3.3115	3.4785
12	3.3140	3.4985	3.6923	3.8960
13	3.6619	3.8833	4.1169	4.3635
14	4.0464	4.3104	4.5904	4.8871
15	4.4713	4.7846	5.1183	5.4736
16	4.9408	5.3109	5.7069	6.1304
17	5.4596	5.8951	6.3632	6.8660
18	6.0328	6.5436	7.0949	7.6900
19	6.6663	7.2633	7.9108	8.6128
20	7.3662	8.0623	8.8206	9.6463
21	8.1397	8.9492	9.8349	10.8038
22	8.9944	9.9336	10.9660	12.1003
23	9.9388	11.0263	12.2271	13.5523
24	10.9823	12.2392	13.6332	15.1786
25	12.1355	13.5855	15.2010	17.0001
26	13.4097	15.0799	16.9491	19.0401
27	14.8177	16.7386	18.8982	21.3249
28	16.3736	18.5799	21.0715	23.8839
29	18.0928	20.6237	23.4948	26.7499
30	19.9926	22.8923	26.1967	29.9599
31	22.0918	25.4105	29.2093	33.5551
32	24.4114	28.2056	32.5683	37.5817
33	26.9746	31.3082	36.3137	42.0915
34	29.8070	34.7521	40.4898	47.1425
35	32.9367	38.5749	45.1461	52.7996
36	36.3950	42.8181	50.3379	59.1356
37	40.2165	47.5281	56.1267	66.2318
38	44.4392	52.7562	62.5813	74.1797
39	49.1054	58.5593	69.7782	83.0812
40	54.2614	65.0009	77.8027	93.0510

The money will be received in two years, so $n = 2$. And because the interest rate is 3%, $1 + r = 1.03$. Now what do we do? We multiply 1.03×1.03:

$$\frac{1}{(1.03) \times (1.03)} = \frac{1}{1.0609} = .942 \text{ or } 94 \text{ cents}$$

So what we really do here is what we've been doing to solve problems in every chapter: (1) write down a formula, (2) substitute numbers into the formula, and (3) solve with arithmetic.

Now it's your turn. If the interest rate were 6% and a dollar will be paid to you in two years, what is the present value of that dollar? Work it out to the nearest cent.

Solution:

$$\frac{1}{(1 + r)^n} = \frac{1}{(1.06)^2} = \frac{1}{1.06 \times 1.06} = \frac{1}{1.1236} = .889 = 89 \text{ cents}$$

Problem:

What is the present value of $100 that will be paid to you in 3 years if the interest rate were 5%? Work it out to the nearest cent.

Solution:

$$\frac{1}{(1 + r)^n} = \frac{1}{(1.05)^3} = \frac{1}{1.05 \times 1.05 \times 1.05} = \frac{1}{1.157625}$$

$$= .8638375 \times \$100 = \$86.38$$

Now you're on your own. Solve each problem in Quick Quiz 8.2.

QUICK QUIZ 8.2

1. If the interest rate is 3%, what is the present value of $1,000 that will be paid to you in three years?

2. If the interest rate is 7%, what is the present value of $2,000 that will be paid to you in four years?

3. If the interest rate is 8%, what is the present value of $1,000 that will be paid to you in three years?

4. If the interest rate is 9%, what is the present value of one dollar that will be paid to you in three years?

5. If the interest rate is 4%, what is the present value of $1,000 that will be paid to you in five years?

Answers to Quick Quiz 8.2

1. $\dfrac{1}{(1+r)^n} = \dfrac{1}{(1.03)^3} = \dfrac{1}{1.03 \times 1.03 \times 1.03} = \dfrac{1}{1.092727}$

   $= .91514 \times \$1,000 = \$915.14$

2. $\dfrac{1}{(1+r)^n} = \dfrac{1}{(1.07)^4} = \dfrac{1}{1.07 \times 1.07 \times 1.07 \times 1.07} = \dfrac{1}{1.310796}$

   $= .7628952 \times \$2,000 = \$1,525.79$

3. $\dfrac{1}{(1+r)^n} = \dfrac{1}{(1.08)^3} = \dfrac{1}{1.08 \times 1.08 \times 1.08} = \dfrac{1}{1.259712}$

   $= .79383 \times \$1,000 = \$793.83$

4. $\dfrac{1}{(1+r)^n} = \dfrac{1}{(1.09)^3} = \dfrac{1}{1.09 \times 1.09 \times 1.09} = \dfrac{1}{1.295029}$

   $= .77218 = 77$ cents

5. $\dfrac{1}{(1+r)^n} = \dfrac{1}{(1.04)^n} = \dfrac{1}{1.21665} = .821929$

   $.821929 \times \$1,000 = \$821.93$

SELF-TEST

The Compound Interest Tables

1. If you were to deposit $12,000 and the bank paid you 6% interest compounded quarterly, how much would the maturity value of your deposit be at the end of nine years?

2. If $1,000 were deposited for 12 years and the interest is 7% compounded annually, how much is the maturity value of that deposit?

3. $3,000 is deposited at an interest rate of 8% compounded quarterly. How much is the maturity value of that deposit after five years?

Present Value

4. If the interest rate is 8%, what is the present value of one dollar that will be paid to you in three years?

5. If the interest rate is 5%, what is the present value of one dollar that will be paid to you in four years?

6. If the interest rate is 11%, what is the present value of one dollar that will be paid to you in four years?

ANSWERS

The Compound Interest Tables

1. $\dfrac{6\%}{4} = 1.5\%$ (36 periods)

   $\$1.7091 \times \$12,000 = \$20,509.20$

2. 7% (12 periods)
    $2.2522 × $1,000 = $2,252.20

3. $\dfrac{8\%}{4}$ = 2% (20 periods)

    $1.4859 × $3,000 = $4,457.70

Present Value

4. $\dfrac{1}{(1+r)^n} = \dfrac{1}{(1.08)^3} = \dfrac{1}{(1.08)\times(1.08)\times(1.08)} = \dfrac{1}{1.259712}$

    = .793 = 79 cents

5. $\dfrac{1}{(1+r)^n} = \dfrac{1}{(1.05)^4} = \dfrac{1}{(1.05)\times(1.05)\times(1.05)\times(1.05)} = \dfrac{1}{1.21551}$

    = .8227 = 82 cents

6. $\dfrac{1}{(1+r)^n} = \dfrac{1}{(1.11)^4} = \dfrac{1}{1.11\times1.11\times1.11\times1.11} = \dfrac{1}{1.5181}$

    = .6587 = 66 cents

We've covered a great deal in these last few chapters. Let's stop for a moment to catch our breath.

Simple and compound interest rates and present value are very basic concepts in business and economics, so you want to be confident that you can work with them before going on in this book. If you've been getting nearly every problem right in the quick quizzes and the problem sets, then I can assure you that you are making excellent progress. If not, then you should review at least some parts of the last two chapters.

9 Depreciation

Machinery, equipment, computer systems, buildings, and other business assets lose value over time. We call that loss depreciation and consider it a cost of doing business.

Why do assets lose value over time? Largely because of wear and tear. A New York City taxi must be replaced every three years. If you don't believe me, try driving *your* car over all those potholes 24 hours a day, seven days a week.

The other main reason why assets lose value over time is that they become obsolete. A perfectly fine computer system must be replaced when a new one comes along. In fact, the field of business communications—faxes, teleconferencing, modems, and E-mail—seems to spawn a new vocabulary every few years, let alone an entirely new set of hardware and software that replaces the old hardware and software.

Depreciation, as a cost of doing business, is 100 percent tax-deductible. Indeed, it is often one of the largest deductions to which a business is entitled.

There are four basic methods of calculating deductions. When you have completed this chapter you will be on great terms with the (1) straight-line method; (2) units-of-production method; (3) sum-of-the-years'-digits method; and the (4) declining-balance method.

1 Straight-Line Method

The straight-line method of depreciation is not only the most frequently used method, but it is also the easiest. This method is based on the assumption that the item being depreciated wears out evenly over its useful life. For example, a cash register is expected to be used for ten years and then put out with the garbage. Under straight-line depreciation it would be depreciated by 10% of its purchase price each year. If it was purchased for $500, then we would depreciate it by $50 a year.

Of course not all of our plant and equipment gets completely used up and then discarded. Often it has some scrap or salvage value when we're finished using it. We'll call that its scrap value. Let's redo our depreciation schedule for that cash register assuming that after ten years it has a scrap value of $50. Using the straight-line method of depreciation, how much should that cash register be depreciated each year for ten years if it has a scrap value of $50 at the end of that period?

Solution:

$$\text{Yearly depreciation} = \frac{\text{cost} - \text{scrap value}}{\text{estimated useful life in years}}$$

$$= \frac{\$500 - \$50}{10}$$

$$= \frac{\$450}{10}$$

$$= \$45$$

Problem:

An office computer costing $17,000 has an estimated life of six years and an estimated scrap value of $800. How much is the annual depreciation?

Solution:

$$\text{Yearly depreciation} = \frac{\text{cost} - \text{scrap value}}{\text{estimated useful life in years}}$$

$$= \frac{\$17,000 - \$800}{6}$$

$$= \frac{\$16,200}{6}$$

$$= \$2,700$$

See? Straight-line depreciation is easy. You'll know that for yourself when you've completed Quick Quiz 9.1.

QUICK QUIZ 9.1

1. An offshore oil rig was built for $500,000 and has an estimated life of 12 years, after which it will have a salvage value of $60,000. Find the annual depreciation.

2. A roomful of office furniture was purchased for $140,000 and has an estimated life of nine years. If it will then have a salvage value of $15,000, what is its annual depreciation?

3. A machine that cost $28,000 has an estimated useful life of seven years and no salvage value. How much is it depreciated each year?

Answers to Quick Quiz 9.1

1. Yearly depreciation $= \dfrac{\text{cost} - \text{scrap value}}{\text{estimated useful life in years}}$

$$= \frac{\$500,000 - \$60,000}{12}$$

$$= \frac{\$440,000}{12}$$

$$= \$36,667$$

2. $\dfrac{\$140,000 - \$15,000}{9} = \dfrac{\$125,000}{9} = \$13,889$

3. $\dfrac{\$28,000}{7} = \$4,000$

2

It's time to introduce a new concept, book value. The book value of an asset is its original cost minus its accumulated depreciation. How much would the book value of the machine in problem 3 be after three years?

It would be $7,000. The machine depreciated by $7,000 per year for three years, so it would have depreciated by a total of $21,000. Using the definition: book value = original cost ($28,000) − accumulated depreciation ($21,000) = $7,000.

How much would the book value of that office furniture in problem 2 be after four years? Work it out right here:

Solution:

$$\text{Book} = \text{original cost} - \text{accumulated depreciation}$$
$$= \$140,000 - 4\,(\$13,889)$$
$$= \$140,000 - \$55,556$$
$$= \$84,444$$

Problem:

Circle Line purchased a $3.8 million sight-seeing boat that had an estimated life of 20 years and a salvage value of $200,000.

1. How much is the boat's annual depreciation?
2. How much is its book value after five years?

Solution:

1. Yearly depreciation = $\dfrac{\text{cost} - \text{scrap value}}{\text{estimated useful life in years}}$

    $= \dfrac{\$3,800,000 - \$200,000}{20}$

    $= \dfrac{\$3,600,000}{20}$

    $= \$180,000$

2. Book value = original cost – accumulated depreciation
    $= \$3,800,000 - 5\,(\$180,000)$
    $= \$3,800,000 - \$900,000$
    $= \$2,900,000$

QUICK QUIZ 9.2

1. Sal's Trucking purchased a tractor-trailer for $70,000. If the tractor-trailer has an estimated life of eight years and a salvage value of $2,000,
    a. How much is its annual depreciation?
    b. How much is its book value after six years?

2. *The New York Times* bought a printing press for $3 million. If the press has an estimated life of seven years and a salvage value of $300,000,
    a. How much is its annual depreciation?
    b. How much is its book value after three years?

3. American Airlines purchased a fleet of Boeing 747s for $720 million. If the fleet has an estimated life of 12 years and a salvage value of $60 million,
    a. How much is its annual depreciation?
    b. How much is its book value after four years?

Answers to Quick Quiz 9.2

1. a. Yearly depreciation = $\dfrac{\$70,000 - \$2,000}{8}$

    $= \dfrac{\$68,000}{8} = \$8,500$

    b. Book value = original cost – accumulated depreciation
        $= \$70,000 - 6(\$8,500)$
        $= \$70,000 - \$51,000$
        $= \$19,000$

2. a. Annual depreciation = $\dfrac{\$3,000,000 - \$300,000}{7}$

    $= \dfrac{\$2,700,000}{7}$

    $= \$385,714$

    b. Book value = original cost – accumulated depreciation
        $= \$3,000,000 - 3(\$385,714)$
        $= \$3,000,000 - \$1,157,142$
        $= \$1,842,858$

3. a. Annual depreciation = $\dfrac{\$720,000,000 - \$60,000,000}{12}$

$= \dfrac{660,000,000}{12} = \dfrac{\$330,000,000}{6}$

$= \$55,000,000$

b. Book value = original cost – accumulated depreciation
$= \$720,000,000 - 4(\$55,000,000)$
$= \$720,000,000 - \$220,000,000$
$= \$500,000,000$

3 Units-of-Production Method of Depreciation

You probably never heard of my Uncle Louie, but the man may have set a record for miles driven in one year. Somehow he put 110,000 miles on his car back in 1951. He worked as a travelling salesman, and every weekend he drove from New York to Boston because he was homesick.

The regular straight-line depreciation schedule just would not work for Uncle Louie's company car. Instead of talking about the expected life of his car in terms of *years,* we need to talk about it in terms of *miles.* Let's say that the expected life of a car is 120,000 miles.

The units-of-production method of depreciation expresses the expected life of an asset in terms of units produced rather than in years. In the case of Uncle Louie's company car, the expected life would then be stated in miles.

To find the amount of depreciation, we follow a two-step method:

1. Unit depreciation = $\dfrac{\text{original cost – salvage value}}{\text{expected life (in units produced)}}$

2. Depreciation amount = unit depreciation × units produced

What are our units? They're miles driven. OK, so Louie gets a $10,000 car with a salvage value of $100 (probably an optimistic figure, considering how Uncle Louie drives). How much has that car depreciated after one year (remember, he drove it 110,000 miles)? Work it out right here:

Solution:

1. Unit depreciation = $\dfrac{\text{original cost – salvage value}}{\text{expected life (in units produced)}}$

$= \dfrac{\$10,000 - \$100}{120,000} = \dfrac{\$\ 9,900}{120,000} = \$.0825$

2. Depreciation amount = unit depreciation × units produced
$= \$.0825 \times 110,000$
$= \$9,075$

So the car depreciated by $9,075 during the year that Uncle Louie put 110,000 miles on it. By the way, how much did the car depreciate for every mile he drove?

It depreciated by $8\frac{1}{4}$¢ per mile. You might imagine a meter ticking away (like the one in taxis) as the car depreciates.

We need great precision when we calculate unit depreciation, so you don't want to do any rounding unless you have to. You might have to if you're using a calculator and you're running out of capacity, but try to carry out your division to at least ten thousandths (that is, four decimal places).

4

Let's step back for a minute and ask ourselves: Why do we have to go through all these moves when the straight depreciation approach is so much easier? The reason why the units-of-production method is better here is because we can estimate the expected life of a machine or a piece of equipment by its use, rather than by its years of service. My Uncle Louie drove as many miles in one year what most people drive in ten. His car might have had an expected life of ten years had a normal person been driving it.

So when we can estimate the expected life in terms of actual use, rather than in years, we use the unit-of-production method. Another reason is that the use of certain machinery and equipment is uneven. An ice cream truck will be idle during the winter, and a heating oil delivery truck will be used much less frequently in the summer.

Problem:

Ford Motor Company has a stamping machine that can stamp out 200,000 car bodies. It cost $4 million, and it has no salvage value. How much has it depreciated after stamping out 50,000 car bodies, and what is its book value at that time?

Solution:

$$\text{Unit depreciation} = \frac{\text{original cost} - \text{salvage value}}{\text{expected life (in units produced)}}$$

$$= \frac{\$4,000,000 - 0}{200,000}$$

$$= \$20$$

$$\text{Depreciation amount} = \text{unit depreciation} \times \text{units produced}$$

$$= \$20 \times 50,000$$

$$= \$1,000,000$$

$$\text{Book value} = \text{original cost} - \text{accumulated depreciation}$$

$$= \$4,000,000 - \$1,000,000$$

$$= \$3,000,000$$

1. A laser printer that cost $25,000 is expected to operate for 20,000 hours, after which it will have a trade-in value of $2,000.
    a. For the first year the printer operated 3,850 hours. Find the depreciation for the year.
    b. Find the book value of the printer after one year.

2. A New York City taxi is purchased new for $16,000 and has a salvage value of $100 after it is driven 100,000 miles.
    a. Find the depreciation when the taxi has been driven for 30,000 miles.
    b. Find the book value of the taxi after 30,000 miles.

3. A tank for holding chemicals has a useful life of 2,000 hours and no salvage value. It cost $90,000.
    a. How much has it depreciated after 1,500 hours?
    b. How much is its book value after 1,500 hours?

Answers to Quick Quiz 9.3

1. a.   Unit depreciation $= \dfrac{\text{original cost} - \text{salvage value}}{\text{expected life (in units produced)}}$

$$= \frac{\$25,000 - \$2,000}{20,000 \text{ hours}}$$

$= \$1.15$

Depreciation amount $=$ unit depreciation $\times$ units produced

$= \$1.15 \times 3,850$

$= \$4,428$

Book value $=$ original cost $-$ accumulated depreciation

$= \$25,000 - \$4,428$

$= \$20,572$

2. a.   Unit depreciation $= \dfrac{\$16,000 - \$100}{100,000}$

$$= \frac{\$15,900}{100,000}$$

$= \$.159$

Depreciation amount $= \$.159 \times 30,000$

$= \$4,770$

  b.   Book value $=$ original value $-$ accumulated depreciation

$= \$16,000 - \$4,770$

$= \$11,230$

3. a.   Unit depreciation $= \dfrac{\$90,000}{2,000}$

$= \$45$

Depreciation amount $= \$45 \times 1,500$

$= \$67,500$

  b.   Book value $=$ original value $-$ accumulated depreciation

$= \$90,000 - \$67,500$

$= \$22,500$

5 The Sum-of-the-Years'-Digits Method

Depreciation is a cost of doing business. It is also a tax deduction. Business firms want to deduct as much as they can as soon as they can. A tax deduction in the current year is worth more than one received in a future year.

The sum-of-the-years'-digits method allows businesses to depreciate their machinery and equipment more in the first year than in the second, and more in the second than in the third. Is this fair? Well, doesn't a car or a truck depreciate more in the first year than in the second? And more in the second than in the third? Don't you think that businesses that use cars, trucks, and other machinery and equipment that depreciates very quickly in the first year or two are entitled to depreciate them faster for tax purposes? Even the Internal Revenue Service agrees.

The key to the sum-of-the-years'-digits method is adding up the years of the estimated life of the asset. Let's say that an asset is expected to last six years. All we do is find the sum of the years: $1 + 2 + 3 + 4 + 5 + 6 = 21$.

How much does our asset depreciate the first year? It depreciates by $\frac{6}{21}$ of the total amount it will depreciate (that is, original cost − salvage value).

And how much will this asset depreciate the second year? It depreciates by $\frac{5}{21}$ × (original cost − salvage value).

And how much will it depreciate the third, fourth, fifth, and sixth years? In the third year, by $\frac{4}{21}$ × (original cost − salvage value); in the fourth by $\frac{3}{21}$ × (original cost − salvage value); in the fifth by $\frac{2}{21}$ × (original cost − salvage value); and finally, in the sixth by $\frac{1}{21}$ × (original cost − salvage value).

Let's do a problem:

A machine is purchased for $100,000, has an expected life of four years, and has a salvage value of $4,000. By how much does it depreciate in the first year, in the second year, in the third year, and in the fourth year?

Solution:

Sum of the years = $1 + 2 + 3 + 4 = 10$

First year: $\frac{4}{10}$ × ($100,000 − $4,000) = $.4 × $96,000 = $38,400$

Second year: $\frac{3}{10}$ × $96,000 = $28,800$

Third year: $\frac{2}{10}$ × $96,000 = $19,200$

Fourth year: $\frac{1}{10}$ × $96,000 = $9,600$

How would you check your results? Just add up the depreciation for the four years and make sure it comes to $96,000: $38,400 + $28,800 + $19,200 + $9,600 = $96,000.

Ready for another one?

A temporary building has a useful life of 15 years. Its original cost is $220,000, and it has a salvage value of $5,000.

1. How much does it depreciate in the first year, and how much is its book value at the end of the first year?

2. How much does it depreciate in the second year, and how much is its book value at the end of the second year?

Solution:

Did you begin by adding 1 + 2 + 3 + 4…all the way up to 15? Well, you'll be happy to learn that there's a shortcut. The sum of the years can be found with this formula:

$$\frac{n\,(n + 1)}{2}$$

The letter n is the estimated years of life of the asset.

Try this formula to see if it works.

Solution:

$$\frac{n\,(n + 1)}{2} = \frac{15\,(15 + 1)}{2} = \frac{15 \times \overset{8}{\cancel{16}}}{\underset{1}{\cancel{2}}} = 120$$

Why didn't I give you this formula *before* you did this problem? Because I wanted you to *appreciate* it. Now you'll know that you can save yourself a lot of addition by using it. But you don't really need the formula for problems that involve assets with estimated lives of just a few years.

Now back to the problem:

$$\text{First year: } \frac{\overset{1}{\cancel{15}}}{\underset{8}{\cancel{120}}} \times (\$220{,}000 - \$5{,}000)$$

$$= \frac{\$215{,}000}{8} = \$26{,}875$$

$$\text{Book value} = \$220{,}000 - \$26{,}875$$
$$= \$193{,}125$$

$$\text{Second year: } \frac{\overset{7}{\cancel{14}}}{\underset{60}{\cancel{120}}} \times (\$215{,}000)$$

$$= \frac{\$1,505,000}{60}$$
$$= \$25,083$$

$$\text{Book value} = \$220,000 - (\$26,875 + \$25,083)$$
$$= \$220,000 - \$51,958$$
$$= \$168,042$$

QUICK QUIZ 9.4

1. A machine that is expected to last 18 years cost $175,000 and has a salvage value of $10,000.
    a. How much does it depreciate in the first year, and how much is its book value at the end of the first year?
    b. How much does it depreciate in the second year, and how much is its book value at the end of the second year?

2. A photocopy machine has an expected life of five years. It cost $4,000, and it has a salvage value of $300.
    a. How much does it depreciate in the first three years?
    b. How much is its book value after three years?

3. The Scarsdale Cleaners purchases a dry cleaning machine for $6,000 that has an estimated life of 16 years and a salvage value of $200.
    a. How much does the machine depreciate in the first five years?
    b. How much is its book value after five years?

Answers to Quick Quiz 9.4

1. a. $\dfrac{n(n+1)}{2} = \dfrac{\overset{9}{\cancel{18}}\,(18+1)}{\underset{1}{\cancel{2}}} = 9 \times 19 = 171$

    First year $= \dfrac{18}{171}$ (original cost − salvage value)

    $$= \dfrac{18}{171}\,(\$175,000 - \$10,000)$$

    $$\text{Depreciation} = \dfrac{18}{171} \times \dfrac{\$165,000}{1}$$

    $$= \dfrac{\$2,970,000}{171}$$

    $$= \$17,368$$
    $$\text{Book value} = \$175,000 - \$17,368$$
    $$= \$157,632$$

    b. $\dfrac{17}{171} \times \dfrac{\$165,000}{1}$

    $$\text{Depreciation} = \dfrac{\$2,805,000}{171}$$

    $$= \$16,404$$
    $$\text{Book value} = \$175,000 - (\$17,368 + \$16,404)$$
    $$= \$175,000 - \$33,772$$
    $$= \$141,228$$

2. a. Sum of years = 5 + 4 + 3 + 2 + 1 = 15

$$\text{First year} = \frac{5}{15} \text{ (original cost – salvage value)}$$

$$\text{Second year} = \frac{4}{15} \text{ (original cost – salvage value)}$$

$$\text{Third year} = \frac{3}{15} \text{ (original cost – salvage value)}$$

$$\text{First three years} = \frac{12}{15} \text{ (\$4,000 – \$300)}$$

$$= \frac{4}{5} \text{ (\$3,700)}$$

$$= .8 \times \$3,700$$
$$= \$2,960$$

$$\text{Book value} = \$4,000 – \$2,960$$
$$= \$1,040$$

3. a. $$\frac{n\,(n+1)}{2} = \frac{\overset{8}{\cancel{16}}\,(16+1)}{\underset{1}{\cancel{2}}} = 8 \times 17 = 136$$

$$\text{First year} = \frac{16}{136} \text{ (original cost – salvage value)}$$

$$\frac{16}{136} \text{ (\$6,000 – \$200)}$$

$$\frac{16}{136} \text{ (\$5,800)}$$

$$\text{Second year} = \frac{15}{136} \text{ (\$5,800)}$$

$$\text{Third year} = \frac{14}{136} \text{ (\$5,800)}$$

$$\text{Fourth year} = \frac{13}{136} \text{ (\$5,800)}$$

$$\text{Fifth year} = \frac{12}{136} \text{ (\$5,800)}$$

$$\frac{16 + 15 + 14 + 13 + 12}{136} \text{ (\$5,800)}$$

$$= \frac{70}{136} \times \$5,800$$

$$= \frac{\overset{35}{\cancel{70}}}{\underset{\underset{17}{\cancel{34}}}{\cancel{68}}} \times \overset{\overset{1,450}{\cancel{2,900}}}{\cancel{\$5,800}}$$

$$= \frac{50,750}{17}$$
$$= \$2,985$$

$$\text{Book value} = \$6,000 – \$2,985$$
$$= \$3,015$$

6   The Declining-Balance Method

The sum-of-the-years'-digits approach took a disproportionate amount of depreciation in the early years of an asset's use. This is called accelerated depreciation. The declining-balance method is another form of accelerated depreciation that takes the largest amount of depreciation in the first year and progressively smaller amounts in succeeding years.

Here is the formula that we'll use:

Annual depreciation = book value of asset × depreciation rate at beginning of year

For the depreciation rate we're going to use straight-line depreciation, just as we did in the first section of this chapter, but to make things interesting, we'll use double the straight-line rate. In fact, we'll do this for the rest of the chapter.

We buy a machine for $10,000 that has an expected life of five years and a salvage value of $500. What is the depreciation for the first year?

Solution:

$$\text{Annual depreciation} = \$10,000 \times \frac{1}{5} \times 2$$

$$= \$10,000 \times \frac{2}{5}$$

$$= \$4,000$$

Why is this called the *declining-balance* method of depreciation? We're about to find out.

Find the depreciation in the second year.

Solution:

$$\text{Annual depreciation} = \$6,000 \times \frac{2}{5}$$

$$= \$2,400$$

Did you follow what we did? We started with the book value at the beginning of the second year, $6,000. Where did the $6,000 come from? The book value at the beginning of the first year was $10,000. The depreciation for the first year was $4,000, so the book value at the end of the first year (or the beginning of the second year) was $10,000 − $4,000 = $6,000.

Now find the depreciation for the third year.

Solution:

$$\text{Annual depreciation} = \$3,600 \times \frac{2}{5} = \$1,440$$

We can keep depreciating until the book value declines to the level of the salvage value. At that point we cannot depreciate any further.

1. An asset is purchased for $25,000, with an expected life of 8 years and a salvage value of $1,000. How much did the asset depreciate for each of the first three years?

2. A machine is purchased for $90,000 and has a salvage value of $6,000. If its expected life is 10 years, by how much does it depreciate over the first four years?

3. A security system is installed for $200,000 that has a salvage value of $3,000. If it has an expected life of 25 years, how much does it depreciate in each of the first five years?

Answers to Quick Quiz 9.5

1.   Annual depreciation (first year) $= \$25,000 \times \dfrac{1}{8} \times 2$

$$= \$25,000 \times \dfrac{1}{4}$$

$$= \$6,250$$

Annual depreciation (second year) $= (\$25,000 - \$6,250) \times \dfrac{1}{4}$

$$= \$18,750 \times \dfrac{1}{4}$$

$$= \$4,687.50$$
$$= \$4,688$$

Annual depreciation (third year) $= (\$18,750 - \$4,688) \times \dfrac{1}{4}$

$$= \$14,062 \times \dfrac{1}{4}$$

$$= \$3,515.50$$
$$= \$3,516$$

2.   Annual depreciation (first year) $= \$90,000 \times \dfrac{1}{10} \times 2$

$$= \dfrac{\$90,000}{5}$$

$$= \$18,000$$

Annual depreciation (second year) $= (\$90,000 - \$18,000) \times \dfrac{1}{5}$

$$= \dfrac{\$72,000}{5}$$

$$= \$14,400$$

Annual depreciation (third year) $= (\$72,000 - \$14,400) \times \dfrac{1}{5}$

$$= \dfrac{\$57,600}{5}$$

$$= \$11,520$$

Annual depreciation (fourth year) $= (\$57,600 - \$11,520) \times \dfrac{1}{5}$

$$= \dfrac{\$46,080}{5}$$

$$= \$9,216$$

Total depreciation for four years $= \$18,000 + \$14,400 + \$11,520 + \$9216$
$$= \$53,136$$

3.   Annual depreciation (first year) $= \$200,000 \times \dfrac{1}{25} \times 2$

$$= \$200,000 \times \dfrac{2}{25}$$
$$= \$200,000 \times .08$$
$$= \$16,000$$

Annual depreciation (second year) $= (\$200,000 - \$16,000) \times .08$
$$= \$184,000 \times .08$$
$$= \$14,720$$

Annual depreciation (third year) $= (\$184,000 - \$14,720) \times .08$
$$= \$169,280 \times .08$$
$$= \$13,542$$

Annual depreciation (fourth year) $= (\$169,280 - \$13,542) \times .08$
$$= \$155,738 \times .08$$
$$= \$12,459$$

Annual depreciation (fifth year) $= (\$155,738 - \$12,459) \times .08$
$$= \$143,279 \times .08$$
$$= \$11,462$$

SELF-TEST

Straight-Line Method

1. A company purchased a piece of equipment for $80,000. If the equipment has an estimated life of 12 years and a salvage value of $3,000,
    a   How much is the annual depreciation?
    b. How much is its book value after two years?
    c. How much is its book value after eight years?

2. A firm purchased a tractor-trailer for $55,000. If the tractor-trailer has an estimated life of nine years and a salvage value of $4,000,
    a. How much is its annual depreciation?
    b. How much is its book value after four years?

Units-of-Production Method

3. Leonard's of Great Neck, a prominent Long Island caterer, built a huge oven that has an expected life of 9,000 hours and no salvage value. It cost $350,000. How much has the oven depreciated after operating for 2,000 hours, and what is its book value at that time?

4. A laser printer that cost $20,000 is expected to operate for 15,000, after which it will have a trade-in value of $1,000.
    a. For the first year the printer operated 3,140 hours. Find the depreciation for the year.
    b. Find the book value of the printer after one year.

The Sum-of-the-Years'-Digits Method

5. A machine is purchased for $200,000, has an expected life of four years, and a salvage value of $5,000. By how much does it depreciate (a) in the first year, (b) in the second year, (c) in the third year, and (d) in the fourth year?

6. A piece of equipment has a useful life of 8 years. Its original cost is $186,000, and it has a salvage value of $3,000.
   a. How much does it depreciate in the first year, and how much is its book value at the end of the first year?
   b. How much does it depreciate in the second year, and how much is its book value at the end of the second year?

The Declining-Balance Method

7. An asset is purchased for $50,000, with an expected life of 10 years and a salvage value of $1,000. How much did the asset depreciate for each of the first three years?

8. A machine is purchased for $75,000 and has a salvage value of $5,000. If its expected life is 7 years, by how much does it depreciate in each of the first four years?

ANSWERS

Straight-Line Method

1. a. Annual depreciation $= \dfrac{\$80,000 - \$3,000}{12} = \dfrac{\$77,000}{12}$

    $= \$6,416.67$

    b. Book value = original cost − accumulated depreciation
    $= \$80,000 - 2(\$6,416.67)$
    $= \$80,000 - \$12,833.34$
    $= \$67,166.66$

    c. Book value $= \$80,000 - 8(\$6,416.67)$
    $= \$80,000 - \$51,333.36$
    $= \$28,666.64$

2. a. Annual depreciation $= \dfrac{\$55,000 - \$4,000}{9} = \dfrac{\$51,000}{9}$

    $= \$5,666.67$

    b. Book value $= \$55,000 - 4 \times \$5,666.67$
    $= \$55,000 - \$22,666.68$
    $= \$32,333.32$

Units-of-Production Method

3. a. Unit depreciation $= \dfrac{\$350,000}{9,000} = \$38.88889$

    Depreciation amount $= \$38.88889 \times 2,000$
    $= \$77,777.78$

    b. Book value $= \$350,000 - \$77,777.78$
    $= \$272,222.22$

4. a. Unit depreciation $= \dfrac{\$20,000 - \$1,000}{15,000} = \dfrac{\$19,000}{15,000} = \$1.266667$

    Depreciation amount $= \$1.266667 \times 3,140 = \$3,977.33$

    b. Book value $= \$20,000 - \$3,977.33$
    $= \$16,022.67$

The Sum-of-the-Years'-Digits Method

5. a. Sum of the years = 1 + 2 + 3 + 4 = 10

$$\text{First year} = \frac{4}{10}\ (\$200{,}000 - \$5{,}000)$$

$$= .4 \times \$195{,}000$$
$$= \$78{,}000$$

   b. Second year = .3 × $195,000
       = $58,500

   c. Third year = .2 × $195,000
       = $39,000

   d. Fourth year = .1 × $195,000
       = $19,500

6. a. Sum of the years = 1 + 2 + 3 + 4 + 5 + 6 + 7 + 8 = 36

$$\text{First year} = \frac{8}{36}\ (\$186{,}000 - \$3{,}000) = \frac{2}{9}\ (183{,}000)$$

$$= .222222 \times \$183{,}000 = \$40{,}666.66$$
$$\text{Book value} = \$186{,}000 - \$40{,}666.66 = \$145{,}333.34$$

$$\text{Second year} = \frac{7}{36}\ (183{,}000) = .1944444 \times \$183{,}000$$

$$= \$35{,}583.33$$

Book value = $145,333.34
            −35,583.33
            $109,750.01

The Declining-Balance Method

7. Annual depreciation (first year) = $50{,}000 \times \dfrac{1}{10} \times 2$

$$= \$50{,}000 \times \frac{1}{5}$$
$$= \$10{,}000$$

Annual depreciation (second year) = $40{,}000 \times \dfrac{1}{5}$
$$= \$8{,}000$$

Annual depreciation (third year) = $32{,}000 \times \dfrac{1}{5}$
$$= \$6{,}400$$

8. Annual depreciation (first year) = $75{,}000 \times \dfrac{1}{7} \times 2$

$$= \$75{,}000 \times \frac{2}{7}$$
$$= \$75{,}000 \times .2857142$$
$$= \$21{,}428.57$$

Annual depreciation (second year) = $75,000.00
                                    −21,428.57
                                    $53,571.43 × .2857142
                                    = $15,306.12

Annual depreciation (third year) = $53,571.43
                                   −15,306.12
                                   $38,265.31 × .2857142
                                   = $10,932.94

Annual depreciation (fourth year) = $38,265.31
                                    −10,932.94
                                    $27,332.37

10 The Balance Sheet

In this chapter and in the one that follows, we will discuss the two greatest accounting concepts of all time—the balance sheet and the income statement. Do you need an extensive background knowledge of accounting to get through this chapter? Some knowledge of accounting certainly wouldn't hurt, but if you pay close attention and work out every problem, you should definitely be able to understand the entire chapter.

I myself am an economist, not an accountant. Do you know the difference between the two professions? An economist and an accountant are both good with numbers, but the economist lacks the accountant's sense of humor.

This chapter is set up differently from the preceding chapters. Because we need to cover a large amount of technical material, and considering the length of the problems you'll be doing, you won't have to take any quick quizzes until we reach the end of the chapter.

1 How the Balance Sheet Is Set Up

A balance sheet is a financial statement that tells you how much a business is worth as of a certain date. It has three basic components: assets, liabilities, and owner's equity.

The assets include what the company owns and what it is owed by others. Typical assets are cash accounts receivable, merchandise inventory, buildings, and equipment.

Liabilities are everything the company owes. Typical liabilities include taxes owed, accounts payable, and notes payable.

The owner's equity (or stockholders' equity if the company is a corporation) is simply the assets minus the liabilities.

So we're left with this set of equations:

1. assets – liabilities = owner's equity
2. assets = liabilities + owner's equity

Assets are divided into current assets and fixed assets. Current assets are either cash or can be converted into cash within a year. Fixed assets are used for more than a year. To simplify our analysis, the only fixed assets we'll be using will be plant and equipment (things like factories and machinery).

Liabilities can be divided into current liabilities, which are due within one year, and long-term liabilities, which are due in more than one year.

The owner's equity tells us how much a business is actually worth. Can a business ever have negative equity?

The answer is yes. If assets – liabilities = owner's equity, what if assets were smaller than liabilities. Then owner's equity would be negative. This can and does happen every day. When it does, then it's a sign that the owner should consider going out of business.

2

Table 10.1 is an example of a balance sheet. It tells us the financial condition of ABC Plumbing Supply as of September 30, 1999.

Notice that current assets ($34,400) and plant and equipment ($128,200) add up to total assets of $162,600. There are no long-term liabilities, so current liabilities ($22,100) are identical to total liabilities ($22,100). And finally, our total liabilities ($22,100) and our owner's equity ($140,500) add up to total assets ($162,600).

3 Vertical Analysis

Are you ready for some vertical analysis? What we'll be doing is looking at each asset as a percentage of total assets. Then we'll look at each liability as a percentage of total assets. And finally, we'll look at the components of owner's equity as a percentage of total assets.

If you have a suspicious nature, you might ask why we don't look at individual liabilities and owner's equity as a percentage of the combined total for liabilities and owner's equity. We could, but because their sum is equal to total assets, let's take *every*thing as a percentage of total assets.

In just a minute we're going to be working out a percentage distribution of all the items on the balance sheet shown in Table 10.1. Do you still remember how to figure out percentage distributions? If you don't, then it would be a good idea to read the accompanying box.

TABLE 10.1

ABC Plumbing Supply
Balance Sheet
September 30, 1999

Assets

Current assets:	
Cash	$ 7,500
Accounts receivable	12,300
Merchandise inventory	14,600
Total current assets	34,400
Plant and equipment:	
Building	121,000
Equipment	7,200
Total plant and equipment	128,200
Total assets	162,600

Liabilities

Current liabilities:	
Accounts payable	9,700
Notes payable	10,000
Wages payable	2,400
Total current liabilities	22,100
Total liabilities	22,100
Owner's equity	140,500
Total liabilities and owner's equity	162,600

OK, let's do some vertical analysis. Take a good look at Table 10.2. To the right of every item you'll find that a percent has been filled in—Table 10.2 lists each item as a percentage of total assets. If you are feeling rusty on percents, see the box called "Review of Percentage Distribution."

Can you guess what comes next? That's right—it's *your* turn. To make things as easy as possible, the balance sheet shown in Table 10.3 has an identical format to the one in Table 10.2. Please work out the percentage distribution right on Table 10.3, just the way I did in Table 10.2.

Check your work with what I've got in Table 10.3A. As we move through this chapter, we'll keep rounding our decimals to tenths.

If you got everything right in Table 10.3, then go directly to the next section. If not, then I want you to give it another shot in Table 10.4. Work out your entire percentage distribution and then check your answers against mine in Table 10.4A.

How did you do? If you're still having trouble, then go back to frame 10 of Chapter 3 and work your way through it and retake Quick Quiz 3.3. Then come back to the beginning of *this* section and work

Review of Percentage Distribution

We haven't done any percentage distribution problems since the last section of Chapter 3, and now a whole bunch of percentage distribution problems are coming up. See if you can do this problem. A firm has five assets: cash: $15,500; accounts receivable: $17,900; merchandise inventory; $23,500; building: $174,000; and equipment: $43,100. What is the percentage share of each of these assets of total assets?

Solution:

$$
\begin{array}{r}
\$\ 15,500 \\
17,900 \\
23,500 \\
174,000 \\
\underline{43,100} \\
\$274,000
\end{array}
$$

$$\text{Cash} = \frac{15,500}{274,000} = 5.6\%$$

$$\text{Accounts receivable} = \frac{17,900}{274,000} = 6.5\%$$

$$\text{Merchandise inventory} = \frac{23,500}{274,000} = 8.6\%$$

$$\text{Building} = \frac{174,000}{274,000} = 63.5\%$$

$$\text{Equipment} = \frac{43,100}{274,000} = 15.7\%$$

Check:

$$
\begin{array}{r}
5.6 \\
6.5 \\
8.6 \\
63.5 \\
\underline{15.7} \\
99.9\%
\end{array}
$$

It's a good practice to check your figures. If they don't add up to 100.0%, then you've got to redo your calculations. In this case we were slightly off at 99.9% because of rounding. Incidentally, in this chapter we'll be rounding all our percentages to the nearest tenth. So, for example, 5.64% is rounded to 5.6% and 8.75% becomes 8.8%.

TABLE 10.2

ABC Plumbing Supply
Balance Sheet
September 30, 1999

Assets

Current assets:			
Cash	$ 7,500	4.6%	
Accounts receivable	12,300	7.6%	
Merchandise inventory	14,600	9.0%	
Total current assets	34,400		21.2%
Plant and equipment:			
Building	121,000	74.4%	
Equipment	7,200	4.4%	
Total plant and equipment	128,200		78.8%
Total assets	162,600		100.0%

Liabilities

Current liabilities:			
Accounts payable	9,700	6.0%	
Notes payable	10,000	6.2%	
Wages payable	2,400	1.5%	
Total current liabilities	22,100		13.6%
Total liabilities	22,100		13.6%
Owner's equity	140,500		86.4%
Total liabilities and owner's equity	162,600		100.0%

out the percentage distributions in Tables 10.3 and 10.4 from scratch. Remember, in math, repetition always helps.

5 | The Current Ratio

When you're running a business, there are always bills that need to be paid. And to pay these bills, you obviously need money. Your current liabilities are everything you owe that must be paid off within a year. And your current assets is the sum of your cash and anything else you own—or are owed—that can be turned into cash within a year.

The current ratio is the ratio of your current assets to your current liabilities:

$$\text{Current ratio} = \frac{\text{current assets}}{\text{current liabilities}}$$

TABLE 10.3

Bill's Photo Supplies
Balance Sheet
March 31, 1998

Assets

Current assets:		
Cash	$ 4,000	_____
Accounts receivable	17,500	_____
Merchandise inventory	26,400	_____
Total current assets	47,900	
Plant and equipment:		_____
Building	195,000	_____
Equipment	24,900	_____
Total plant and equipment	219,900	
Total assets	267,800	_____

Liabilities

Current liabilities:		
Accounts payable	17,000	_____
Notes payable	4,000	_____
Wages payable	2,600	_____
Total current liabilities	23,600	
Total liabilities	23,600	_____
Owner's equity	244,200	_____
Total liabilities and owner's equity	267,800	_____

Look all the way back to Table 10.2 and figure out the current ratio of ABC Plumbing Supply.

Solution:

$$\text{Current ratio} = \frac{\text{current assets}}{\text{current liabilities}} = \frac{\$34,400}{22,100} = 1.6$$

And now find the current ratio for Bill's Photo Supplies (Table 10.3) and Steve's Restaurant (Table 10.4).

Solutions:

$$\text{Bill's Photo Supplies} = \frac{47,900}{23,600} = 2.0$$

$$\text{Steve's Restaurant} = \frac{17,700}{32,800} = 0.5$$

Of the three businesses we have just looked at, it appears that Bill's Photo Supplies, with a current ratio of 2.0, is in the best financial shape. The larger the current ratio, the better the financial condition of the firm. A ratio of at least 2:1 or 2.0 is considered desirable.

TABLE 10.3A

ANSWERS TO TABLE 10.3

Bill's Photo Supplies
Balance Sheet
March 31, 1998

Assets

Current assets:			
Cash	$ 4,000	1.5%	
Accounts receivable	17,500	6.5%	
Merchandise inventory	26,400	9.9%	
Total current assets	47,900		17.9%
Plant and equipment:			
Building	195,000	72.8%	
Equipment	24,900	9.3%	
Total plant and equipment	219,900		82.1%
Total assets	267,800		100.0%

Liabilities

Current liabilities:			
Accounts payable	17,000	6.3%	
Notes payable	4,000	1.5%	
Wages payable	2,600	1.0%	
Total current liabilities	23,600		8.8%
Total liabilities	23,600		8.8%
Owner's equity	244,200		91.1%
Total liabilities and owner's equity	267,800		100.0%

6   The Acid Test Ratio

The formula for the acid test ratio is similar to that of the current ratio, but liquid assets are substituted for current assets. Liquid assets are cash and anything that can quickly be converted into cash. For most businesses, that would be accounts receivable. The formula is:

$$\text{Acid test ratio} = \frac{\text{liquid assets}}{\text{current liabilities}}$$

Problem:

How much would the acid test ratio be for a firm that had $20,000 in cash, $35,000 in accounts receivable, and $40,000 in current liabilities?

Solution:

$$\text{Acid test ratio} = \frac{\text{liquid assets}}{\text{current liabilities}}$$

$$= \frac{\$55,000}{40,000} = \frac{11}{8} = 1.375 = 1.4$$

TABLE 10.4

Steve's Restaurant
Balance Sheet
January 1, 1999

Assets

Current assets:		
Cash	$ 12,100	_____
Accounts receivable	1,400	_____
Merchandise inventory	4,200	_____
Total current assets	17,700	
Plant and equipment:		
Building	153,500	_____
Equipment	16,700	_____
Total plant and equipment	170,200	
Total assets	187,900	

Liabilities

Current liabilities:		
Accounts payable	7,900	_____
Notes payable	20,000	_____
Wages payable	4,900	_____
Total current liabilities	32,800	
Total liabilities	32,800	

Owner's equity	155,100	_____
Total liabilities and owner's equity	187,900	

Do you think this is a good acid test ratio? Yes, it certainly is. An acid test ratio of at least 1:1, or 1, is considered desirable.

Let's do one more.

Find the acid test ratio of a firm with current liabilities of $55,000, $12,000 in cash, and $17,000 in accounts receivable.

Solution:

$$\frac{\$29,000}{55,000} = .5$$

7 Horizontal Analysis

Everything we've done so far involved vertical analysis, because we were examining a single balance sheet from top to bottom. Now we'll be doing a comparative analysis of two balance sheets that belong to the same firm. A balance sheet gives us a snapshot of a firm's financial condition at a certain point in time. By doing a comparative analysis of two balance sheets, we can see how a firm's financial condition has changed over time.

TABLE 10.4A

ANSWERS TO TABLE 10.4

Steve's Restaurant
Balance Sheet
January 1, 1999

Assets

Current assets:			
Cash	$ 12,100	6.4%	
Accounts receivable	1,400	0.7%	
Merchandise inventory	4,200	2.2%	
Total current assets	17,700		9.4%
Plant and equipment:			
Building	153,500	81.7%	
Equipment	16,700	8.9%	
Total plant and equipment	170,200		90.6%
Total assets	187,900		

Liabilities

Current liabilities:			
Accounts payable	7,900	4.2%	
Notes payable	20,000	10.6%	
Wages payable	4,900	2.6%	
Total current liabilities	32,800		17.5%
Total liabilities	32,800		
Owner's equity	155,100		82.5%
Total liabilities and owner's equity	187,900		

Table 10.5 is a comparative analysis of the two balance sheets of Malimar Kennels. Four columns of figures are shown. The two lefthand columns show the company's balance sheets for 1997 and 1998. The next column to the right shows the amount of increase or decrease in each item between 1997 and 1998. Let's look at cash. Cash rose from $7,500 in 1997 to $9,000 in 1998, so the amount of increase was $1,500. Accounts receivable fell from $19,100 in 1997 to $18,200 in 1998. By convention, negative numbers are placed in parentheses, so the decline of 900 is shown this way: (900).

Much of the work in this chapter requires using percentages, to which Chapter 3 was devoted. In Table 10.5 we computed a whole series of percentage changes in the righthand column. If you need some help with percentage changes, please read the box on Finding Percentage Changes.

Was the financial condition of Malimar Kennels better in 1998 than in 1997? We went over two measurements of financial conditions a couple of pages back. Do you recall what they are?

TABLE 10.5

Malimar Kennels
Comparative Balance Sheet
July 1, 1997 and 1998

	1998	1997	Increase (Decrease) Amount	Percent*
Assets				
Current assets:				
Cash	$ 9,000	$ 7,500	$1,500	20.0
Accounts receivable	18,200	19,100	(900)	−4.7
Merchandise inventory	26,900	22,800	4,100	18.0
Total current assets	54,100	49,400	4,700	9.5
Plant and equipment:				
Building	77,000	79,000	(2,000)	−2.5
Equipment	12,500	14,000	(1,500)	−10.7
Total plant and equipment	89,500	93,000	(3,500)	−3.8
Total assets	143,600	142,400	1,200	−0.8
Liabilities				
Current liabilities:				
Accounts payable	16,400	18,700	(2,300)	−12.3
Notes payable	10,000	7,500	2,500	33.3
Wages payable	3,200	4,800	(1,600)	−33.3
Total current liabilities	29,600	31,000	(1,400)	
Total liabilities	29,600	31,000	(1,400)	−4.5
Owner's equity				
Total liabilities and owner's equity	114,000	111,400	2,600	2.3

*In horizontal analysis, the percentages do not add up vertically.

There's the current ratio and the acid test ratio. Figure the current ratios for 1997 and 1998.

Solution:

$$1997: \text{current ratio} = \frac{\text{current assets}}{\text{current liabilities}}$$

$$= \frac{\$49,400}{31,000} = 1.6$$

$$1998: \frac{\$54,100}{29,600} = 1.8$$

Now let's do the acid test ratios for 1997 and 1998:

Finding Percentage Changes

To find a percentage change, just use this formula:

$$\text{Percentage change} = \frac{\text{change}}{\text{original number}}$$

Problem: Find the percentage change if we go from 4,000 to 5,000.

Solution:

$$\text{Percentage change} = \frac{\text{change}}{\text{original number}} = \frac{1{,}000}{4{,}000}$$

$$= \frac{1}{4} = .25^\dagger = 25\% \quad 4\overline{)1.00} \quad .25 = 25\%$$

Just follow these three steps: (1) Write down the formula; (2) substitute numbers into the formula; and (3) solve by dividing the bottom number (or denominator) into the top number (or numerator).

If this still isn't clear to you, then go back to frame 6 of Chapter 3, which goes over this operation in greater detail.

---

†Remember that when we convert a decimal into a percent, we simply move the decimal point two places to the right, .25. and tack on a percent sign, 25%.

Solution:

$$1997: \text{acid test ratio} = \frac{\text{liquid assets}}{\text{current liabilities}}$$

$$= \frac{\$26{,}000}{31{,}000} = .8$$

$$1998: \frac{\$27{,}200}{29{,}600} = .9$$

What can we say about the financial condition of Malimar Kennels in 1997 and 1998? According to the current ratio, there was some improvement between 1997 and 1998, because it went from 1.6 to 1.8. But a ratio of less than 2 is not good.

Similarly, the acid test ratio rose from .8 in 1997 to .9 in 1988. Maybe nothing to write home about, but if an acid test ratio of 1 is considered desirable, in 1998 Malimar Kennels just missed that mark.

What I did for the comparative balance sheets of Malimar Kennels, I'd like you to do for the comparative balance sheets of Sue Ann's Party Supplies in Table 10.6. Actually, we'll work in stages. First, fill in the two righthand columns in Table 10.6.

How did you do? Check your work against mine in Table 10.6A.

TABLE 10.6

Sue Ann's Party Supplies
Comparative Balance Sheet
July 1, 1997 and 1998

	1998	1997	Increase (Decrease) Amount	Percent
Assets				
Current assets:				
Cash	$ 46,400	$ 41,800	_____	_____
Accounts receivable	73,600	70,200	_____	_____
Merchandise inventory	29,100	32,700	_____	_____
Total current assets	149,100	144,700	_____	_____
Plant and equipment:				
Building	36,500	37,000	_____	_____
Equipment	4,200	4,500	_____	_____
Total plant and equipment	40,700	41,500	_____	_____
Total assets	189,800	186,200	_____	_____
Liabilities				
Current liabilities:				
Accounts payable	15,100	16,800	_____	_____
Notes payable	5,000	7,000	_____	_____
Wages payable	2,200	1,400	_____	_____
Total current liabilities	22,300	25,200	_____	_____
Total liabilities	22,300	25,200	_____	_____
Owner's equity				
Total liabilities and owner's equity	167,500	161,000	_____	_____

Next we're going to do a little analysis. Find the current ratios for Sue Ann's Party Supplies in 1997 and in 1998. Was the firm's financial condition desirable in both years? How desirable? Did the financial condition of the firm improve or deteriorate between 1997 and 1998?

Solutions:

$$1997: \text{current ratio} = \frac{\text{current assets}}{\text{current liabilities}}$$

$$= \frac{\$144,700}{25,200} = 5.7$$

$$1998: \frac{\$149,100}{22,300} = 6.7$$

Judging from the current ratios in 1997 and 1998, the firm is in excellent financial condition. Indeed, the ratio rose from 5.7 in 1997 to 6.7 in 1998. So the financial condition actually improved.

TABLE 10.6A

ANSWERS TO TABLE 10.6

Sue Ann's Party Supplies
Comparative Balance Sheet
July 1, 1997 and 1998

	1998	1997	Increase (Decrease) Amount	Percent
Assets				
Current assets:				
Cash	$ 46,400	$ 41,800	4,600	11.0%
Accounts receivable	73,600	70,200	3,400	4.8
Merchandise inventory	29,100	32,700	(3,600)	(11.0)
Total current assets	149,100	144,700	4,400	3.0
Plant and equipment:				
Building	36,500	37,000	(500)	(1.4)
Equipment	4,200	4,500	(300)	(6.7)
Total plant and equipment	40,700	41,500	(800)	(1.9)
Total assets	189,800	186,200	3,600	1.9
Liabilities				
Current liabilities:				
Accounts payable	15,100	16,800	(1,700)	(10.1)
Notes payable	5,000	7,000	(2,000)	(28.6)
Wages payable	2,200	1,400	800	57.1
Total current liabilities	22,300	25,200	(2,900)	(11.5)
Total liabilities	22,300	25,200	(2,900)	(11.5)
Owner's equity				
Total liabilities and owner's equity	167,500	161,000	6,500	4.0

What about the acid test ratios?

$$1997: \text{acid test ratio} = \frac{\text{liquid assets}}{\text{current liabilities}}$$

$$= \frac{\$112,000}{25,200} = 4.4$$

$$1998: \frac{\$120,000}{22,300} = 5.4$$

Any acid test ratio over one is considered desirable, so Sue Ann's Party Supplies is in very good financial shape. The acid test ratio, which rose from 4.4 in 1997 to 5.4 in 1998 showed improvement in the firm's already excellent financial condition.

8 Word Problems

We're finally ready to put together most of what you've been learning about balance sheets in the form of word problems. Let's see how you do.

Problem:

If current liabilities are 25% of current assets, how much is the current ratio?

Solution:

$$\text{Current ratio} = \frac{\text{current assets}}{\text{current liabilities}} = \frac{1.00}{.25} = 4$$

Here's another problem:

The current ratio is 3, and the three components of current assets are cash, $4,000; accounts receivable, $8,000, and merchandise inventory, $3,000. How much are current liabilities?

Solution:

$$3 = \frac{\$15,000}{\text{current liabilities}}$$

$$3 \times \text{current liabilities} = \$15,000$$

$$\text{current liabilities} = \$5,000$$

Now I'm going to throw the entire kitchen sink at you:

The Ace Trucking Company has these assets: cash, $38,000; accounts receivable, $104,000; building, $95,000; equipment, $230,000. It has these liabilities: wages payable, $5,500; accounts payable, $27,200, taxes payable, $13,000; notes payable over one year, $36,000.

Find the following: (1) total assets; (2) total liabilities; and (3) owner's equity. Then find (4) accounts receivable as a percentage of total assets; and (5) taxes payable as a percent of total assets.

Solution:

1.	$ 38,000	2.	$ 5,500	3.	$467,000
	104,000		27,200		−81,700
	95,000		13,000		$385,300
	230,000		36,000		
	$467,000		$81,700		

4. $\dfrac{\$104,000}{467,000} = 22.3\%$

5. $\dfrac{\$13,000}{467,000} = 2.8\%$

SELF-TEST

1. A company has these assets: cash, $15,000; accounts receivable, $20,000; merchandise inventory, $5,000; building, $45,000; equipment, $10,000. It has these liabilities: wages payable, $3,000; accounts payable, $5,000; taxes payable, $1,000; notes payable over one year, $10,000.

   Find the following: (a) total assets, (b) total liabilities, and (c) owner's equity. Then find (d) cash as a percentage of total assets and (e) accounts payable as a percentage of total assets.

2. Ace Taxi has these assets: cash, $13,300; accounts receivable, $4,500; building, $32,000; equipment, $78,200. It has these liabilities: wages payable, $500; accounts payable, $2,400; notes payable, $3,000.

   Find these: (a) the current ratio, and (b) the acid test ratio. (c) How desirable is the firm's current ratio and its acid test ratio?

3. Lefty's Friendly Tavern has a current ratio of 2.5. If its current assets are $50,000, how much are its current liabilities?

4. The Cranford Grocery has total liabilities of $35,000 and the owner's equity is $15,000. If its cash is 20% of its total assets, how much cash does it have?

5. Goniff and Shyster, a law firm, has an owner's equity of $75,000. If its only assets are $15,000 in cash and $80,000 in accounts receivable, how much are its total liabilities as a percentage of its assets?

ANSWERS

1. a. $15,000
      20,000
      5,000
      $40,000 current assets
      45,000
      10,000
      $95,000 total assets

   b. $ 3,000
      5,000
      1,000
      10,000
      $19,000 total liabilities

   c. $95,000
      −19,000
      $76,000 owner's equity

   d. $\dfrac{\$15,000}{\$95,000} = \dfrac{15}{95} = \dfrac{3}{19} = 15.8\%$

   e. $\dfrac{\$5,000}{95,000} = \dfrac{1}{19} = 5.3\%$

2. $13,300
   4,500
   $17,800 current assets

   $ 500
   2,400
   3,000
   $5,900 current liabilities

   a. Current ratio $= \dfrac{17,800}{5,900} = 3.0$

   b. Acid test ratio $= \dfrac{17,800}{5,900} = 3.0$

   c. Current ratio is over 2 and acid ratio is over 1; both are desirable ratios.

3. Current ratio $= \dfrac{\$50,000}{\text{current liabilities}} = 2.5$

    $\$50,000 = 2.5 \times$ current liabilities
    $\$20,000 =$ current liabilities

4. Total assets = total liabilities + owner's equity
    $\qquad\qquad = \$35,000 \qquad + \$15,000$
    $\qquad\qquad = \$50,000$
    $\qquad \text{cash} = .2 \times \$50,000$
    $\qquad\qquad = \$10,000$

5. Total assets – owner's equity = total liabilities
    $\$15,000 + \$80,000 - \$75,000 =$ total liabilities
    $\$95,000 - \$75,000 =$ total liabilities
    $\$20,000$

    $$\frac{\$20,000}{95,000} = \frac{20}{95} = \frac{4}{19} = 21.1\%$$

11 The Income Statement

In the preceding chapter we analyzed the balance sheet, the first of the two greatest accounting concepts of all time. Now we'll work on the second—the income statement.

The balance sheet gives us a snapshot view of a company's finances on a particular date. Often it will be the first day of the year, the last day of the year, the first day of a quarter, or the last day of a quarter.

The income statement covers a company's finances over a period of time. Almost always that time period is either a year or a quarter. The basic setup of an income statement is this: Sales – cost = net income, or profit.

Remember that in the last chapter we had just one self-test, and that was at the end of the chapter. We'll follow the same format here.

1 How the Income Statement Is Set Up

Before we even *begin* to deal with the numbers in an income statement, let's look at the very simplified statement in Table 11.1.

Let's work our way down Table 11.1.

Gross sales – returns and allowances = net sales

Cost of goods sold = beginning inventory – ending inventory + purchases

Net sales – cost of goods sold = gross profit

TABLE 11.1

Revenue:
  Gross sales
− Returns and allowances
= Net sales

Cost of goods sold:
  Beginning inventory
− Ending inventory
+ Purchases
= Cost of goods sold
    Gross profit

Operating expenses:
  Salaries
  Rent
  Utilities
  Depreciation
    Total operating expenses

Net income

Operating expenses = salaries + rent + utilities + depreciation

Gross profit − operating expenses = net income

Those are the basic relationships of the income statement. But we'll need numbers to go with the words. We'll introduce those numbers in the next section.

2   Vertical Analysis

A firm's income statement gives us a lot of very useful information, but its bottom line is net income, which every business owner wants to know. At the top of the income statement we start with sales, subtract all our costs, and what's left over is our net income.

Three very useful formulas are used in preparing income statements:

1. Total sales − returns and allowances = net sales
2. Net sales − cost of goods sold = gross profit
3. Gross profit − operating expenses = net income

We're going to complete an income statement step by step. We'll begin with Table 11.2. How much are net sales?

Net sales are $975,700. Use the information in Table 11.3 to find gross profit.

In Table 11.3 fill in cost of goods sold and then gross profit.

TABLE 11.2

Revenue:	
Gross sales	$985,400
Returns and allowances	9,700
Net sales	

TABLE 11.3

Net sales	$975,700
Cost of goods sold:	
Beginning inventory, 1/1	27,600
Ending inventory, 12/31	24,900
Purchases	390,100
Cost of goods sold	
Gross profit	

To find the cost of goods sold, we take our beginning inventory, $27,600, and subtract our ending inventory, $24,900. During the year we used up $2,700 of inventory. Actually we sold that $2,700 of inventory, along with the $390,100 of goods that we purchased during the year. So cost of goods sold was $2,700 plus $390,100 = $392,800.

Now we employ the second equation we listed: Net sales – cost of goods sold = gross profit: $975,000 – $392,800 = $582,900.

Are you ready to move on to Table 11.4? This will finally bring us down to the bottom line, net income.

First, how much are total operating expenses, and second, how much is net income?

Total operating expenses are $149,200. Then we use our third equation: Gross profit – operating expenses = net income: $582,900 – $149,200 = $433,700.

You have just completed your first vertical analysis of an income statement. Just remember the three equations, do the subtraction, and you're home free.

If we were to combine Tables 11.2, 11.3, and 11.4 into one table, we'd end up with something like Table 11.5. Fill in the numbers for net sales, cost of goods sold, gross profit, total operating expenses, and net income. Then check your results with mine in Table 11.5A.

That was so much fun, let's do another one! Fill in Table 11.6, and then check your work with mine in Table 11.6A.

There must be some mistake. Did you also get a negative number for net income? How could that be?

TABLE 11.4

Gross profit	$582,900
Operating expenses:	
Salaries	107,600
Rent	24,000
Utilities	11,200
Depreciation	6,400
Total operating expenses	

TABLE 11.5

Harry's Grocery
Income Statement
July 1, 1996 to September 30, 1996

Revenue:	
Gross sales	$1,231,600
Returns and allowances	24,200
Net sales	_____
Cost of goods sold:	
Beginning inventory, 7/1	174,700
Ending inventory, 9/30	186,500
Purchases	538,100
Cost of goods sold	_____
Gross profit	_____
Operating expenses:	
Salaries	185,200
Advertising	63,800
Rent	36,000
Utilities	15,200
Depreciation	12,900
Total operating expenses	_____
Net income	_____

There is only one way that net income could be negative—when the firm has lost money. How often does that happen? Most new firms go out of business within a couple of years after they were started. Why? Because they were losing money. And quite often you'll read about established firms losing money, especially during recessions.

Our analysis of income statements more or less parallels our analysis of balance sheets in the last chapter. What we're going to do next is a percentage distribution table. Using the data from Table 11.5A, we want to calculate each item as a percentage of net sales. I've done just that in Table 11.7 for Harry's Grocery.

TABLE 11.5A

ANSWERS TO TABLE 11.5

Harry's Grocery
Income Statement
July 1, 1996 to September 30, 1996

Revenue:	
Gross sales	$1,231,600
Returns and allowances	24,200
Net sales	1,207,400
Cost of goods sold:	
Beginning inventory, 7/1	174,700
Ending inventory, 9/30	186,500
Purchases	538,100
Cost of goods sold	526,300
Gross profit	681,100
Operating expenses:	
Salaries	185,200
Advertising	63,800
Rent	36,000
Utilities	15,200
Depreciation	12,900
Total operating expenses	313,100
Net income	368,000

This information can be very useful to the owners of a business. What percentage of our net sales do we spend on salaries or advertising? What percentage of net sales are returns and allowances?

What I've done for Harry's Grocery, I'd like you to do for the Strand Bookstore. Just fill in the percentage of net sales for every item in Table 11.8. Be sure you use *net* sales and not *gross* sales. In other words, the percentage for your gross sales will be over 100%, while your percentage for net sales will be 100%. After you've done this, check your work with mine in Table 11.8A.

---

4 The Operating Ratio

Business owners usually have a pretty good idea of how well their companies are doing. But sometimes they'd like to have some hard numbers backing up their seat-of-the-pants estimates. In this section, and in the next two, we'll take up three tools that measure just how good business is.

The first of these measures, the operating ratio, is found by using this formula:

TABLE 11.6

The Strand Bookstore
Income Statement
January 1, 1997 to March 31, 1997

Revenue:	
Gross sales	$1,486,200
Returns and allowances	79,800
Net sales	_____
Cost of goods sold:	
Beginning inventory, 1/1	153,600
Ending inventory, 3/31	160,200
Purchases	781,900
Cost of goods sold	_____
Gross profit	_____
Operating expenses:	
Salaries	378,400
Advertising	197,800
Rent	84,000
Utilities	31,300
Depreciation	28,700
Total operating expenses	_____
Net income	_____

$$\text{Operating ratio} = \frac{\text{cost of goods sold} + \text{operating expenses}}{\text{net sales}}$$

Find the operating ratio of a firm that has net sales of $500,000, operating expenses of $100,000, and a cost of goods sold of $300,000.

Solution:

$$= \frac{\$300,000 + \$100,000}{\$500,000} = \frac{\$400,000}{\$500,000} = \frac{4}{5} = .8$$

Now use Table 11.7 to find the operating ratio for Harry's Grocery.

Solution:

$$\text{Operating ratio} = \frac{\text{cost of goods sold} + \text{operating expenses}}{\text{net sales}}$$

$$= \frac{526,300 + 313,100}{1,207,400} = \frac{839,400}{1,207,400} = .695 = .7$$

Do you think there may be a shortcut? If we were to use the figures we already calculated for cost of goods sold as a percent of net sales (43.6%) and for operating expenses (25.9%), all we need to do is add

TABLE 11.6A

ANSWERS TO TABLE 11.6

The Strand Bookstore
Income Statement
January 1, 1997 to March 31, 1997

Revenue:	
Gross sales	$1,486,200
Returns and allowances	79,800
Net sales	1,406,400
Cost of goods sold:	
Beginning inventory, 1/1	153,600
Ending inventory, 3/31	160,200
Purchases	781,900
Cost of goods sold	775,300
Gross profit	631,100
Operating expenses:	
Salaries	378,400
Advertising	197,800
Rent	84,000
Utilities	31,300
Depreciation	28,700
Total operating expenses	720,200
Net income	(89,100)

them: 43.6 + 25.9 = 69.5%. And then convert that number from a percent into a decimal: 69.5% = .695. Then, we round that to .7.

Now find the operating ratio for the Strand Bookstore.

Solution:

Cost of goods sold (55.1%) + operating expenses (51.2) = 106.3%, or 1.1.

So the operating ratio of the Strand Bookstore is 1.1. What does this mean? It means that the sum of the cost of goods sold and the operating expenses is greater than net sales. It means that the firm is losing money.

Now we can generalize. What you really want to see is a low operating ratio—the lower the better. What does an operating ratio of 1 indicate? It indicates that the firm is just breaking even. That's not so great either, but it's better than an operating ratio of more than 1 because then the firm is losing money.

TABLE 11.7

Harry's Grocery
Income Statement
July 1, 1996 to September 30, 1996

		Percent of Net Sales
Revenue:		
Gross sales	$1,231,600	102.0
Returns and allowances	24,200	2.0
Net sales	1,207,400	100.0
Cost of goods sold:		
Beginning inventory, 7/1	174,700	14.5
Ending inventory, 9/30	186,500	15.4
Purchases	538,100	44.6
Cost of goods sold	526,300	43.6
Gross profit	681,100	56.4
Operating Expenses		
Salaries	185,200	15.3
Advertising	63,800	5.3
Rent	36,000	3.0
Utilities	15,200	1.3
Depreciation	12,900	1.1
Total operating expenses	313,100	25.9
Net income	368,000	30.5

5 Gross Profit Margin Ratio

This second measure of a company's performance is found with this formula:

$$\text{Gross profit margin ratio} = \frac{\text{net sales} - \text{cost of goods sold}}{\text{net sales}}$$

Using the data from Table 11.3, find the gross profit margin ratio for Harry's Grocery.

Solution:

$$\frac{\$1,207,400 - 526,300}{\$1,207,400} = \frac{\$681,100}{\$1,207,400} = .564 = .6$$

Can you think of any shortcuts? First of all, because we already have the gross profit in the table, we could use this formula:

$$\text{Gross profit margin ratio} = \frac{\text{gross profit}}{\text{net sales}}$$

But there's an even shorter shortcut. We also happen to know that gross profit is 56.4% of net sales. As a decimal, that comes to .564, which, rounded, is .6.

TABLE 11.8

The Strand Bookstore
Income Statement
January 1, 1997 to March 31, 1997

		Percent of Net Sales
Revenue:		
Gross sales	$1,486,200	_____
Returns and allowances	79,800	_____
Net sales	1,406,400	_____
Cost of goods sold:		
Beginning inventory, 1/1	153,600	_____
Ending inventory, 3/31	160,200	_____
Purchases	781,900	_____
Cost of goods sold	775,300	_____
Gross profit	631,100	_____
Operating expenses:		
Salaries	378,400	_____
Advertising	197,800	_____
Rent	84,000	_____
Utilities	31,300	_____
Depreciation	28,700	_____
Total operating expenses	720,200	_____
Net income	(89,100)	_____

You may ask why we need these formulas when we can simply take the information we need directly from the table. There are two reasons why we need the formulas. First, they help us understand the relationships between net sales and other important variables like cost of goods sold and operating expenses. And second, we may not always have a table to work with. For instance, suppose we know that net sales are $400,000, and that the cost of goods sold is $300,000. How much is the gross profit margin ratio?

Solution:

$$\text{Gross profit margin ratio} = \frac{\text{net sales} - \text{cost of goods sold}}{\text{net sales}}$$

$$= \frac{\$400,000 - \$300,000}{\$400,000} = \frac{\$100,000}{\$400,000}$$

$$= \frac{1}{4} = .25$$

This number could, of course, be rounded to .3, but I'd just as soon leave it. There is no agreed upon convention for rounding these ratios.

TABLE 11.8A

ANSWERS TO TABLE 11.8

The Strand Bookstore
Income Statement
January 1, 1997 to March 31, 1997

		Percent of Net Sales
Revenue:		
Gross sales	$1,486,200	105.7%
Returns and allowances	79,800	5.7
Net sales	1,406,400	100.0
Cost of goods sold:		
Beginning inventory, 1/1	153,600	10.9
Ending inventory, 3/31	160,200	11.4
Purchases	781,900	55.6
Cost of goods sold	775,300	55.1
Gross profit	631,100	44.9
Operating expenses:		
Salaries	378,400	26.9
Advertising	197,800	14.1
Rent	84,000	6.0
Utilities	31,300	2.2
Depreciation	28,700	2.0
Total operating expenses	720,200	51.2
Net income	(89,000)	−6.3

Some people like to round to one decimal, as we've been doing up to now, and others like to round to two decimals. Either way is correct.

One last problem: Use Table 11.8A to find the gross margin profit ratio for the Strand Bookstore.

Solution:

$$44.9\% = .449 = .4 \text{ or } .45$$

Incidentally, a common rounding error is to round from .449 to .45, and then to round further to .5. If the original number is .449 and we were to round to one decimal place, we would round to .4.

6   Profit Margin on Net Sales

The formula we use here is:

$$\text{Profit margin on net sales} = \frac{\text{net income}}{\text{net sales}}$$

How much would the profit margin on sales be for Harry's Grocery? Use Table 11.7.

Solution:

$$\frac{\$368,000}{\$1,207,400} = .3047 = .3$$

Again, we could take a shortcut and use 30.5% from the table, which, rounded, comes to .3.

And finally, find the profit margin on sales for the Strand Bookstore from Table 11.8A.

Solution:

It comes to −.1, or, if you prefer, −.06.

Obviously a profit margin on net sales of minus *anything* is not good. What we would hope for, then, would be a high profit margin on sales. Harry's Grocery had one of .3, or, 30.5% to be more exact. So it would be fair to say that Harry's Grocery had a far better quarter than the Strand Bookstore.

7 Horizontal Analysis

When the business owner asks herself "How am I doing?" we might ask her: In comparison to *what?* And she might answer: In comparison to last year. Or perhaps last quarter.

Let's return to Harry's Grocery. In Table 11.9, we show the store's income statements for the third quarters of 1996 and 1997. Basically, we want to know if the store is doing better or worse in 1997 than it was in 1996.

See if you can fill in the two righthand columns of the table. Then check your work with mine in Table 11.9A.

In general, would you say that Harry's did better or worse in the third quarter of 1997 than it did in the third quarter of 1996? Clearly, it did much better in 1997. In fact, virtually everything went up. Net sales were up 12.2%, and, most important of all, net income rose by 5.3%.

In the third quarter of 1996, the operating ratio of Harry's was .8. How much was it in the third quarter of 1997?

Solution:

$$\text{Operating ratio} = \frac{\text{cost of goods sold + operating expenses}}{\text{net sales}}$$

$$= \frac{\$598,600 + \$368,800}{\$1,354,800} = \frac{\$967,400}{\$1,354,800} = .7$$

We can see, then, that the firm's operating ratio fell from .8 in the third quarter of 1996 to .7 in 1997. The lower the operating ratio, the better, so we can say that this decline is good news for Harry's.

TABLE 11.9

Harry's Grocery
Comparative Income Statements
July 1 to September 30, 1996 and 1997

	1996	1997	Increase (Decrease) Amount	Percent*
Revenue:				
Gross sales	$1,231,600	1,387,200	_____	_____
Returns and allowances	24,200	32,400	_____	_____
Net sales	1,207,400	1,354,800	_____	_____
Cost of goods sold:				
Beginning inventory	174,700	196,100	_____	_____
Ending inventory	186,500	199,200	_____	_____
Purchases	538,100	601,700	_____	_____
Cost of goods sold	526,300	598,600	_____	_____
Gross profit	681,100	756,200	_____	_____
Operating expenses:				
Salaries	185,200	214,600	_____	_____
Advertising	63,800	88,500	_____	_____
Rent	36,000	36,000	_____	_____
Utilities	15,200	16,800	_____	_____
Depreciation	12,900	12,900	_____	_____
Total operating expenses	313,100	368,800	_____	_____
Net income	368,000	387,400		

* In horizontal analysis, the percentages do not add up vertically.

Next comes the gross profit margin ratio. In the third quarter of 1996, it was .6 (actually .564). How much was it for Harry's in the first quarter of 1997?

Solution:

$$\text{Gross profit margin ratio} = \frac{\text{gross profit}}{\text{net sales}}$$

$$= \frac{\$756,200}{\$1,354,800} = .558 = .6$$

We can see that the gross profit margin ratio was virtually unchanged. And finally we come to the profit margin on net sales. In 1996, it was .3. Please use Table 11.9A to find it in the third quarter of 1997.

TABLE 11.9A

ANSWERS TO TABLE 11.9

Harry's Grocery
Comparative Income Statements
July 1 to September 30, 1996 and 1997

	1996	1997	Increase (Decrease) Amount	Percent*
Revenue:				
Gross sales	$1,231,600	1,387,200	155,600	12.6%
Returns and allowances	24,200	32,400	8,200	33.9
Net sales	1,207,400	1,354,800	147,400	12.2
Cost of goods sold:				
Beginning inventory, 7/1	174,700	196,100	21,400	12.2
Ending inventory, 9/30	186,500	199,200	12,700	6.8
Purchases	538,100	601,700	63,600	11.8
Cost of goods sold	526,300	598,600	72,300	13.7
Gross profit	681,100	756,200	75,100	11.0
Operating expenses:				
Salaries	185,200	214,600	29,400	15.9
Advertising	63,800	88,500	24,700	38.7
Rent	36,000	36,000	—	—
Utilities	15,200	16,800	1,600	10.5
Depreciation	12,900	12,900	—	—
Total operating expenses	313,100	368,800	55,700	17.8
Net income	368,000	387,400	19,400	5.3

* In horizontal analysis, the percentages do not add up vertically.

Solution:

$$\text{Profit margin on net sales} = \frac{\text{net income}}{\text{net sales}}$$

$$= \frac{\$387,400}{\$1,354,800} = .3$$

So the profit margin on net sales remained the same. Now we'll move on to the Strand Bookstore.

Fill in the two righthand columns of Table 11.10 and then compare your answers with mine in Table 11.10A.

In general, how did the Strand Bookstore do in the first quarter of 1998 compared to the first quarter of 1997? Clearly, it did a lot better.

In the first quarter of 1997, the Strand Bookstore had an operating ratio of 1.1, which was not good at all. Use Table 11.10 or 11.10A to find its operating ratio in the first quarter of 1998.

TABLE 11.10

The Strand Bookstore
Comparative Income Statements
January 1 to March 31, 1997 and 1998

	1997	1998	Increase (Decrease) Amount	Percent*
Revenue:				
Gross sales	$1,486,200	$1,743,400	_____	_____
Returns and allowances	79,800	86,500	_____	_____
Net sales	1,406,400	1,656,900	_____	_____
Cost of goods sold:				
Beginning inventory	153,600	166,300	_____	_____
Ending inventory	160,200	164,400	_____	_____
Purchases	781,900	831,700	_____	_____
Cost of goods sold	775,300	833,600	_____	_____
Gross profit	631,100	823,300	_____	_____
Operating expenses:				
Salaries	378,400	382,600	_____	_____
Advertising	197,800	204,300	_____	_____
Rent	84,000	88,000	_____	_____
Utilities	31,300	32,700	_____	_____
Depreciation	28,700	28,700	—	—
Total operating expenses	720,200	736,300	_____	_____
Net income	(89,000)	97,000	_____	_____

* In horizontal analysis, the percentages do not add up vertically.

Solution:

$$\text{Operating ratio} = \frac{\text{cost of goods sold} + \text{operating expenses}}{\text{net sales}}$$

$$= \frac{\$833,600 + \$736,300}{\$1,656,900} = \frac{\$1,569,900}{\$1,656,900} = 0.9$$

We can see that the operating ratio fell from 1.1 to .9. This was a vast improvement, because an operating ratio of more than 1 means the firm is losing money, and an operating ratio of 1 means that it's breaking even. At .9, it's making money. So we can see from looking at the firm's operating ratio that it went from losing money in the first quarter of 1997 to making a profit in the first quarter of 1998.

One down, two to go. In 1997, the Strand Bookstore had a gross profit margin ratio of .45. How much was it in 1998?

TABLE 11.10A

ANSWERS TO TABLE 11.10

The Strand Bookstore
Comparative Income Statements
January 1 to March 31, 1997 and 1998

	1997	1998	Increase (Decrease) Amount	Percent*
Revenue:				
Gross sales	$1,486,200	$1,743,400	257,200	17.3%
Returns and allowances	79,800	86,500	6,700	8.4
Net sales	1,406,400	1,656,900	250,500	17.8
Cost of goods sold:				
Beginning inventory	153,600	166,300	12,700	8.3
Ending inventory	160,200	164,400	4,200	2.6
Purchases	781,900	831,700	49,800	6.4
Cost of goods sold	775,300	833,600	58,300	7.5
Gross profit	631,100	823,300	192,200	30.5
Operating expenses:				
Salaries	378,400	382,600	4,200	1.1
Advertising	197,800	204,300	6,500	3.3
Rent	84,000	88,000	4,000	4.8
Utilities	31,300	32,700	1,400	4.5
Depreciation	28,700	28,700	—	—
Total operating expenses	720,200	736,300	16,100	2.2
Net income	(89,000)	87,000	176,000	—

* In horizontal analysis, the percentages do not add up vertically.

Solution:

$$\text{Gross profit margin ratio} = \frac{\text{gross profit}}{\text{net sales}}$$

$$= \frac{\$823,300}{\$1,656,900} = .496 = .5$$

There was some improvement here. Finally we come to the profit margin on net sales. In 1997, it was –.06. How much was it in 1998?

$$\text{Profit margin on net sales} = \frac{\text{net income}}{\text{net sales}}$$

$$= \frac{\$87,000}{\$1,656,900} = .053 = .05$$

The change in the profit margin on net sales was a major turn-around for the firm, because it went from a loss of .06 to a profit of .05.

8   Word Problems

Now we're going to put most of what we've been doing in this chapter into the form of word problems. Here comes the first one:

If your company had an operating ratio of .8, net sales of $400,000, and a cost of goods sold of $100,000, how much are your operating expenses?

Solution:

$$.8 = \frac{\$100,000 + \text{operating expenses}}{\$400,000}$$

$$.8 \times \$400,000 = \$100,000 + \text{operating expenses}$$
$$\$320,000 = \$100,000 + \text{operating expenses}$$
$$\$220,000 = \text{operating expenses}$$

Here's a three-part problem for you to solve:

Eyelab Opticians had net sales of $3.4 million; cost of goods sold was $1.8 million; and operating costs were $1.4 million.

1. How much was its operating ratio?
2. How much was its gross profit margin?
3. How much was its profit margin on net sales?

Solution:

$$\text{Operating ratio} = \frac{\text{cost of goods sold} + \text{operating expenses}}{\text{net sales}}$$

1. $$\frac{\$1.8 \text{ million} + \$1.4 \text{ million}}{\$3.4 \text{ milion}} = \frac{3.2}{3.4} = .94 \text{ or } .9$$

$$\text{Gross profit margin} = \frac{\text{gross profit}}{\text{net sales}}$$

$$\text{Gross profit} = \text{net sales} - \text{cost of goods sold}$$

2. $$\frac{\$1.6 \text{ million}}{\$3.4 \text{ million}} = .47 \text{ or } .5$$

$$\text{Profit margin on net sales} = \frac{\text{net income}}{\text{net sales}}$$

$$\text{Net income} = \text{gross profit} - \text{operating costs}$$

3. $$\frac{\$.2 \text{ million}}{\$3.4 \text{ million}} = .059 \text{ or } .6$$

SELF-TEST

1. Raleigh Motors had a beginning inventory of $400,000 on January 1, and an ending inventory of $420,000 on December 31. If its purchases of cars to sell were $1,000,000, then how much were its cost of goods sold during the year?

2. The Phoenix Corporation had net sales of $2,000,000, its cost of goods sold was $1,600,000, and its operating expenses were $500,000.
    a. How much was its gross profit?
    b. How much was its net income?

3. The George Washington Motor Lodge had net sales of $4,000,000, gross profit of $2.1 million, and these expenses: salaries and wages of $550,000; utilities of $230,000, advertising of $75,000; and depreciation of $45,000. How much was its net income?

4. The Sixth Street Garage had a net income of $35,000. If its operating expenses were $380,000, how much was its gross profit?

5. The Fleetwood Lounge had net sales of $970,000; cost of goods sold was $320,000; and operating expenses were $280,000.
    a. How much was its operating ratio?
    b. How much was its gross profit margin?
    c. How much was its profit margin on net sales?

6. In 1996, the operating expenses of the Top 40 CD Store was $175,000 and the gross profit was $240,000. In 1997, the operating expenses rose to $200,000 and the gross profit rose to $290,000. By what percentage did net income change from 1996 to 1997?

ANSWERS

1. $1,000,000
    −20,000
    $980,000

2. $2,000,000
    −1,600,000
    400,000 gross profit
    −500,000
    (100,000) net income

3. $550,000 $2,100,000
    230,000   −900,000
    75,000 $1,200,000 net income
    45,000
    $900,000

4. $ 35,000
        380,000
        $415,000

5. a. $\dfrac{\$320,000 + \$280,000}{\$970,000} = \dfrac{\$600,000}{\$970,000} = .62$ or .6

    b. $\dfrac{\$970,000 - \$320,000}{\$970,000} = \dfrac{\$650,000}{\$970,000} = .67$ or .7

    c. $970,000   \dfrac{\$370,000}{\$970,000} = .38 = .4$
        −600,000
        $370,000

6.   1996   1997 $\dfrac{25,000}{65,000} = .3846 = +38.5\%$
        $240,000 $290,000
        −175,000   −200,000
        65,000   90,000

Part IV   Statistics and Graphing Techniques

12 Basic Statistical Measures

When you think of statistics, do you visualize column after column of numbers, complex formulas, and graphs that could pass for abstract art? Well, then, your worries are over. Because in this chapter and the next, all that we'll be doing is organizing and analyzing some numbers. You'll probably find these last two chapters easy, and you might even have fun working your way through them.

We'll return to our old format of having self-tests after covering each basic concept. And you may even use a calculator.

1 The Mean

You might not realize it, but you've probably calculated the mean many times. If you received 90, 65, and 80 on three exams, how much is your average (to the nearest tenth)?

Solution:

$$90 + 65 + 80 = 235$$
$$\frac{235}{3} = 78.3$$

So to figure out the mean, or average, add the values and divide by the number of values.

Problem:

The Lewis family opened a camera store just outside Cincinnati. At the end of the day, Peggy Jo had sales of $895.32, Savannah had sales of $808.74, Cameron had sales of $796.15, and Martin had sales of $743.91. How much was their mean sales?

Solution:

$$\begin{array}{r} \$895.32 \\ 808.74 \\ 796.15 \\ \underline{743.91} \\ \$3,244.12 \end{array} \qquad \begin{array}{l} \$\,811.03 \\ \overline{4)\$3244.12} \end{array}$$

Do this set of problems.

1. If the Kmart in downtown Louisville had these sales in 1995, how much was its average monthly sales?

January	$1,972,356.12
February	1,416,903.43
March	2,006,431.09
April	2,013,463.98
May	2,134,802.00
June	2,397,164.48
July	2,247,935.82
August	2,190,838.17
September	2,462,190.29
October	2,530,145.60
November	2,096,873.55
December	2,889,403.74

2. The Brooks Cleaning Service had a profit of $8,304.17 in the first quarter, a profit of $25,850.02 in the second quarter, a loss of $5,930.75 in the third quarter, and a profit of $12,835.18 in the fourth quarter. How much was its average quarterly profits?

3. At the Henrietta Weight Watcher's Center outside Rochester, New York, 28 people who made New Year's resolutions to lose weight reported these weekly losses for the first ten weeks of the year:

    98 pounds
    91 pounds
    88 pounds
    84 pounds
    73 pounds
    69 pounds
    62 pounds
    54 pounds
    50 pounds
    45 pounds

How much was their mean weight loss per week?

Solutions:

1. $\dfrac{\$26{,}358{,}508.27}{12} = \$2{,}196{,}542.36$

2.
$$
\begin{array}{r}
\$\ 8{,}304.17 \\
25{,}850.02 \\
\underline{12{,}835.18} \\
\$46{,}989.37 \\
\underline{-5{,}930.75} \\
\$41{,}058.62
\end{array}
\qquad
\dfrac{\$41{,}058.62}{4} = \$10{,}264.66
$$

3. $\dfrac{714}{10} = 71.4$ pounds per week

2

Do you know what a weighted average is? Well, believe it or not, a weighted average that follows you around all through college. It's called your grade point average, or GPA.

Virtually every college, when computing GPAs, calls A's 4, B's 3, C's 2, D's 1, and F's 0. Suppose that one semester you got all C's. Then your grade point average was 2, or 2.0. And if you got all A's? Then it would be a perfect 4.0.

But you must consider the number of credits you received for each course. Some courses are four credits, most happen to be three, some are two, one, or even some strange numbers like half a credit or one and a half credits.

Here's how you did last term:

Course	Credits	Grade
Intro to Accounting	4	D
Macroeconomics	3	C
Oral Communications	2	A
Intro to Psychology	3	B
Marketing	3	B
	15	

What we want to do now is to figure out your weighted average, or grade point average. Accounting really pulled your average down. In fact, without accounting, your GPA would have been just below B. Try to figure out your GPA. Remember, A is 4, B is 3, C is 2, and D is 1. You'll need to multiply the credits by the grade, add up these numbers, and then divide by the total numbers of credits. Work it out right on this page and then check your work with my solution.

Course	Credits	Grade	
Intro to Accounting	4	D	$4 \times 1 =$ 4
Macroeconomics	3	C	$3 \times 2 =$ 6
Oral Communications	2	A	$2 \times 4 =$ 8
Intro to Psychology	3	B	$3 \times 3 =$ 9
Marketing	3	B	$3 \times 3 =$ 9
	15		36

$$\frac{36}{15} = 2.4$$

QUICK QUIZ 12.1

1. We want to find the weighted mean hourly wage of the Schwartz family. Denise Schwartz worked 46 hours, earning $18.40 an hour. David Schwartz worked 39 hours, earning $17.83 an hour. And Evan Schwartz worked 24 hours, earning $10.53 an hour.

2. The Shady Rest Pet Cemetery had 21 sales representatives who worked on straight commission. Two reps sold 2 burial plots each, 4 reps sold 3 plots each, 5 reps sold 4 plots each, 5 reps sold 5 plots each, 4 reps sold 6 plots each, and one rep sold 7 plots. What is the weighted average sales of the reps?

3. In Alpha Company, 8 recruits were 17 years old, 12 were 18 years old, 7 were 19 years old, 4 were 20 years old, 2 were 21 years old, and one was 22 years old. What is the weighted average of their ages?

Answers to Quick Quiz 12.1

1.

	Hours		Hourly Earnings		Total Earnings	
Denise	46	×	$18.40	=	$ 846.40	
David	39	×	17.83	=	695.37	
Evan	24	×	10.53	=	252.72	
	109				$1,794.49	

$$\frac{\$1,794.49}{109} = \$16.46$$

2.

Number of Plots		Number of Reps		Total Sales
2	×	2	=	4
3	×	4	=	12
4	×	5	=	20
5	×	5	=	25
6	×	4	=	24
7	×	1	=	7
		21		92

$$\frac{92}{21} = 4.4 \text{ plots}$$

3.

Age		Number of Recruits	Total Years of Age
17	×	8	136
18	×	12	216
19	×	7	133
20	×	4	80
21	×	2	42
22	×	1	22
		34	629

$$\frac{629}{34} = 18.5 \text{ years old}$$

3 | **The Median**

The median of a highway is the strip that runs down the middle of the highway, dividing the traffic going one way from the traffic going the other way. The median in a group of children standing in size places is the child standing smack in the middle. If we arranged a group of numbers in order of size, the median would be the middle number. You can't miss it. For example, how much is the median in this group of numbers?

7, 15, 29, 31, 50

The median is 29. What if the numbers were not in order of size? You need to put them in order of size and then find the median. For instance, find the median in this group:

84, 37, 96, 115, 22, 9, 53

Solution:

9, 22, 37, 53, 84, 96, 115
The median is 53.

What if there are an even number of terms? See if you can find the median here, doing a bit of averaging:

14, 22, 34, 38, 59, 71

Solution:

The median would be exactly *halfway* between the third number, 34, and the fourth number, 38. So the median is 36.

QUICK QUIZ 12.2 In each of these problems, find the median:

1.   13, 19, 27, 31, 40, 62, 88, 115, 119

2.   46, 29, 103, 55, 17, 3, 149

3.   15, 19, 30, 37, 48, 61

4.   101, 2, 16, 90, 43, 112

Answers to Quick Quiz 12.2

1.   40

2.   3, 17, 29, 46, 55, 103, 149
     46

3. $\frac{30 + 37}{2} = \frac{67}{2} = 33.5$

4.   2, 16, 43, 90, 101, 112
     $\frac{43 + 90}{2} = \frac{123}{2} = 61.5$

4 The Mode

The mode is the most frequent value in a set of numbers. What's the mode in this set?

17, 31, 14, 29, 17, 28, 15, 63

The mode is 17 because that number occurs twice and each of the others occurs only once.

What's the mode in this distribution?

4, 19, 13, 29, 19, 17, 31, 34, 13, 39, 19, 12

The mode is 19, because it occurs *three* times, while 13 happens to occur twice. Three wins over two every time.

Sometimes we have *bimodal* distributions, when two different numbers are both modes. Pick out the two modes here:

2, 9, 15, 2, 19, 7, 9, 6

Obviously 2 and 9 are the modes in this bimodal distribution. Now let's see what you can do with this distribution:

16, 8, 9, 12, 17, 13, 0, 12, 4, 5, 11, 26, 17, 10, 4, 15, 8, 23, 4, 29, 36, 17, 3, 8, 0, 33

It takes a bit of work, but the answers are 4, 8, and 17. We call this a *trimodal* distribution because there are *three* modes.

Can there be a distribution with *more* than three modes? Yes! Will you encounter any in this chapter? No!

QUICK QUIZ 12.3

In each problem, find the mode or the modes.

1. 16, 13, 0, 9, 14, 22, 76, 13

2. 10, 17, 0, 4, 12, 17, 9, 4, 10, 5, 0, 10, 4, 17, 20, 3, 12, 14, 6, 23, 4, 15, 9

3. 7, 12, 15, 19, 12, 18, 34, 63, 56, 73, 15, 33, 106, 29, 47, 27, 35

4. 0, 19, 13, 24, 15, 12, 5, 13, 24, 11, 16, 3, 62, 5, 35, 40, 10, 28

Answers to Quick Quiz 12.3

1.	13	2.	4
3.	12 and 15	4.	5, 13, and 24

---

5 The Range

The range of a distribution of numbers is the difference between the highest and lowest values. For instance, find the range of this array of numbers:

14, 16, 17, 23, 45, 119, 186, 209

The range would be found this way: 209 – 14 = 195.

What if the numbers are not in order? Put them in order first, and then find the range. See what you can do with this group of numbers:

19, 36, 94, 37, 53, 12, 115, 29, 16, 5, 80

Solution:

5, 12, 16, 19, 29, 36, 37, 53, 80, 94, 115

115 – 5 = 110

Do you really need to put all the numbers in order to figure out the range? Not really. All you need to do is find the highest number and the lowest number, and then do the subtraction. Why do I put the numbers in order? Because we'll often want to find the mean, median, and mode, as well as the range, and putting the values in numerical order makes those jobs a lot easier.

QUICK QUIZ 12.3

Please find the range for each of these numerical distributions:

1. 95, 73, 56, 49, 42, 34, 28, 23, 14, 8

2. 15, 67, 35, 90, 9, 88, 32, 105, 77, 29

3. 50, –5, 0, 17, 39, 116, 12, –19, 46, 2

4. 15, 27, 4, 18, 75, 13, –1, 60, –10, 43, 37, 65, 9

Answers to Quick Quiz 12.4

1. 95 – 8 = 87
2. 105 – 9 = 96
3. 116 – (–19) = 116 + 19 = 135
4. 75 – (–10) = 75 + 10 = 85

Did these last two problems throw you because they contained negative numbers? If that's the case, then review Chapter 7, especially the first two sections, which show you how to add and subtract negative numbers.

---

6 | Finding the Mean, Median, Mode, and Range

Have you had a blood test lately? Don't get alarmed; I'm not suggesting that there's anything wrong with you. I'm trying to draw an analogy between a blood test and the statistical analysis we've been doing so far in this chapter.

The mean, median, mode, and the range are to statistics what the blood test is to medicine. By analyzing just a blood sample, they can test you for all types of afflictions. And we can find out a lot of interesting things about a group of numbers by finding the mean, median, mode, and range.

We'll start you off with an easy one: Find the mean, median, mode, and range for this distribution:

14, 39, 17, 12, 18, 9, 6, 15, 32, 14, 6, 2

Solution:

$$\text{Mean} = \frac{184}{12} = 15.3$$

Median: 2, 6, 6, 9, 12, 14, 14, 15, 17, 18, 32, 39

Median = 14

Mode = 6, 14

Range = 39 − 2 = 37

I want to point out a couple of things. First, you can see why we need to put the numbers in order. Second, you want to be sure not to leave out any of the numbers. You can make sure by crossing out each number as you put the numbers in order. So you would have crossed out the 2, then the 6, then the next 6, then the 9, and so forth. What I do is start with the numbers below 10, then I look for numbers between 10 and 19, then the twenties, then the thirties, and so forth.

Here's another group of numbers for which I'd like you to find the mean, median, mode, and range:

15, 8, 26, −4, 15, 3, 0, 23, 10, −15, 35

Solution:

$$\text{Mean} = \frac{116}{11} = 10.5$$

Median: −15, −4, 0, 3, 8, 10, 15, 15, 23, 26, 35

Median = 10

Mode = 15

Range = 35 − (−15) = 50

Remember that zero is a number. When we found the mean, zero had to be averaged in.

For each of these numerical distributions, find the mean, median, mode, and range.

1. Here are the number of cars sold each month by Tricky Dick's Used Car Dealership:

   January: 15
   February: 9
   March: 14
   April: 16
   May: 14
   June: 12
   July: 19
   August: 18
   September: 15
   October: 11
   November: 15
   December: 10

2. Pathmark listed these quarterly profit (and loss) figures over the last three years. Each is rounded to the nearest million dollars: 12, 4, 9, –3, 7, –5, 2, 15, 7, 0, 12, 3.

3. In the 1998 Superbowl, Joe Montana completed passes for this yardage: 4, 16, 11, 28, 5, 11, 7, 38, 6, 15, 3, 18, 7, 9, 15, 4, 11, 9, 2, 13, 6, 5, 19.

1. Mean: $\dfrac{168}{12}$ = 14 cars

   Median: 9, 10, 11, 12, 14, 14, 15, 15, 15, 16, 18, 19

   Median: $\dfrac{14 + 15}{2} = \dfrac{29}{2}$ = 14.5 cars

   Mode = 15 cars
   Range = 19 – 9 = 10 cars

2. Mean: $\dfrac{63}{12}$ = \$5.25 million or \$5.3 million

   Median: –5, –3, 0, 2, 3, 4, 7, 7, 9, 12, 12, 15

   Median = $\dfrac{417}{2}$ = \$5.5 million

   Mode = \$7 million, \$12 million
   Range: 15 – (–5) = 15 + 5 = \$20 million

3. Mean: $\dfrac{262}{23}$ = 11.4 yards

   Median: 2, 3, 4, 4, 5, 5, 6, 6, 7, 7, 9, 9, 11, 11, 11, 13, 15, 15, 16, 18, 19, 28, 38
   Mode: 11 yards
   Range: 38 – 2 = 36 yards

13 Basic Graphing Techniques

Congratulations! Twelve down, one to go. If you can count and draw a little, you will not find this last chapter too challenging. In fact, you'll be surprised at how easy it is to read and draw graphs.

The whole idea is to take raw data, combine it in some meaningful way, and then draw a picture, or graph, of this information. We'll begin by compiling frequency distributions, and then we'll start drawing graphs.

By the end of the chapter, you will know how to compile a frequency distribution and to draw bar graphs, line graphs, and pie charts.

1 Frequency Distribution

Have you ever gotten a call from someone doing market research? Or maybe a questionnaire in the mail? They may want to know what toothpaste you use, which breakfast cereals you tried during the last year, or which TV programs you watch. Market research firms and their corporate clients are constantly gathering data that provides them with a pretty accurate picture of our likes and dislikes and our consumption patterns. All this data is tabulated and analyzed to help companies advertise and market their goods and services.

One of the most useful statistical tools is the frequency distribution, which organizes raw data into a more manageable format. For instance, Mark, Maggie, and Mary Pat Jared decided it would be a good idea to do a survey of their neighborhood to determine if it was a good location for a lemonade stand, although they were open to the possibility of selling other soft drinks as well. The following are the responses to the question in their survey: What is your favorite cold beverage?

soda beer lemonade water beer soda lemonade orange juice soda beer water soda beer grape juice lemonade soda water lemonade limeade water lemonade beer soda grape juice soda beer lemonade water lemonade soda soda lemonade water lemonade.

Let's organize this data into a frequency distribution.

Beverage	Tally	Frequency
soda	||||| ||||	9
beer	|||||		6
lemonade	||||| ||||	9
water	|||||		6
orange juice			1
grape juice	||	2
limeade			1

QUICK QUIZ 13.1

Use the data in these problems to do your own frequency distributions:

1. The Riccio Development Corporation was interested in building off-campus housing in Madison for students attending the University of Wisconsin. The corporation did a survey of students, asking them how much they would pay for a 20 × 20 studio apartment, which they would share with another student. The results of the survey are shown here:

   How much would you be willing to pay for a 20 × 20 studio apartment (to the nearest $50/month) that you would share with another student?

   $250 $200 $300 $250 $300 $250 $200 $350 $300 $150 $300 $250 $200 $350 $400 $250 $350 $150 $250 $200 $350 $300 $200 $250 $400 $250 $350 $300 $250 $250 $200 $350 $300 $400 $250 $350 $200 $300 $250 $250

2. Forty people, selected at random, who attended an Atlanta Falcons game, were asked how far they had traveled to reach the stadium. Arrange this data in a frequency distribution using intervals of (a) less than 10 miles; (b) 10 to 19 miles; (c) 20 to 29 miles; (d) 30 to 39 miles; (e) 40 to 49 miles; and (f) 50 miles and more.

   Responses to question: How many miles did you travel to get to the stadium?

   4, 12, 9, 72, 55, 6, 21, 10, 46, 35, 7, 19, 68, 24, 11, 17, 43, 28, 14, 2, 15, 88, 7, 26, 9, 4, 1, 54, 116, 20, 5, 79, 38, 3, 1, 80, 23, 4, 2, 4

3. Jinx and Dana Adams ran a market research firm based in Springfield, Massachusetts. Their firm was hired by a real estate developer who was interested in building an 80-lane bowling alley in downtown Springfield. Using the data below, draw up a frequency distribution, using intervals of 0, 1, 2, 3, 4, and over 4 times per month.

Responses to question: If a large bowling alley were built in downtown Springfield, how many times a month would you bowl?

1, 0, 1, 0, 0, 4, 1, 0, 3, 6, 1, 0, 0, 4, 0, 2, 5, 0, 0, 0, 4, 2, 1, 1, 0, 8, 3, 0, 0, 3, 0, 1, 0, 0, 2, 4, 0, 0, 4, 0, 1, 1, 4, 0, 4, 0, 3, 2, 0, 0, 0, 1, 0, 0, 3, 1, 0, 10, 2, 0, 1, 1, 0, 4, 0, 6, 0, 3, 0, 4, 0, 1, 0, 0, 8, 1, 2, 0, 4, 1, 4, 0, 0, 0, 0, 0, 5, 0, 1, 1, 4, 0, 10, 6, 0, 0, 3, 1, 4, 2, 1, 4, 0, 2, 0, 1, 1, 4, 4, 0, 2, 1, 2

Answers to Quick Quiz 13.1

1. **Frequency Distribution of Data from Problem 1**

Rent	Tally	Frequency
$150	II	2
200	IIIII II	7
250	IIIII IIIII III	13
300	IIIII III	8
350	IIIII II	7
400	III	3

2. **Frequency Distribution of Data from Problem 2**

Miles	Tally	Frequency
under 10	IIIII IIIII IIIII	15
10–19	IIIII II	7
20–29	IIIII I	6
30–39	II	2
40–49	II	2
50 and over	IIIII III	8

3. **Frequency Distribution of Data from Problem 3**

Times per month	Tally	Frequency
0	IIIII IIIII IIIII IIIII IIIII IIIII IIIII IIIII IIII II	47
1	IIIII IIIII IIIII IIIII III	23
2	IIIII IIIII	10
3	IIIII II	7
4	IIIII IIIII IIIII I	16
over 4	IIIII IIII	9

2 Bar Graphs

Now that we've gotten our data organized into frequency distributions, what do you do with it? We draw graphs. But don't worry, I promise you that these graphs will be very easy to draw and easy to read.

You've often seen bar graphs in newspapers and newsmagazines. They are used to present data so that the observer can get the picture in just a couple of seconds. I've placed the data we gathered in the table on page 00 into the graph shown in Figure 13.1.

This happens to be a *vertical* bar graph. This same data can also be used to draw a *horizontal* bar graph, which you'll find drawn in Figure 13.2.

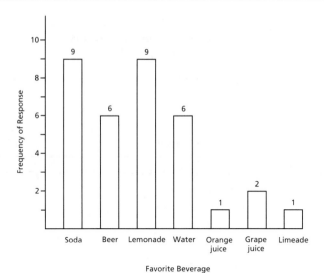

FIGURE 13.1

Now I'd like you to try your hand at drawing graphs. Use the frequency distribution in Table 13.1 for your data. Draw a horizontal bar graph in Figure 13.3.

You can check your work in Figure 13.3 by comparing it to mine in Figure 13.3A. Are you ready to draw some more bar graphs? I've got three for you to draw in Quick Quiz 13.2.

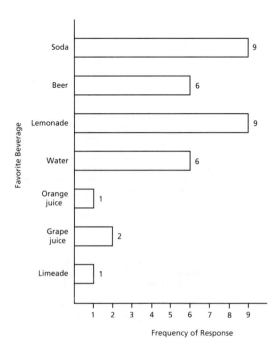

FIGURE 13.2

TABLE 13.1

**Poll of Prospective Voters
October 12, 1992**

Candidate	Frequency
Bush	396
Clinton	414
Perot	163
undecided	182

FIGURE 13.3

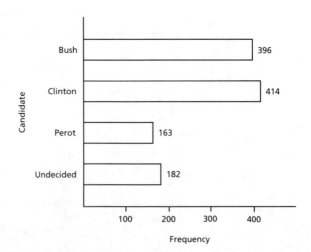

FIGURE 13.3A

QUICK QUIZ 13.2   Use the space provided to draw each graph.

1. Draw a vertical bar graph, using the data from problem 1 of Quick Quiz 13.1.

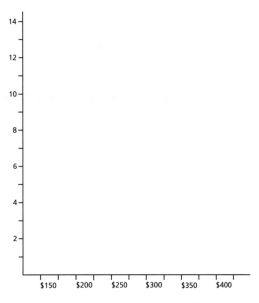

2. Draw a vertical bar graph, using the data from problem 2 of Quick Quiz 13.1.

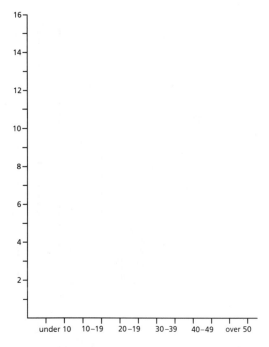

3. Draw a horizontal bar graph, using the data from problem 3 of Quick Quiz 13.1.

Answers to Quick Quiz 13.2

1.

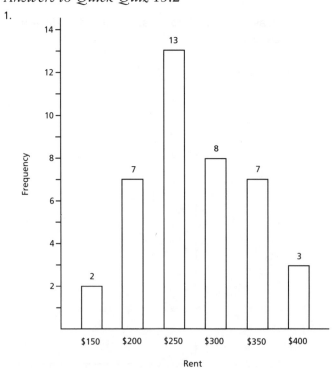

2.

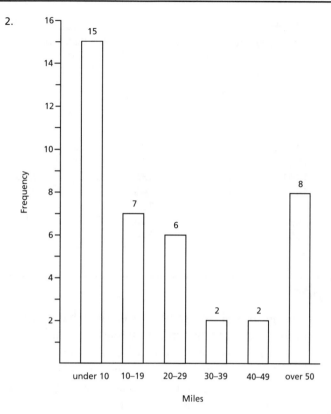

3.

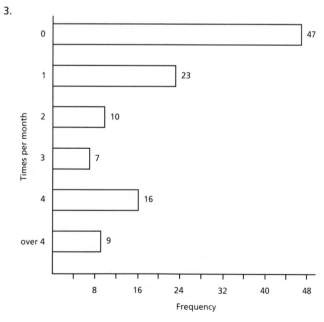

TABLE 13.2

Quarterly Profits of the Inland Empire Bancorp
1990–1994 (in millions of dollars)

Year	Quarter	Sales	Year	Quarter	Sales
1990	I	106	1992	III	180
1990	II	113	1992	IV	196
1990	III	118	1993	I	204
1990	IV	121	1993	II	216
1991	I	123	1993	III	234
1991	II	138	1993	IV	256
1991	III	145	1994	I	289
1991	IV	151	1994	II	302
1992	I	163	1994	III	316
1992	II	174	1994	IV	331

3   Line Graphs

Line graphs show trends better than bar graphs. Once you try to show more than eight or ten numbers, line graphs become much more appropriate. For instance, Table 13.2 lists the quarterly sales figures of the Inland Empire Bancorp. The fastest growing financial company west of the Rockies, Inland Empire is based in Mukilteo, Washington, and is owned entirely by Sayeed Ramadan, Krishna Singh, and Sen Wing Chien, three college roommates, who have built up the company from scratch. Figure 13.4 is a line graph showing the profits listed in Table 13.2.

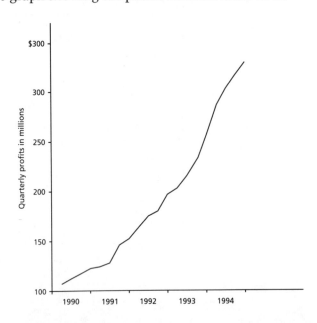

FIGURE 13.4

TABLE 13.3

Beginning of the Month Inventory at Holt GM, 1994

January	216
February	198
March	181
April	184
May	153
June	142
July	177
August	164
September	141
October	144
November	229
December	256

Now it's your turn. Boris Fleck, Michelle Eldridge, and Meredith Jagutis run a GM dealership in Holt, Michigan. The number of cars on their lot varies widely from month to month, as you can see from Table 13.3. Draw a line graph based on this data in Figure 13.5.

Check your work in Figure 13.5 with what I drew in Figure 13.5A. Now draw some more line graphs.

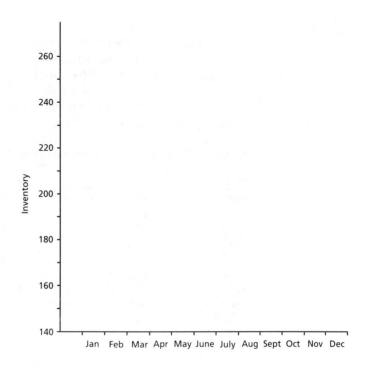

FIGURE 13.5

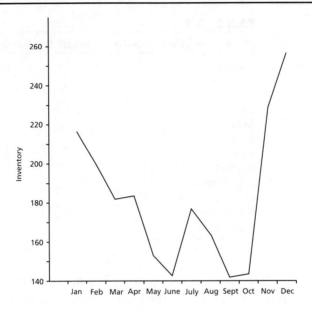

FIGURE 13.5A

QUICK QUIZ 13.3

1. The Lynchburg Historical Directory, edited by Massey Whorley, Kaye Whorley, and Jeannette McFarland, provides tourists and native Virginians with a great wealth of information about Amherst, Bedford, Campbell, and Appomattox Counties. The annual sales of the directory over a 20-year period are shown in the following table. Use this information to draw a line graph in the chart provided, showing sales from 1975 to 1994.

Annual Sales of the Lynchburg Historical Directory, 1975–1994

Year	Sales	Year	Sales
1975	413	1985	538
1976	422	1986	541
1977	463	1987	560
1978	496	1988	566
1979	492	1989	573
1980	503	1990	582
1981	520	1991	604
1982	526	1992	615
1983	531	1993	604
1984	520	1994	622

2. Judy Ruiz manages the telemarketing sales group of the Hamilton County Appliance Corporation. The table shows the quarterly sales of her group from 1989 through 1994. Use the space provided to draw a line graph for this period.

Quarterly Telemarketing Sales of Hamilton County Appliance Corporation, 1989–1994, in Thousands of Dollars

Year	Quarter	Sales	Year	Quarter	Sales
1989	I	296	1992	I	366
	II	291		II	353
	III	304		III	403
	IV	337		IV	380
1990	I	322	1993	I	371
	II	349		II	399
	III	301		III	441
	IV	385		IV	425
1991	I	376	1994	I	418
	II	348		II	427
	III	399		III	456
	IV	370		IV	412

Answers to Quick Quiz 13.3

1.

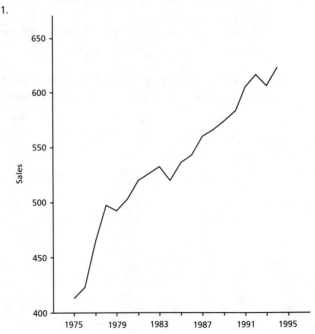

2.

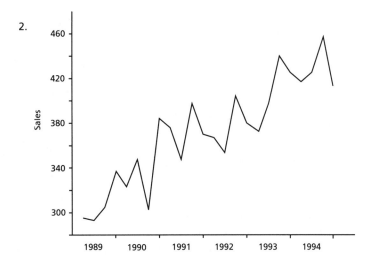

4 Pie Charts

Believe it or not, we're beginning the last section of the last chapter in this book. Congratulations for hanging in there. Pie charts are also called circle graphs. When you buy pizza, you can buy a whole pie, or you can buy it by the slice. If you bought one slice, it would be $\frac{1}{8}$ of an 8-slice pie.

A circle can also be divided into percentage slices because 100% would equal the entire circle. If a publisher sells 10% of its books by mail order, 40% through college bookstores, and 50% through regular trade bookstores, divide up the circle in Figure 13.6 by percentage share.

You don't have to use very special drafting equipment to do this, except perhaps a ruler or straightedge.

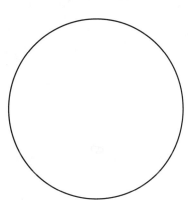

FIGURE 13.6

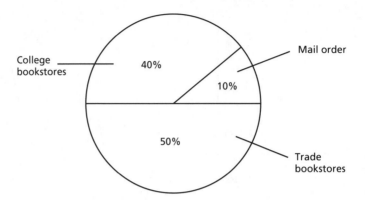

FIGURE 13.7

5

How up are you on percentage distribution, which was the last topic in Chapter 3? I guess we're about to find out.

If Haruhiko Kawaguchi has 8 red beads, 4 blue beads, 3 white beads, 2 yellow beads, and 1 green bead,

> a. What is the percentage distribution of Haruhiko's beads?
> b. Draw a pie chart showing this percentage distribution.

Solution:

a.
$$
\begin{array}{l}
8 \\
4 \\
3 \\
2 \\
\underline{1} \\
18
\end{array}
$$

$\text{red} = \dfrac{8}{18} = \dfrac{4}{9}$ $9\overline{)4.0^40^40}$ $.4\ 4\ 4 = 44.4\%$

$\text{blue} = \dfrac{4}{18} = \dfrac{2}{9}$ $9\overline{)2.0^20^20}$ $.2\ 2\ 2 = 22.2\%$

$\text{white} = \dfrac{3}{18} = \dfrac{1}{6}$ $6\overline{)1.0^40^40^40}$ $.1\ 6\ 6\ 6 = 16.7\%$

$\text{yellow} = \dfrac{2}{18} = \dfrac{1}{9}$ $9\overline{)1.0^10^10}$ $.1\ 1\ 1 = 11.1\%$

$\text{green} = \dfrac{1}{18}$

$$
\begin{array}{r}
.0555 = 5.6\% \\
18\overline{)1.0000} \\
-90xx \\
\hline
100 \\
-90 \\
\hline
100 \\
-90 \\
\hline
\end{array}
$$

b.

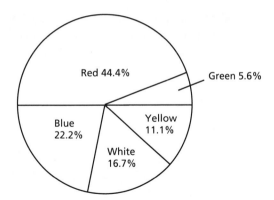

FIGURE 13.8

You're about to take the last quick quiz of the last chapter in this book. All right, then: Take a deep breath and begin.

QUICK QUIZ 13.4   For each of the following items, (a) compute the percentage distribution, and (b) draw a pie chart showing this percent distribution in the space provided.

1. Stacia Perry dispatches 5,000 freight containers a day for United Parcel Service. Fifteen hundred are sent by air, 2,300 go by rail, and the rest by truck.

2. Kostas Tsiskakis runs a TV shoppers' club with 45,000 members. Women under 40 total 4,500; 7,900 are women over 40; 12,800 are men under 40; and the remainder of members consists of men over 40.

3. The Sandy Hampton Detective Agency handled 40 cases last year. Twelve involved missing persons, 18 involved matrimonial disputes, 6 involved business disputes, and 4 involved murders.

Answers to Quick Quiz 13.4

1. a. Air = $\dfrac{1500}{5000} = \dfrac{15}{50} = \dfrac{30}{100} = 30\%$

   Rail = $\dfrac{2300}{5000} = \dfrac{23}{50} = \dfrac{46}{100} = 46\%$

   Truck = $\dfrac{1200}{5000} = \dfrac{12}{50} = \dfrac{24}{100} = 24\%$

b.

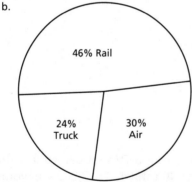

2. a. Women under 40 = $\dfrac{4,500}{45,000} = \dfrac{45}{450} = \dfrac{1}{10} = \dfrac{10}{100} = 10\%$

   Women over 40 = $\dfrac{7,900}{45,000} = \dfrac{79}{450} = \dfrac{7.9}{45}$

$$
\begin{array}{r}
.1755 = 17.6\% \\
45\overline{)7.9000} \\
-4\ 5\text{xxx} \\
\hline
3\ 40 \\
-3\ 15 \\
\hline
250 \\
-225 \\
\hline
250 \\
-225 \\
\hline
\end{array}
$$

$$\text{Men under 40} = \frac{12,800}{45,000} = \frac{128}{450} = \frac{64}{225}$$

```
          .284 = 28.4%
225)64.000
   -45 0xx
    19 00
   -18 00
     1 000
      -900
       100
```

```
 4,500
 7,900
12,800
──────
25,200

45,000
-25,200
──────
19,800
```

$$\text{Men over 40} = \frac{19,800}{45,000} = \frac{198}{450} = \frac{99}{225} = \frac{33}{75} = 1125$$

```
         .44 = 44%
25)11.000
  -10 0xx
    1 00
   -1 00
```

b.

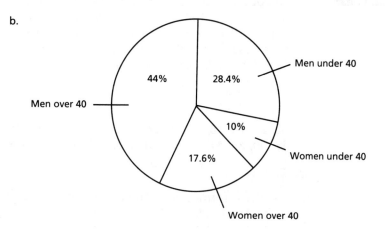

3. a. $\frac{12}{40} = \frac{6}{20} = \frac{3}{10} = 30\%$ missing persons

$\frac{18}{40} = \frac{9}{20} = 45\%$ matrimonial disputes

$\frac{6}{40} = \frac{3}{20} = 15\%$ business disputes

$\frac{4}{40} = \frac{1}{10} = 10\%$ murders

b.

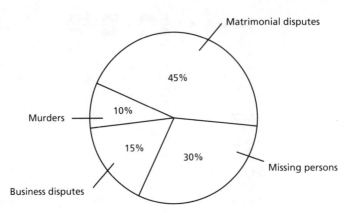

Matrimonial disputes

45%

Murders — 10%

15%

30%

Missing persons

Business disputes

SELF-TEST

Frequency Distributions

1. The people attending a retirement workshop were asked to estimate their incomes to the nearest thousand dollars. Using the data shown below, arrange this data in a frequency distribution using intervals of (a) less than $20,000; (b) $20,000–$39,999; (c) $40,000–$59,999; (d) $60,000–$79,999; (e) $80,000–$99,999; and (f) $100,000 and greater.

   Response to question: How much is your income to the nearest thousand dollars?

   62, 23, 78, 18, 142, 97, 46, 25, 88, 15, 34, 75, 195, 72, 28, 45, 60, 54, 33, 90, 29, 41, 68, 80, 105, 75, 215, 42, 17, 36, 82, 65

Bar Graphs

2. Use the information in the table to draw a vertical bar graph in the space provided.

   Graduates of the University of Texas Attending the 1997 Alumni Dinner, by Decade of Graduation

Decade	Frequency
1920s	31
1930s	84
1940s	159
1950s	235
1960s	342
1970s	416
1980s	319
1990s	140

Line Graphs

3. The information in the table shows the annual sales of cars at Titusville Ford from 1975 through 1994. Draw a line graph of this data using the space provided.

Annual Sales of Titusville Ford, 1975–1994, in Thousands of Dollars

Year	Sales	Year	Sales
1975	$4,616	1985	$6,932
1976	4,873	1986	6,553
1977	5,234	1987	6,745
1978	5,004	1988	6,993
1979	5,312	1989	7,129
1980	5,750	1990	7,240
1981	5,914	1991	7,052
1982	6,487	1992	6,824
1983	6,926	1993	6,681
1984	7,038	1994	6,473

4. Of the people who came into Sharon's Boutique one day, 48 made no purchase, 29 spent less than $10, 23 spent between $10 and $25, 14 spent more than $25 but less than $100, and 4 spent more than $100.

   a. What is the percentage distribution of customers by how much they spent?
   b. Draw a pie chart showing this percentage distribution.

ANSWERS

1. FREQUENCY DISTRIBUTIONS

Income	Tally	Frequency
under $20,000	III	3
$20,000–39,999	IIIII II	7
40,000–59,999	IIIII	5
60,000–79,999	IIIII III	8
80,000–99,999	IIIII	5
100,000 and over	IIII	4

2.

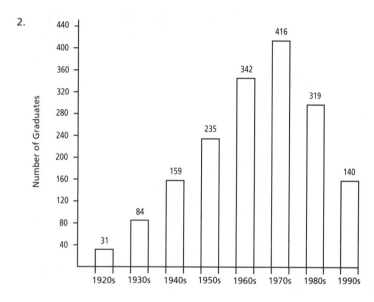

3.

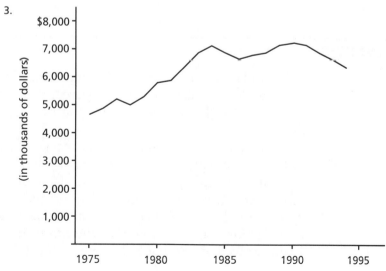

4. a.

$$\text{No purchase} = \frac{48}{118} = 40.7\%$$

$$\text{Spent less than } \$10 = \frac{29}{118} = 24.6$$

$$\text{Spent } \$10 - \$25 = \frac{23}{118} = 19.5$$

$$\text{Spent more than } \$25, \text{ less than } \$100 = \frac{14}{118} = 11.9$$

$$\text{Spent more than } \$100 = \frac{4}{118} = \underline{3.4\%}$$

$$100.1\%$$

b.

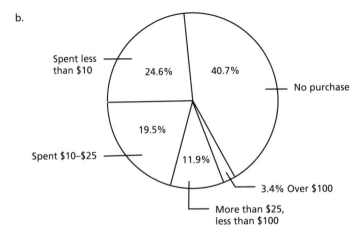

LAST WORD

Congratulations on your having completed this book. But why stop here? With the skills you have mastered, you can continue in business, in math, or in both subjects. And you can continue studying on your own.

John Wiley & Sons offers a wide range of Self-Teaching Guides, or STGs, one of which you've just completed. You'll find a partial listing right after the title page in the front of the book. For business skills, I recommend *Statistics* by Donald Koosis and *Accounting Essentials* by Neal Margolis and N. Paul Harmon. Other books you might want to consider for math skills are *All the Math You'll Ever Need*, which I wrote, as well as two books I wrote with Peter Selby: *Practical Algebra* and *Quick Algebra Review*.

Glossary

acid test ratio   Liquid assets divided by current liabilities.

APR (Annual Percentage Rate)   True annual interest rate charged by sellers.

APR formula $\dfrac{2 \times \text{number of payment periods in one year} \times \text{finance charge}}{\text{amount of loan} \times (\text{total number of payments} + 1)}$

assets   What a company owns and what it is owed by others.

balance sheet   Financial statement listing assets, liabilities, and equity on a particular date.

bar graph   Vertical or horizontal bars are used to depict a frequency distribution.

book value   Cost of asset less accumulated depreciation.

cash discount   Savings resulting from early payment to supplier.

chain discount   Two or more trade discounts that are applied in a series.

compound interest   Interest that is calculated periodically and then added to the principal.

cost of goods sold   Beginning inventory + net purchases – ending inventory.

cost ratio $\dfrac{\text{cost of goods available for sale at cost}}{\text{cost of goods available for sale at retail}}$

current assets   Cash or assets that can be converted into cash within one year.

current liabilities   A company's debts that are due within one year.

current ratio   Current assets divided by current liabilities.

decimal point   Point located between units and tenths. Example: 3.14.

declining-balance method   Depreciation each year is calculated by book value beginning each year times the rate.

denominator   The lower part of a fraction. *Example:* $\frac{2}{3}$, of which 3 is the denominator.

depreciation   The aging and obsolescence of an asset. The decline in value over the useful life of an asset.

end of month (EOM) discount   Discount you receive if bill is paid by tenth day of the month after the date of the bill.

equation   Mathematical statement that shows equality for numbers or expressions or both.

equity   A company's assets minus its liabilities.

exact interest, exact time   Simple interest based on a 365-day year.

first-in, first-out (FIFO) inventory method   Based on two assumptions: (1) The oldest inventory is sold first; and (2) The current inventory is what was acquired most recently.

fixed assets   Assets that are used for more than one year.

fraction   Expresses a part of a whole number. *Example:* $\frac{7}{10}$ expresses 7 parts out of 10.

frequency distribution   Table showing number of times each variable occurs.

gross profit   Net sales – cost of goods sold = gross profit.

gross profit margin ratio $\dfrac{\text{net sales} - \text{cost of goods sold}}{\text{net sales}}$

horizontal analysis   A method of financial analysis where a total in one period is compared to that total in the previous period. *Example:* Sales in period 2 is compared to sales in period 1.

improper fraction   Fraction with numerator that is equal to or larger than denominator. *Examples:* $\frac{3}{3}$, $\frac{18}{5}$.

income statement   Sales – costs = net income for one quarter, two quarters, or one year.

installment buying   Paying off a purchase over a period of months or years.

installment loan   Retail loan repaid over time.

interest   Payment for use of money over a specified time period: Principal × rate × time.

interest turnover   The number of times that a business firm replaces its inventory over a specific period of time.

inventory turnover at retail $\dfrac{\text{net sales}}{\text{average inventory at retail}}$

inventory turnover at cost $\dfrac{\text{net sales}}{\text{average inventory at cost}}$

last-in, first-out (LIFO) inventory method Based on two assumptions: (1) The newest inventory is sold first; and (2) The current inventory is what was acquired earliest.

liabilities Everything a company owes.

line graph Comparison of variable made over time by single line rising and falling.

list price Suggested retail price paid by customers.

markdown Percent of original price by which selling price is reduced.

markup The percent of cost or selling price by which selling price is raised.

maturity value The money you get when a loan matures. Interest + principal.

mean Average of two or more numbers.

median The middle number in an array that begins with the lowest number and ends with the highest.

mixed number Number written as a whole number and a proper fraction. *Examples:* $5\frac{1}{8}$, $2\frac{1}{2}$

mode The most frequent value in a set of numbers.

negative number A number with a value of less than zero; a number with a negative sign. *Examples:* -2, $-\frac{3}{4}$.

net decimal equivalent The percent of the list price that the retailer pays after taking all available discounts.

net income Cost of goods sold – operating expenses = net income.

numerator The upper part of a fraction. *Example:* $\frac{2}{3}$, of which 2 is the numerator.

operating ratio $\dfrac{\text{cost of goods sold + operating expenses}}{\text{net sales}}$

ordinary dating method discount Cash discount if supplier is paid within the discount period.

ordinary interest, exact time Simple interest based on a 360-day year.

owner's equity Company's assets minus its liabilities.

percent Stands for hundredths. *Example:* 27 percent is 27 parts of 100, or $\frac{27}{100}$.

percentage distribution The parts of 100 in each class or category. *Example:* A store that has an inventory of 80 windows and 20 doors has an inventory of 80 percent ($\frac{80}{100}$) windows and 20 percent ($\frac{20}{100}$) doors.

pie charts Circular charts whose slice sizes are in proportion to percentage share of each slice.

present value How much a dollar received at some date in the future is worth today.

present value formula   Present value of dollar received n years from now = $\frac{1}{(1+r)^n}$.

principal   Amount of money that was originally deposited, borrowed, or loaned.

profit margin on net sales $\frac{\text{net income}}{\text{net sales}}$

promissory note   A promise to pay a certain sum of money on a specific date.

proper fraction   Fraction with denominator that is larger than numerator. *Example:* $\frac{3}{5}$.

range   The difference between the highest and lowest values in a distribution of numbers.

receipt of goods (ROG) discount   Discount period begins the day the goods are received.

retail method of estimating inventory   The cost ratio times ending inventory at retail equals the ending cost of inventory.

salvage value   Cost of asset minus accumulated depreciation.

scrap value   Same as salvage value.

simple discount note   A note, or loan, from which the bank deducts interest in advance.

simple interest   Money paid for the use of principal. *Example:* 4 percent simple interest on a one-year $1,000 loan would be $40.

simple interest formula   Interest = principal × rate × time.

straight-line method   Method of depreciation that spreads an equal amount of depreciation each year over the life of the asset.

sum-of-the-years'-digits method   Depreciation each year is calculated by multiplying cost (less residual value) times a fraction. Numerator is number of years of useful life remaining. Denominator is sum of the years of estimated life.

units-of-production method   Estimates depreciation by amount of usage of asset.

vertical analysis   Total on a financial statement as compared to other totals. *Example:* Current assets as a percent of total assets.

weighted average inventory method   Calculates an average cost of all inventory remaining.

Index

5